Touring the West Country

CONTENTS

The delightful little cove of Chapel Porth, near St Agnes, Cornwall, takes its name from an ancient chapel which once stood in a secluded valley near the sea.

INTRODUCTION

The West Country is an area of great natural beauty, famed for its delightful villages, its coastline of tall cliffs and its long stretches of sand where surfers lie in wait for the Atlantic rollers. Wherever you go in this part of the country there are great things to be seen, including Dartmoor, Lorna Doone's Exmoor, the Mendips, the Forest of Dean, the Cotswolds and Thomas Hardy's Dorset. There are man-made wonders too, such as Brunel's bridge over the Avon Gorge and the daunting Stonehenge, marvellous cathedrals and great houses. There are beautiful cities too, from the Georgian elegance of Bath to the charm of Wells, England's smallest city. This book reveals these treasures and more through its carefully planned motoring tours which provide the ideal way to explore this fascinating region. Each self-contained circular tour can be completed within a day and includes magnificent colour pictures to give a foretaste of what is to come.

As well as the tours the book contains 30 pages of invaluable town plans to guide you around the West Country's popular towns. There is also a large scale, 3 miles to the inch atlas of the region. *Touring the West Country* is just one in a series of six colourful *Regional Guides* which embrace the rich history and varied countryside of Britain. The other five in the series are: *Touring South and South East England, Touring Wales, Touring Central England and East Anglia, Touring the North Country* and *Touring Scotland.* The six regions covered by the series are shown on the adjacent map.

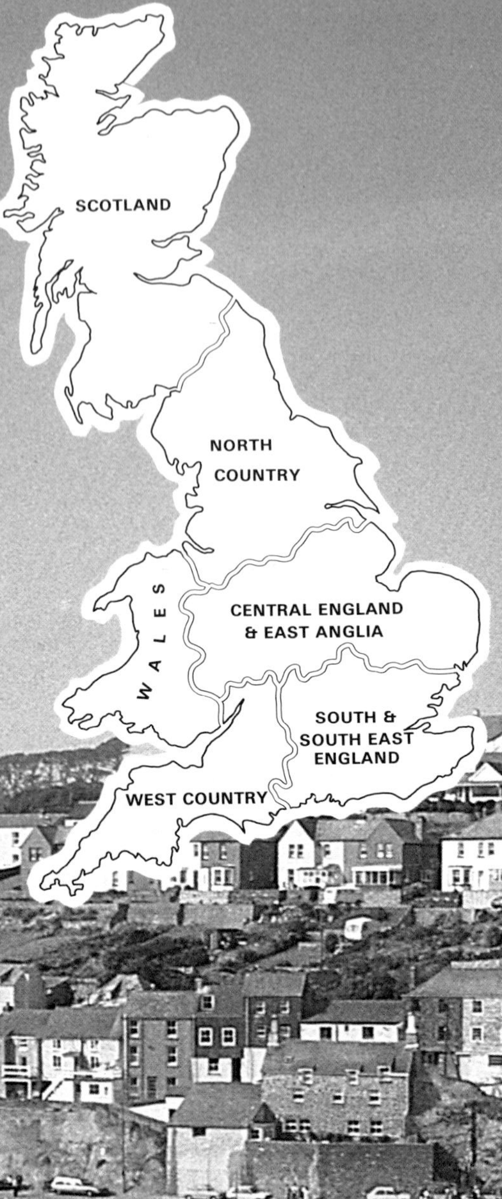

SCOTLAND

NORTH COUNTRY

W A L E S

CENTRAL ENGLAND & EAST ANGLIA

SOUTH & SOUTH EAST ENGLAND

WEST COUNTRY

ABOUT THE TOURS

The tours in this guide have been designed for clarity. Each tour occupies two pages and has a clear map accompanying the text. All the places described in the text are shown in **black** on the tour maps and are described as they occur on the road, linked in sequence by route directions. This precise wayfinding information is set in *italic*.

Castles, stately homes and other places of interest described in the tours are not necessarily open to the public or may be open only at certain times. It is therefore advisable to check the opening times of any place before planning a stop there. Properties administered by the National Trust, National Trust for Scotland and the Ancient Monument Scheme (NT, NTS and AM) are generally open most of the year, but this should be checked with the relevant organisation, as should precise opening times.

The Automobile Association's guide *Stately Homes, Museums, Castles and Gardens in Britain* is the most comprehensive annual publication of its kind and describes over 2,000 places of interest, giving details of opening times and admission prices, including many listed in this book.

Sprawling up the cliff in typical Cornish style, Mevagissey promotes a sense of timelessness in its quaint narrow streets, colour-washed cottages and busy harbour.

HOW TO FIND THE TOURS

All the motor tours in the book are shown on the key map below
and identified by the towns where they start. The tours are
arranged in the book in alphabetical order by start town name.
Page numbers are also given on page vii. Each tour begins at a
well-known place, but it is possible to join or leave at any point if
more convenient.

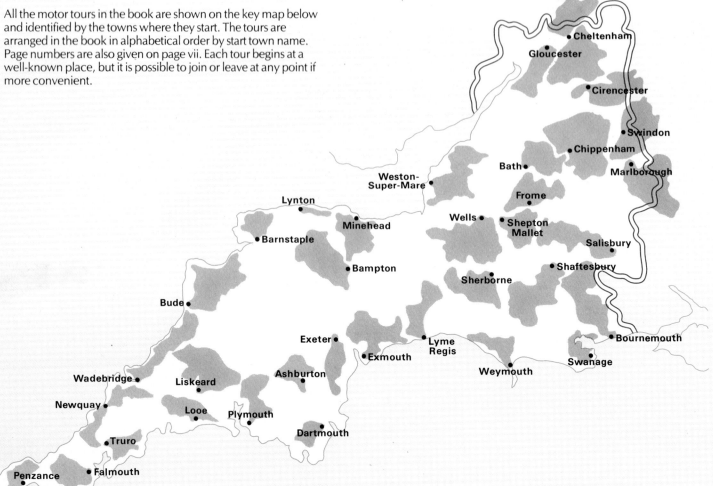

MAPS		Marshland	⋯⋯	TEXT	
Main Tour Route	══	Memorial/Monument	m	AM	Ancient Monument
Detour/Diversion from Main Tour Route	▬▬	Miscellaneous Places of Interest & Route Landmarks	■	c	*circa*
Motorway	═══	National Boundary	⋯⋯	NT	National Trust
Motorway Access		National Trust Property	NT	NTS	National Trust for Scotland
Motorway Service Area		National Trust for Scotland Property	NTS	OACT	Open at Certain Times
Motorway and Junction Under Construction		Non-gazetteer Placenames	*Thames/Astwood*	PH	Public House
A-class Road	A68	Notable Religious Site	✝	RSPB	Royal Society for the Protection of Birds
B-class Road	B700	Picnic Site	Ⓟ		
Unclassified Road	unclass	Prehistoric Site		SP	Signpost (s)'(ed)
Dual Carriageway	A70	Racecourse	⬭		
Road Under Construction	====	Radio/TV Mast			
Airport	✈	Railway (BR) with Station	━●━		
Battlefield	✕	Railway (Special) with Station	┿┿┿		
Bridge		River & Lake			
Castle	◫	Woodland Area			
Church as Route Landmark	✝	Scenic Area			
Ferry	Ⓥ	Seaside Resort			
Folly/Tower		Stately Home	🏛		
Forestry Commission Land	♣	Summit/Spot Height	KNOWE HILL 209 ▲		
Gazetteer Placename	Zoo/Lydstep		KNOWE HILL 209 ▲		
Industrial Site (Old & New)		Viewpoint	☀		
Level Crossing	LC				
Lighthouse	⚲				

TOURING
THE WEST COUNTRY

Motor Tours
Pages 2-79

DARTMOOR NATIONAL PARK (EAST), Devon

The south-eastern edge of the vast national park that surrounds Dartmoor proper is a kinder country than the wild, high plateau farther inland. Here are wind-haunted heathlands clad with bracken and heather, where granite outcrops raise strange weathered silhouettes against the sky and the remains of prehistoric settlements survive underfoot. Country lanes strung with picturesque villages of thatch and stone lead into lush river valleys.

ASHBURTON, Devon

Once an important tin and cloth centre on a popular coaching route, Ashburton makes an ideal base from which to tour this side of the national park. Its narrow streets and old tile-hung houses impart their own particular charm to the town, and the fine local church features a characteristic Devon stair turret. The local museum includes American Indian antiques.

From Ashburton follow SP 'Buckland' along an unclassified road and shortly turn left across the River Ashburn. Ascend, and pass beneath the slopes of Buckland Beacon.

BUCKLAND BEACON, Devon

At the summit of this 1,282ft hill, which commands good all-round views, is the Ten Commandments Stone, carved by a local stonemason.
Continue to Buckland-in-the-Moor.

BUCKLAND-IN-THE-MOOR, Devon

Although visited by many people as one of the county's show villages, Buckland-in-the-Moor remains unspoilt. Its 15th- and 16th-century church contains a notable rood-screen, and the church clock has an unusual dial on which the hours are marked by the letters 'My Dear Mother' instead of numbers.

Continue and in 1 mile at a T-junction, turn left SP 'Widecombe'. Descend into the attractive East Webburn Valley and cross the river, then ascend to another T-junction. Turn right, and in 1 mile enter Widecombe-in-the-Moor.

WIDECOMBE-IN-THE-MOOR, Devon

Probably the best known and by far the most commercialized of the Dartmoor villages, Widecombe stands at 800ft and is dominated by the 120ft tower of its fine 14th-century church - often referred to as the Cathedral of the Moor. Adjacent are the Church House (NT) and the green, where the Widdecombe Fair of song fame is held on the second Tuesday in September.

Leave by the 'Bovey Tracey' road, bearing right past the green, and ascend on to open moorland. Later pass 1,560ft Rippon Tor on the right and enjoy magnificent views over South Devon to Torbay. To the left are 1,350ft Saddle Tor and the famous Haytor Rocks (1,490ft).

BELOW THE HIGH MOOR

Below the desolate summits of the high moor is a gentler country, where small rivers tumble through deep wooded valleys, and mellow old towns maintain a pace of life long gone elsewhere in England. Here were the tin, wool, and market centres of Dartmoor - the focuses of Devonshire life.

Ancient farmsteads shelter in many of Dartmoor's deep coombs.

HAYTOR ROCKS, Devon

These rocks rise 100ft above the surrounding moorland heights and form one of the most spectacular crags in the national park. They are easily accessible by car, simple to climb, and afford superb views as far as the coast and the rich, cultivated lowlands of Devon. During the 19th century stone worked from nearby quarries was loaded on to a tramway and hauled some 6 miles to a canal wharf at Teigngrace by horses. The route is still visible in places.

The church at Widecombe-in-the-Moor.

Descend to the Bovey Valley and after 3 miles at crossroads by the Edgemoor Hotel turn left, and in ½ mile turn left again on to the B3344 SP 'Manaton'. Shortly pass the Yarner Wood National Nature Reserve on the left.

YARNER WOOD NATIONAL NATURE RESERVE, Devon

This reserve protects the mature stands of oak, holly, birch, and rowan that make up an unspoilt woodland rich with birdlife. A nature trail has been laid out here, and details are available from the entrance lodge.

Continue a winding climb across the slopes of Trendlebere Down and enter dense woodland surrounding Becka Falls.

BECKA FALLS, Devon

Best seen after heavy rain, these falls are created by the picturesque Becka Brook as it leaps and plunges 70ft down a series of great boulders.
Continue on the B3344 to Manaton.

MANATON, Devon

Once the home of novelist John Galsworthy, Manaton is a scattered hamlet with a typical 15th-century church. A notable feature of the latter is its fine rood-screen, which extends right across the building. There is a pleasant green surrounded by trees and overlooked by the thatched Church House. About 1½ miles south west of Manaton is Hound Tor, where there is a medieval settlement of long houses inhabited from Saxon times to cAD1300. Bowerman's Nose, an outcrop of rock weathered into a curiously distinctive shape, can be seen ¾ mile to the south.

Continue for ¾ mile from Manaton Church and at a T-junction turn right on to the unclassifed 'North Bovey' road. Descend steeply, and after 1½ miles cross the River Bovey. Ascend into North Bovey.

NORTH BOVEY, Devon

Many people consider this east Dartmoor village to be the most picturesque in Devon. The River Bovey countryside that surrounds it is enchanting, and the unspoilt village green is complemented by the delightful Ring of Bells Inn. Inside the church is a fine screen with statuettes.

Follow SP 'Postbridge' and in ½ mile at crossroads turn left. In ¾ mile meet a T-junction and turn left on to the B3212 SP 'Princetown'. Later ascend on to open moorland, passing an unclassified left turn leading to Grimspound and 1,737ft Hameldown Tor.

GRIMSPOUND, Devon

This fine example of a Bronze-Age shepherd settlement consists of 24 small hut circles in a walled enclosure with a paved entrance. Sir Arthur Conan Doyle used the brooding atmosphere of the area in *The Hound of the Baskervilles*.

Continue on the B3212 and climb to a road summit of 1,426ft near the Warren House Inn.

WARREN HOUSE INN, Devon

A traditional welcome in the form of a peat fire that has been burning continuously for over 100 years waits here. The inn takes its name from one of the park's many rabbit warrens. A footpath leads to the headstream of the West Webburn and the remains of artificial ravines dug by tin miners long ago.

Continue to the village of Postbridge.

Buckland-in-the-Moor's cottages are built to weather the roughest storms.

POSTBRIDGE, Devon
A small touring centre for the moor, Postbridge derives its name from a bridge that once carried the earliest Dartmoor post road between Exeter and south Cornwall across the East Dart River. A few yards south is the largest and by far the most impressive of Dartmoor's clapper bridges. This primitive-looking structure is massively constructed from huge granite slabs, and is thought to have been built when the inner moor was opened up for mining and farming some time during the 13th century.

Beyond the bridge a detour can be taken from the main route by turning left along an unclassified road and passing Bellever Wood to reach Bellever picnic site and nature trail.

BELLEVER, Devon
Numerous hut circles and other prehistoric monuments survive in this area. Also here are 2 fascinating nature trails laid out for visitors by the Forestry Commission.

Continue with the B3212 and reach the edge of Two Bridges.

TWO BRIDGES, Devon
An hotel and little else stands at this junction of the only 2 major routes across central Dartmoor. North east is Crockern Tor, where the so-called Tinners' Parliament met at irregular intervals to enact special laws governing the stannary towns where tin was valued and taxed. Wistman's Wood, a forest nature reserve some 1½ miles north near the West Dart River, features a mature stand of rare dwarf oaks.

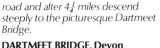

Turn left on to the B3357 'Ashburton' road and after 4¼ miles descend steeply to the picturesque Dartmeet Bridge.

DARTMEET BRIDGE, Devon
Here, where the East and West Dart Rivers join forces to descend through a deep valley to Dartmouth, is one of the most popular beauty spots in the national park. Footpaths which wind through the valley allow some of the spectacular gorge-like scenery to be seen at close range.

Continue on an unclassified road and ascend (1 in 5) to the neighbourhood of 1,250ft Sharp Tor for fine views down the valley, and continue to Poundsgate. Descend steeply to cross the river at Newbridge, where there is a picnic site, and enter the woods of Holne Chase. In ½ mile turn right on to an unclassified road. (A detour from the main route to the River Dart Country Park can be made here by continuing forward for 1¾ miles).

RIVER DART COUNTRY PARK, Devon
Oak coppice, marshland, and valley bogs make up the varied landscape of this country park, which adjoins Holne Woods (NT) and occupies both banks of the River Dart.

Continue on the main route and in ½ mile turn right again to Holne.

HOLNE, Devon
In 1819 the attractive late-Georgian rectory was the birthplace of the novelist Charles Kingsley. Holne Church dates from c1300 and houses a good screen featuring a wealth of detail. An hour glass is incorporated in the carved pulpit. A fine walk leads west of the village along the Sandy Way to the source of the River Avon.

Follow SP 'Buckfastleigh' along a narrow road and in ½ mile bear right. In a further ½ mile descend (1 in 5), and at the bottom keep left. In 1⅓ miles meet crossroads and turn left SP 'Buckfast, Totnes'. In ¼ mile bear right then immediately left, and in ¾ mile enter Buckfast village to pass the famous abbey.

BUCKFAST ABBEY, Devon
Buckfast Abbey was founded in the 10th century, refounded 2 centuries later, and rebuilt on the old foundations by the Benedictine monks themselves between 1907 and 1938. A magnificent mosaic pavement has been laid inside the church. Near by is the House of Shells museum, which demonstrates the use of shells in arts and crafts.

Continue for ¼ mile to meet a T-junction. A short detour can be made from the main route by turning right into Buckfastleigh here.

BUCKFASTLEIGH, Devon
A long flight of steps leading to the church in this old wool town affords excellent views. Inside the church, which has an Early-English chancel, is a notable Norman font.

DART VALLEY RAILWAY, Devon
The northern terminus of this revived steam line, originally built in 1872 to serve the mining and farming industries, is in Buckfastleigh. Great Western rolling stock and a number of locomotives from that company can be seen here. The 14-mile round trip to Totnes BR station affords excellent views of the superb Dart Valley countryside.

Follow the main route by turning left at the T-junction before the detour. Cross the River Dart by Dart Bridge, turn left again, and in 1¾ miles meet a T-junction. Turn left then shortly right to re-enter Ashburton.

ALONG THE EXE VALLEY

From its wild moorland source the Exe struggles through a mile of peat before finding its deep valley to the fertile lands of North-east Devon. All along its route are little red-stone villages that burst into activity once a week when the local hunt meets.

BAMPTON, Devon

This small market town is situated by the River Batherm near its junction with the Exe. Ponies culled from the wild herds that roam the moor are sold in the October Pony Fair. The excellence of the limestone quarried to the south of the town is almost legendary. Today these quarries are of geological rather than commercial interest, and their situation affords fine views of the town. St Michael's Church, built c1300, was rebuilt with a north aisle in the 15th century. Inside are notable carved rood and tower screens and a pulpit dating from the 16th-century.

Leave Bampton on the B3222 SP 'Dulverton', and at Exe Bridge turn right A396 then almost immediately left to rejoin the B3222. Cross the River Exe and proceed through the valley of the River Barle to Dulverton.

DULVERTON, Somerset

The River Barle is spanned here by an attractive 3-arched bridge and is known for its excellent trout and salmon fishing. Dulverton itself is a shopping centre and the general administrative centre for the south-east area of Exmoor, a status that makes it a prime touring base. Everywhere is the sight and sound of water, a fact succinctly commented upon by Lord Tennyson in 1891 when he called Dulverton 'a land of bubbling streams'. Fine views of the town are available from the shade of a giant sycamore, which is some 250 years old and obscures a modest church. Local painters exhibit their works each summer in Exmoor House by the bridge.

Turn left on to the B3223 'Lynton' road and enter the Exmoor National Park.

EXMOOR NATIONAL PARK (SOUTH), Devon & Somerset

Much of this tour runs through the southern area of the Exmoor National Park, a place of dense mixed forests and wild open moors dominated in the north by the River Exe and in the south by the River Barle. Once a year the Exmoor ponies are herded and culled, some being freed and others taken to be sold at the famous local pony fairs. Pure-bred Exmoors are bay, dun, or brown, with no white or other markings of any kind, and have a characteristic oatmeal colour to the muzzle and inside ears. These animals, untainted by domestic stock, are hardy, agile creatures. The possibilities for recreation in the park are unlimited. Superb walks start from almost any point along the route, and those worried about getting lost in the vast expanse of the moor can follow specially marked trails. Care must be taken to avoid the deep, sphagnum- filled bogs; broken-in Exmoor ponies are good for trekking the moor because they know the area and recognize the smell of the boglands. The only other large herd animal found here is the red deer, a lovely, shy animal which is best sought for in secluded spots during the early morning or late evening.

Continue on the B3223. After 4½ miles reach a left turn leading to Tarr Steps for a pleasant detour from the main route.

TARR STEPS, Somerset

Tarr Steps (AM, NT) is the local name for a superb old clapper bridge. Situated on the edge of Exmoor, near Dulverton, it spans the tumbling River Barle and comprises 20 piers topped by a stone footway raised some 3ft above water level. The piers are large blocks of stone placed on the river bed, and the top is made up of several giant slabs that must have taken incredible effort to position. This fascinating monument to the ingenuity of ancient man is believed to have been built before the Norman Conquest. A car-park is provided on the approach.

Back on the main route, continue along the B3223 to reach Winsford Hill and the Caratacus Stone, on the right.

Tarr Steps' enormous slabs have been washed away many times, but have always been replaced in their original positions.

WINSFORD HILL & THE CARATACUS STONE, Somerset

Heather-clad Winsford Hill (NT) rises between Exmoor's two major rivers. Its wooded lower slopes rise to a clear summit from which the marked contrast between the River Barle woodlands and the empty slopes that rise from the Exe can be truly appreciated. The Caratacus Stone, an inscribed tablet on the hill, is thought to date from the dark ages of paganism that followed the departure of the Romans. Its inscription is ambiguous because it is incomplete, and is translated as either 'Kinsman of Caratacus' or 'Caranacus'.

Continue 1¼ miles beyond the Winsford Hill road summit to a left turn that offers a pleasant detour to Withypool.

WITHYPOOL, Somerset

Beautifully situated on the River Barle and much favoured by game anglers, this tiny village has one of the two legal commons existing in the national park (the other is at Brendon). A fine old bridge spans the river here, and nearby Withypool Hill features a stone circle among neolithic burial mounds.

Continue on the main route and after 1½ miles at crossroads turn right on to an unclassified road and descend into Exford.

Exmoor is a beautiful mixture of rolling farmland and open moor.

EXFORD, Somerset

Hunting and horses are the bread and butter of this well-kept Exe-Valley village. The kennels of the Devon and Somerset Stag Hounds are based here, and horses are very much in evidence at all times. Exford's annual Horse Show is generally held on the 2nd Wednesday in August. The nucleus of the village is an attractive grouping of cottages, shops, and hotels around the local cricket and football field. Other buildings are dotted amid the rural outskirts, and the modest little church contains an interesting 15th-century screen.

Follow the B3224 'Lynton' road for 1 mile, rejoin the B3223, and continue to Simonsbath.

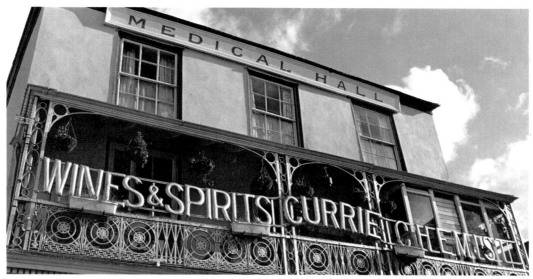

The Medical Hall in South Molton.

Dulverton's Market House dates from 1866.

SIMONSBATH, Somerset

Sited 1,100ft above sea level, Simonsbath is the highest village in the park and stands at the centre of what used to be the Royal Exmoor Forest. Deer were once commonplace here, but today these timid creatures are rarely seen. The 100-year-old church administers the largest parish in the park.

Turn left on to an unclassified road SP 'South Molton' and climb to 1,500ft. After 8 miles join the B3226, and in 1½ miles join the A361 and proceed to South Molton.

SOUTH MOLTON, Devon

Known to have existed as a Saxon colony cAD700, this lovely little town lies just south of Exmoor and is an agricultural centre for the region. Between the Middle Ages and the mid-19th century it became a thriving wool town; it was also a coach stop on the route to Barnstaple and Bideford, and the nearest town to the iron and copper mines of North Molton. A square of elegant Georgian houses is complemented by the town's grand 18th-century Guildhall and 19th-century Assembly Rooms, all built with the profits from wool and minerals. Disaster struck when the industries collapsed, and the town's population was reduced by half. Since 1961 it has been the centre for a busy livestock market. Opposite the square an avenue of pollarded lime trees leads to the local church, which houses an excellently-carved pulpit and carries a 15th-century tower. A small museum behind the Guildhall displays examples of pewterware, a cider press, and an intriguing old fire engine dating from 1736. Also of interest here is the Quince Honey Farm.

Continue on the A361 'Bampton, Taunton' road and cross the rivers Mole and Yeo to Bish Mill. Branch right on to the B3221 SP 'Tiverton' and continue through woodland and hilly farming country to Tiverton.

TIVERTON, Devon

This prosperous industrial and agricultural town stands on the River Exe and its tributary, the River Lowman. After the conquest of the south-west in the 7th century it became one of the first Saxon settlements, and later during the 17th- and 18th-century heyday of the clothing industry the town became the principal industrial area in the county. Architecturally, the town has benefited greatly from the prosperity of its inhabitants. Rich wool merchants have bequeathed such fine buildings as St Peter's Church, Blundell's School, and three sets of almshouses. The church, particularly noted for the richly-carved Greenway Chapel and its organ, stands in front of a 12th-century castle (open) which preserves its towers and gateway despite being incorporated in a private house. Blundell's School is famous in having taught such illustrious persons as R D Blackmore, author of *Lorna Doone*, and Frederick Temple, Archbishop of Canterbury from 1896 to 1902. St George's Church was built in 1773 and is reputed to be one of the finest Georgian churches in Devon. Also of interest is the large and very comprehensive museum, including a GWR locomotive, housed in a 19th-century school building. The 19th-century Grand Western Canal begins at the south-east edge of the town and extends for 11 miles. It was originally intended to link the Bristol Channel with the English Channel, but the project was never completed. The towpath now forms a famous scenic walk and there are horsedrawn barge trips.

From Tiverton take the A396 'Bampton' road and continue to Bolham. Turn right here for a short detour to Knightshayes Court.

KNIGHTSHAYES COURT, Devon

The 19th-century house (open) that stands here is pleasant enough to look at, but it is totally put in the shade by some of the most beautiful gardens in Devon. Protected by both the National Trust and Knightshayes Garden Trust, the grounds have a woodland theme and are particularly noted for their splendid rhododendrons.

On the main route, continue along the A396 for the return to Bampton.

Exford is the most important stag hunting centre on Exmoor.

THE COMBES AND GOLDEN BAYS OF NORTH DEVON

Delightful combes tumble down to the Atlantic, bold headlands guarded by lonely lighthouses jut out between sweeps of sandy beaches and everywhere in this sea-bound corner of Devon echoes with the cries of wheeling seagulls.

Combe Martin Bay

BARNSTAPLE, Devon
Onetime harbour on the estuary of the River Taw and an ancient trading centre, Barnstaple thrives now as north Devon's major market town. The wool trade brought prosperity to Barnstaple in the 18th century and its predominantly Georgian architecture reflects this period of growth. One good example is the attractive colonnaded Exchange by the river, called Queen Anne's walk. Here stands the Tome Stone where any verbal bargains struck were considered binding. Barnstaple's pleasant narrow streets are always busy, but there is an oasis of quiet at the centre. Here the large church, St Anne's Chapel and Horwood's Almshouses and School stand in the leafy churchyard. Within the Chapel is a museum of local history (OACT). On Tuesdays and Fridays the Victorian Pannier Market off the High Street bustles with traders selling delicious Devonshire produce under its high glass roof and fine wrought iron pillars.

Follow SP 'Ilfracombe A361' along the Taw estuary to Braunton.

BRAUNTON, Devon
Practically a small town, but alleged to be the largest village in England, Braunton is certainly of ancient origin. The first church was built by the Irish saint, Brannock, when a dream decreed that he must build a church wherever he first met a sow and her piglets — Braunton fitted the bill. This legend is substantiated by a carving of a sow and her litter on the church roof above the font. The church interior is high and spacious, elaborately Jacobean

with much gilt decoration. To the left of the road to Saunton lie Braunton Burrows — about 3-4 square miles of sand dunes that have been turned into a nature reserve. A nature trail runs through the dunes and a great variety of wild flowers flourish here. Backing on to the Burrows on the seaward side is Saunton Sands, where vast expanses of sand are exposed when the tide goes out.

At the traffic signals in Braunton turn left on to the B3231, SP 'Croyde', and continue through Saunton, round the headland of Saunton Down to Croyde.

CROYDE, Devon
There is a unique museum of local gems and shells at the edge of the village, and in the craft workshop demonstrations of gem cutting and polishing can be seen. To the west of the village the National Trust cliffland of Baggy Point shelters the northern side of Croyde Bay, a magnificent bathing and surfing beach lying round the corner from Saunton Sands.

From Croyde village continue on the Woolacombe road to Georgeham.

GEORGEHAM, Devon
Several old thatched cottages and a stream flowing near the church make a pleasing picture in Georgeham. The church has suffered a great many changes since its first construction in the 13th century, but the Victorians were the last to tamper with it and they attempted to restore its medieval character. Interesting monuments inside include one presumed to represent Manger St

Aubyn — a 13th-century knight who fought in the 1st Crusade.

Remain on the B3231 and in 1¾ miles turn left on to an unclassified road, SP 'Woolacombe Steep Hill', then descend to Woolacombe and follow the Esplanade, SP 'Mortehoe', and continue to Mortehoe.

MORTEHOE, Devon
Rocky terrain characterises Mortehoe — the granite beneath emerging erratically by the roadsides. One of Thomas à Becket's murderers is reputed to have lived here prior to the bloody crime in 1170. Whether or not this is true, a relative of the murderer, Sir William de Tracy, was certainly vicar of the parish in the 14th century and he lies in a tomb-chest in the south chapel. A path from the village leads to the grassy promontory of Morte Point (NT) from where Lundy Island can be seen lying out to sea.

Continue on the unclassified road and in 2 miles join the B3343, SP 'Ilfracombe', then cross the bridge for Turnpike Cross. Here bear left, then take the next turning left B3231 SP 'Lee'. After 1½ miles pass the unclassified road on the left, which leads to Lee.

LEE, Devon
A picture-postcard combe opens on to Lee Bay where the rocks are veined with marble. The tiny hamlet has pretty cottages and gardens overflowing with red and purple fuchsias, but best loved is Three Old Maids Cottage — a white, thatched 17th-century 'show' cottage (not open). It was

the prototype of the many dwellings that sprang up in the 1800s as show cottages belonging to the rich.

The main tour continues to Ilfracombe.

ILFRACOMBE, Devon
In 1874 the railway came to Ilfracombe and the town's future as a holiday resort was established. It subsequently grew rapidly around the harbour and continued to straggle out to become north Devon's largest holiday town. The conical rock called Lantern Hill at the mouth of the harbour is a reminder of Ilfracombe's long history as a port. St Nicholas' Chapel has perched on top of it since the 13th century, with a light burning from its window to guide in ships.

Leave Ilfracombe on the A399 Combe Martin road and later pass the unclassified road, on the right, to Chambercombe Manor.

CHAMBERCOMBE MANOR, Devon
Set in a pretty, sheltered combe, Chambercombe (OACT), with its cobbled courtyard and uneven roofs, resembles a rambling farm building and informal romantic gardens, including a water garden, surround the house.
Much of the furniture is 17th-century and there is a tiny chapel, just 10ft long, that has not been changed since it was licensed in 1404. Well in keeping with the atmosphere of the house is the tale of a corpse walled up in a secret chamber whose spirit still haunts the manor.

Continue on the A399 and in ½ mile pass Hele Mill.

This trinket at Arlington Court came from Barbados in the 19th century when shellwork was a flourishing export

The Boudoir, Arlington Court, was used by the lady of the house as a study

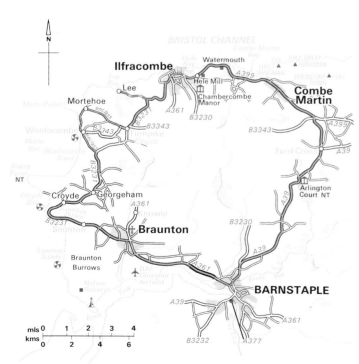

HELE MILL, Devon
Having stood derelict for over 30 years, 16th-century Hele Mill (OACT) has been restored to working order and its 18ft wheel again powers the production of wholemeal flour. Inside several items of mill machinery are on display.

Remain on the coast road and later pass Watermouth (left).

WATERMOUTH, Devon
Greatly commercialised yet still lovely is the inlet at Watermouth where yachts and small pleasure craft ride at anchor. Watermouth Castle (OACT) offers a wide range of family entertainments.

Continue into Combe Martin.

COMBE MARTIN, Devon
Combe Martin derived its name from Martin de Turribus — an adventurer who came over with William the Conqueror and won this piece of land. The village straggles along the main road running through an old mining valley, flanked by abandoned silver and lead mine workings up on the hillsides. Along the main street stands the Pack of Cards Inn, a curious place built in the 18th century by a gambling man.

The inn looks like a house of cards with its curious sloping roofs.

Continue on the A399 and after 2 miles turn right on to the B3229, SP 'Kentisbury Ford'. At Ford Cross (Kentisbury Ford) go forward on to the A39, SP 'Barnstaple'. In 1¼ miles pass, on the left, the road to Arlington Court.

ARLINGTON COURT, Devon
The Chichester family owned the estate from 1384 until 1949, when Miss Rosalie Chichester died and left it to the National Trust. This great lady spent her entire life in the house, and her tastes and personality are reflected in practically every item. She was an avid collector — not necessarily of things of any great value — but of objects that caught her fancy. Consequently the rooms are filled with fascinating treasures such as model ships, seashells from the 7 oceans of the world, birds, butterflies, fans, jewels and trinkets. All her possessions were lovingly arranged with the furniture she inherited and the Trust has sensitively preserved the individuality of her home.

Continue on the A39 which climbs to high ground before the long, gradual descent to Barnstaple.

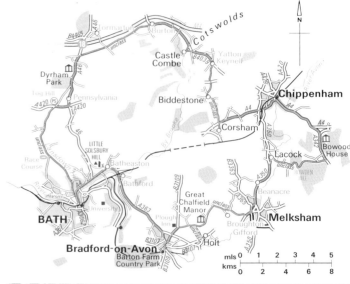

FROM THE CITY OF ELEGANCE

High in the hills that provided the stone for Britain's most elegant city are the Cotswold wool towns. Sturdy manor houses and fine churches seem to grow from the mellow rock, and everywhere are the grass-grown scars of old quarry workings.

BATH, Avon

Justly spoken of as England's most elegant city, Bath is a spa resort of Georgian terraces, crescents, and squares arranged round spacious landscaped parks in the Avon Valley. Warm local stone is set off by trim lawns and mature trees, and the source of the city's prosperity still bubbles into cisterns and baths built by the Romans some 2,000 years ago. Many centuries after the invaders left *Aquae Sulis* to salvage their crashing empire, the dandified high society of Georgian England resumed the sophisticating process. Beau Nash and other arbiters of fashion came here to gossip with royalty and 'take the waters', and the legions of the wealthy occupied magnificent houses built for them by John Wood and his son. Bath today mainly reflects the cultured tastes of the 17th and 18th centuries, but it also contains relics from more distant periods. The ancient baths themselves receive half a million gallons of water at a constant 49°C each day, and their history is interestingly related in an associated museum. Overlooking the baths is the city's splendid 15th-century Abbey Church, while near by is the Pump Room (open) where people came to cure everything from boredom to gout. Rebuilt in 1795, this popular meeting place offers a choice of coffee or spa water in a genteel atmosphere heightened by chandelier lighting, chamber music, and the occasional sedan chair. The work of the Woods is everywhere, but some of the best examples can be seen in the Circus, the superb Royal Crescent (No. 1 is open), and

the Assembly Rooms (open). A very good museum of costume is housed in the latter. Several museums and similar foundations can be visited in the city, and amongst these are the Holburne of Menstrie Museum, the Victoria Art Gallery and the Bath Carriage Museum.

Leave Bath on the A4 'Chippenham' road and follow the Avon Valley to Batheaston, with views of Little Solsbury Hill to the left.

LITTLE SOLSBURY HILL, Avon

A fine Iron-Age hillfort (NT) featuring ramparts faced with dry-stone walling, stands on this flat-topped 625ft hill.

Beyond Batheaston branch right on to the A363 'Bradford-on-Avon' road. Skirt Bathford and climb along wooded slopes before crossing pleasant farmland to reach Bradford-on-Avon.

BRADFORD-ON-AVON & BARTON FARM COUNTRY PARK, Wilts

The disused Kennet and Avon Canal connects here with the River Avon, which itself is spanned by a 17th-century bridge incorporating a small contemporary lock-up. A tall but tiny Saxon church rescued from obscurity here in the 19th century has turned out to be one of the most important buildings of its age in Britain. Old weavers' cottages stand in Dutch Barton Street, and Barton Farm Country Park contains a superbly preserved 14th-century tithe barn (AM). The Park itself is an unspoilt area of country between the canal and the river.

Bradford-on-Avon's tithe barn houses a collection of agricultural machinery beneath its enormous roof timbers.

Leave the town on the B3109 'Chippenham, Corsham' road. After 1 mile reach the Plough Inn and turn right on to an unclassified road SP 'Great Chalfield, Holt'. After another 1 mile branch left on to a narrow road through attractive farmland. The road to the right offers a pleasant detour to Holt.

John Wood the Younger built Bath's magnificent Royal Crescent, which is a half-ellipse of 30 houses, between 1767 and 1774. The overall style is based on the drawings of the architect Palladio.

HOLT, Wilts

Local weavers once brought their disputes to The Courts to be settled, but this 17th-century building now enjoys a peaceful retirement amid fine gardens (NT). Features of the latter include topiary work, a lily pond, and an arboretum.

Proceed for 1 mile to Great Chalfield Manor.

GREAT CHALFIELD MANOR, Wilts

Built in the 15th century, this magnificent stone-built house (NT) features a great hall and is encircled by a moat.

Continue to a T-junction and turn right (no SP) to enter Broughton Gifford. Pass the large village green on the left, then bear left on to the 'Melksham' road. Proceed for 1¼ miles and turn left on to the B3107. After ½ mile at the edge of meet a roundabout and take the 1st exit A350 SP 'Chippenham'. For Melksham town centre take the 2nd exit.

MELKSHAM, Wilts

The River Avon is spanned here by an 18th-century bridge, and an attractive group comprising a converted tithe barn and 17th- and 18th-century houses stands near the church. Nowadays the town is an expanding industrial centre.

Continue with SP 'Chippenham A350', passing through Beanacre with 17th-century Beanacre Manor on the left. Proceed for 1¼ miles and turn right on to the unclassified 'Lacock' road to enter Lacock, then turn right SP 'Bowden Hill, Calne'.

LACOCK, Wilts

A wide architectural range from medieval times to the 18th century has been preserved in the stone, half-timbered, and thatched buildings of this delightful village (NT). Its abbey was the last religious house to be suppressed at the Dissolution in 1539, and was later converted into a private dwelling incorporating many of its medieval buildings. Over the centuries its ancient structure has acquired an octagonal Tudor tower and 17th-century gothic hall. The abbey gatehouse contains a museum of work by W H Fox-Talbot, a 19th-century pioneer of photography who once owned the abbey. Elsewhere in the village is a great tithe barn with 8 massive bays, and a small 14th-century lock-up known as the Cruck House.

About ¼ mile past Lacock Abbey cross the River Avon and begin the ascent of 580ft Bowden Hill. Proceed, with fine views of the Avon Valley, and meet a T-junction on the outskirts of Sandy Lane. Turn left on to the A342 and continue for 1⅓ miles to pass the entrance to Bowood House.

BOWOOD HOUSE, Wilts

The magnificent Georgian house of Bowood, with its superb art collection, is complemented by its extensive grounds, laid out by Capability Brown.

Descend to join the A4, and drive along the Avon Valley to Chippenham.

CHIPPENHAM, Wilts

Situated on the River Avon near the edge of the Cotswold Hills, this pleasant industrial town was a market centre for centuries. Several attractive half-timbered houses and an old lock-up are preserved here.

Leave Chippenham on the A4 'Bath' road, and proceed for 3⅓ miles. Meet crossroads and turn left on to an unclassified road for Corsham, on the edge of the Cotswold Hills.

THE COTSWOLDS

The Cotswolds extend from north of Bath to north of Oxfordshire, nowhere exceeding 30 miles in breadth but rising to 1,000ft in some places. From the 12th century the whole area benefited from the profits of wool, and a legacy of that wealth survives in the beautiful old cottages, houses, mansions, and churches which are such a feature of the district.

CORSHAM, Wilts

This developing town has an old heart of Bath limestone and a scattering of buildings from various periods. Of particular note are the 16th-century Flemish Cottages and 17th-century Hungerford Almshouses. Magnificent Corsham Court (open) was extended in Georgian times and shows work by architect John Nash and by Capability Brown, better known as a brilliant landscape gardener. Inside are good pieces of Chippendale furniture and superb paintings.

Leave Corsham with SP 'Chippenham' and after ½ mile meet crossroads. Drive forward over the A4 on to the 'Biddestone, Yatton Keynell' road, and proceed for 1¾ miles to enter Biddestone.

BIDDESTONE, Wilts

Stone houses surround an attractive green and pond in this pretty Cotswold village. The 17th-century manor house (not open) has a brick gazebo, or garden house, and can be seen from the road.

Bear right on to the 'Yatton Keynell' road and after ¾ mile cross the main road SP 'Castle Combe'. After another 1¼ miles enter Yatton Keynell, turn left on to the B4039 and follow SP 'Castle Combe'. Proceed for 1¾ miles, and turn left again on to an unclassified road for Castle Combe village. Parking in the village is severely restricted, so it is advisable to stop at one of the car parks along this road and walk.

Weathered stone houses are grouped around an ancient market cross in Castle Combe.

CASTLE COMBE, Wilts

Built of Cotswold stone deep in a stream-threaded combe, this old weaving centre is acknowledged as one of England's most picturesque villages. Numerous old buildings unalloyed by the brashness of concrete and brick present a homogeneous completeness round the canopied 13th-century market cross. Close to the centre is the 17th-century manor house, now an hotel. The village was transformed into a harbour (by means of damming the stream) for a scene in the film ''Dr. Doolittle''.

Return to the B4039 and turn left SP

Winter sunlight on Biddestone Village.

'Acton Turville'. Proceed for 2⅓ miles to pass through Burton, and at the end of the village turn left on to the unclassified 'Pucklechurch' road. Continue for 4¼ miles and meet crossroads. Turn left here on to the A46 SP 'Bath' and in ¾ mile pass on the right the entrance to Dyrham Park.

DYRHAM PARK, Avon

Dyrham Park (NT) was built on the site of a Tudor house between 1692 and 1702 for William Blathwayt, Secretary of State and Secretary for War. Dyrham is barely glimpsed in its vale from the entrance gate, and disappears altogether as the drive descends a steep hillside of rough pasture dotted with trees before it turns along the valley floor to the house. The east front, which then greets the visitor, is a great wall of Bath stone blocking the valley with neat rows of tall, narrow many-paned windows. The interior is laid out as apartments, late 17th-century rooms of sensible and sober taste, influenced by the Dutch — William often went to the Netherlands on business. The furniture, paintings and pottery he collected are all still part of the house. A Dutch-style garden of parterres, terraces and detailed formal designs surrounded Dyrham until about 1800, when it fell to the 'modern' taste for landscaped gardens — the style of 'Capability' Brown, which survives today.

Proceed for 1¾ miles, pass through Pennsylvania, then in ½ mile meet traffic lights and turn right on to the A420 'Bristol' road. In ¾ mile reach the start of a descent, meet crossroads, and turn left on to an unclassified road (no SP). In 1 mile descend steeply, then near the top of the following ascent turn left SP 'Lansdown, Bath'. Reach the top of a 700ft ridge and pass Bath racecourse. Return to Bath.

BOURNEMOUTH, Dorset

Queen of the South Coast resorts, Bournemouth has grown into one of the largest and most popular seaside towns in the country. Its 6 miles of superb sandy beach backed by spectacular cliffs first became popular about the middle of the last century when Dr Granville recommended its mild sunny climate to invalids. Attractive parks and gardens, theatres and the world famous symphony orchestra offer a wide range of entertainment. The town also has 2 notable museums. In the Russell Coates Museum is the Henry Irving theatrical collection, a magnificent display of butterflies and moths, oriental art and a freshwater aquarium. Its geological terrace has exhibits covering 2,600 million years. Finally, the Big Four Railway Museum houses a working model railway and a large collection of nameplates and other relics.

Leave the town centre on the A338, SP 'Ringwood'. In 2¾ miles, at the roundabout, take the 3rd exit on to the A3060, SP 'Christchurch'. At the next roundabout, take the 2nd exit, SP 'Tuckton'. At the end turn left, then at the roundabout turn left again and cross the River Stour to pass Tucktonia.

TUCKTONIA, Dorset

Tucktonia (OACT) is a Britain in Miniature, containing over 200 scale models of historic buildings, all linked by a network of model railways, roads, rivers and canals. Among the models are Hadrian's Wall, London's most famous sights and a typical Cornish fishing village complete with boats.

At the next traffic signals turn right on to the A35, SP 'Lyndhurst', and at the next roundabout take the B3059 into Christchurch.

CHRISTCHURCH, Dorset

According to legend, Christ himself gave the town its name by his miraculous intervention in the building of the great Norman priory in the 12th century. Until then it had been called Twynham,

CRANBORNE CHASE AND THE AVON VALLEY

The well-wooded slopes of the lovely Avon Valley lead up to the spacious chalklands of the rolling Wiltshire Downs and on to the scattered beech woods of Cranborne Chase, a centuries-old forest where King John loved to hunt fallow deer and where, later, smugglers and poachers found refuge from the law.

Harvest time above Cranborne

an old word meaning the meeting place of 2 rivers. Near the priory, on the banks of the mill stream, stand the ruins of the Norman castle and hall, built of rough blocks of local Purbeck marble. The Red House Museum has an interesting collection of Iron-Age finds, mostly from nearby Hengistbury Head.

At the end of Christchurch High Street keep left and cross the River Avon, then at the mini-roundabout turn left B3347 into Stony Lane. At the next roundabout take the 2nd exit on to the Sopley road. Continue along the valley of the Avon to Ringwood.

RINGWOOD, Hants

The attractive, tree-clad valley of the River Avon leads to Ringwood, an old market town lying just inside the Hampshire border between 2 ancient tracts of woodland, the New Forest and the Forest of Ringwood. Among the many old houses is one called the Monmouth House (not open), where the ill-fated Duke, illegitimate son of Charles II, stayed during his rebellion against James II.

Leave on the A338 Salisbury Road. To the right of the road, beyond Blashford, is Moyles Court.

MOYLES COURT, Hants

Today a school is housed in this attractive 17th-century manor (open by appointment) with a tragic history. Two of Monmouth's rebels, fugitives from the Battle of Sedgemoor, were sheltered here by the 70-year-old lady of the manor, Dame Alicia Lisle. The bloodthirsty Judge Jeffries condemned her to be burned alive, but the sentence was commuted to the more merciful

one of beheading and her execution took place at Winchester, in September 1685.

Continue on the A338 and at Ibsley turn left SP 'Alderholt'. In ½ mile pass Harbridge church and turn left and in another ¾ mile turn right, SP 'Fordingbridge'. In 1 mile turn left on to the wooded Cranbourne road. At the edge of Alderholt bear left, and later join the Verwood road. In 1 mile turn left into Batterby Drove and continue to Verwood. Here turn right on to the B3081. In 1½ miles, turn left with the Wimborne St Giles road, and in 1¾ miles turn left again on to the B3078, SP 'Wimborne Minster'. After 1½ miles turn right SP 'Wimborne St Giles', and pass on the right Knowlton Church ruins and Knowlton Rings.

KNOWLTON RINGS, Dorset

In the quiet, wooded countryside lies a mysterious pagan site dating back to Neolithic times. Knowlton Rings consists of a number of circles and henge monuments, guarded by banks and ditches. Two of the rings can be seen clearly from the road: the Central Circle (AM) in the middle of which stand the lonely ruins of a Norman church; and to the east, the so-called Great Barrow, a 20ft mound crowned by a circle of trees.

Continue, over the River Allen, then at the T-junction turn right for Wimborne St Giles. From the village follow SP 'Cranborne' and later keep forward on to the B3081. In ½ mile turn right on to an unclassified road then in ¾ mile turn left on to the B3078 for Cranborne.

CRANBORNE, Dorset

Brick and timber houses scattered round a green, a 13th-century church with medieval wall paintings and a stone manor house make Cranborne a picturesque sight. Formerly it was the busy market centre of the Chase, to which it gave its name, and the place where the Chase Court sat. The medieval manor, Cranborne House, was rebuilt by the 1st Earl of Salisbury, who turned it into a charming Jacobean house. The lovely gardens (OACT) were laid out at the same time and there is also a garden centre.

In Cranborne turn left on to the Martin road, then in ¼ mile bear right to Boveridge. Nearly 2 miles beyond the Hampshire border at the T-junction, turn left for Martin.

MARTIN, Hants

The thatched cottages of Martin cluster in the valley of the Allen Water at the foot of the downs. To the south-west of the village, 2 ancient boundaries can be seen crossing Martin Down. The oldest

Christchurch stands between the Avon and Stour, which meet in the town's harbour

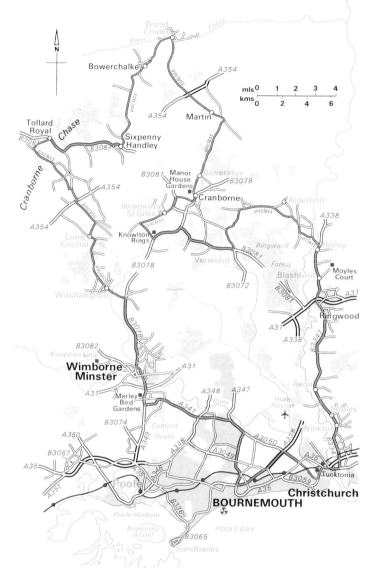

century the inn was the headquarters of a notorious smuggler, Isaac Gulliver, who had married the landlord's daughter. He and his band of 50 men successfully ran contraband from the deep chines of the Dorset coast. Deer poachers also felt safe in Sixpenny Handley and used one of the tombstones in the churchyard with impunity as a hiding place for their stolen carcases.

At Sixpenny Handley turn right on to the B3081 and continue to Tollard Royal.

TOLLARD ROYAL, Wilts
Tollard, hidden in a hollow of the downs, within the old hunting preserve of Cranborne Chase, was designated 'royal' in the 12th century by King John. His house, a lofty medieval stone building on the site of the royal hunting lodge was restored by General Sir Pitt Rivers, whose family had acquired the estate. He also laid out a charming pleasure garden, Larmer Gardens, ornamented with statues and little temples. 'Larmer' means wych elm; until 1894 there was an elm tree here which was reputed to be the place where King John's huntsmen gathered, but it has now been replaced by an oak.

At the telephone kiosk turn left, SP '13th-century church', then immediately bear right and climb on to Cranborne Chase.

CRANBORNE CHASE, Dorset & Wilts
Once a vast area of unbroken woodland, Cranborne Chase stretched across the downs from Shaftesbury in Dorset to Salisbury in Wiltshire. The Chase has long since disappeared, but many fine beech trees survive, to remind one of the vanished forest. It was a royal hunting ground even before the Normans, but it is most strongly associated with King John, who jealously guarded his right to hunt the fallow deer by stringent laws. As royalty became less addicted to hunting deer, these laws allowed the Chase to become the unsavoury haven of all kinds

of smugglers, poachers and wrongdoers, until, in 1830, Parliament put a stop to it all by a special Act.

After 1 mile, at the T-junction, turn left and re-enter Dorset. In another mile bear right and, at the next T-junction, turn right. Reach the A354, turn right then immediately left on to the Moor Crichel road. In 1½ miles, turn right for the village of Long Crichel. Here turn left, SP 'Witchampton', and at the next T-junction, turn left then immediately right, then right again for Witchampton. Later turn right on to the B3078 to Wimborne Minster.

WIMBORNE MINSTER, Dorset
The minster or 'mission' church at the centre of this old market town on the River Stour was built by the Normans on the site of a Saxon nunnery founded by St Cuthberga, sister of King Ine of Wessex. High on the outside wall of the 15th-century west tower a quarter-jack, in the form of a gaily painted Grenadier Guard, strikes the quarter hours. He is part of a 14th-century astronomical clock which can be seen inside the tower. The 16th-century Priest's House near the minster has been converted into an interesting museum of local history. To the north west is Kingston Lacy House (NT) a fine classical structure set in formal gardens and surrounded by 254 acres of parkland.

Follow signs Bournemouth A349, and cross the River Stour. After passing the Willett Arms PH the Merley Bird Gardens lie to the right of the road.

MERLEY BIRD GARDENS, Dorset
Exotic birds are housed in spacious aviaries set in the secluded walled gardens here. The house was built in the 18th century for Ralph Willett, a man who had made his fortune in the West Indies.

After another ½ mile, turn left on to the A341, SP 'Bournemouth'. In 3 miles, at the roundabout, take the 2nd exit and follow SP 'Bournemouth Town Centre'.

of these is part of Grim's Ditch, marking the southern edge of a Bronze and Iron-Age cattle ranch. More prominent is the 6ft rampart of Bokerley Dyke, a Romano-British defence against the invading Saxons.

Continue on the unclassified road and in 1½ miles cross the main road, SP 'Broad Chalke'. After entering Wiltshire climb to over 600ft, with fine downland views, then descend to Broad Chalke and follow SP 'Bowerchalke'.

BOWERCHALKE, Wilts
Watercress beds, rich emerald-green, continually fed by little trickling streams, line the approaches to this tiny downland village, tucked away on a tributary of the River Ebble. The views from here and from the road to Sixpenny Handley of the rolling downs and their belts of beech wood are particularly lovely.

Continue on the road, SP '6d Handley', to Sixpenny Handley.

One of the many monuments in Wimborne's minster: this, to Anthony Etricke, lies in the south choir aisle

SIXPENNY HANDLEY, Dorset
The famous abbreviated signpost 'To 6d Handley' conjures up an idyllic picture that the village scarcely lives up to, perhaps because it was almost totally rebuilt during 1892 in the aftermath of a disastrous fire. It is set in the lovely countryside of Cranborne Chase, however, and its history is colourful. In the 18th

BUDE, Cornwall

One of Bude's main attractions is its huge surfing beach, where strong winds that have caused hundreds of wrecks over the centuries provide a constant supply of rollers ideal for the sport. The town itself is sheltered from the full force of the weather by ridges of downland between it and the sea. Visitors interested in sun and sea bathing are catered for by Summerleaze beach, a sheltered area of sand at the mouth of the River Neet. Here a large swimming pool is naturally refilled every high tide. A notable 3-mile scenic walk extends along clifftops south of Bude, visiting Compass Point and Efford Beacon for their excellent views. Bude Castle was built in 1840 and now houses the local council offices.

Leave by the A3072 'Bideford' road. After 1¼ miles turn left on to the A39, pass the edge of Stratton, and drive to Kilkhampton.

KILKHAMPTON, Cornwall

The main feature of the village is the 12th- to 15th-century church, which contains no fewer than 157 carved bench-ends dating from the 16th century. The Norman doorway is elaborately carved, and there is a splendid barrel roof. Three miles east are the Tamar lakes with various leisure facilities.

Continue for 3 miles. A detour from the main route can be made by turning left here on to an unclassified road to reach Morwenstow.

MORWENSTOW, Cornwall

Henna Cliff rears 450ft above the waves about ¼ mile from Morwenstow village church, on the other side of a grassy coomb. It is the highest cliff in Cornwall and forms part of an awesome range that once proved useful to the wreckers, who signalled ships on to the rocks in order to plunder their cargoes. The Norman church itself stands a little aloof from the tiny village, and features attractive Romanesque zig-zag work over the porch and carved bench ends. During the 19th century the local vicar, Robert Hawker, wrote the ballad *Song of the Western Man*.

Continue on the A39 for 2 miles to Welcombe Cross. A detour can be made from the main route to reach Welcombe and Welcombe Mouth by turning left on to an unclassified road.

WELCOMBE, Devon

Situated near the Cornish border, this village stands in a remote glen that leads to a wild stretch of cliff-bound coast at Morwenstow Bay. The cliff strata here has been violently contorted by unimaginable stresses to form really spectacular coastal scenery. A fine waterfall can be seen at Marsland Mouth, and picturesque Welcombe Cove is well worth visiting.

A small stream tumbles into Bideford Bay at Buck's Mills.

NORTH DEVON CLIFFTOPS

Bude's long beach is a brief calm before the great geological storm that lies ahead. Just north are soaring cliffs violently twisted and fractured by massive forces, where small streams from the lush hinterland plunge hundreds of feet to the shore as waterfalls, or dash over boulder beds through deep wooded ravines.

Atlantic waves break constantly on Bude's magnificent beach, creating ideal conditions for surfers.

From Welcombe Cross proceed on the A39 for 1 mile to pass the West Country Inn, then branch left on to an unclassified road SP 'Elmscott'. Cross a short stretch of moorland to reach Tosberry Cross, and bear left then right for Stoke, 3 miles further on.

STOKE, Devon

Hartland's 14th-century church stands here, raising its magnificent tower 128ft into the air to form a local landmark. Inside are a carved Norman font and a fine screen.
Continue for ½ mile and descend steeply to Hartland Quay.

HARTLAND QUAY, Devon

The quay that stood here has long since been washed away by storms, but the rocky shore is a constant attraction. Some of the most exciting shorescapes of the north Devon and Cornwall coasts are formed by the strangely twisted and fractured strata of the local cliffs. The interesting Hartland Quay Museum has sections on geology, natural and coastal history, and shipwrecks. A clifftop path leads 1 mile south to Speke's Mill Mouth waterfall, perhaps the most spectacular of several cliff waterfalls in the district.

Return to Stoke and follow SP 'Hartland, Bideford'. After ½ mile a road to the left leads to Hartland Point.

HARTLAND POINT, Devon

Although only 3 miles from Hartland Quay, the beautiful 350ft cliffs here are red instead of grey. This spectacular coast has an ugly history and has been the death of many a helpless and storm-battered ship. Because of this the point carries a small white lighthouse which emits the strongest light of any on Britain's coast.
Return to Hartland.

HARTLAND, Devon

To the west of this pleasant village is the 18th-century house of Hartland Abbey. The abbey itself was founded in the 12th century and has entirely vanished. A coomb leads from here to the sea.

From Hartland proceed on the B3248 'Bideford, Clovelly' road for 3 miles and turn left on to an unclassified road. After another ¼ mile turn left again on to the B3237 and drive to the carpark for Clovelly.

CLOVELLY, Devon

Clovelly is one of the West Country's most picturesque fishing villages. No cars are allowed here because the steep cobbled street, lined with lovely old houses, descends 400ft to the sea in a series of steps. Donkeys are used to transport visitors' luggage, and zig-zag steps allow pedestrian access down the wooded cliffs to the tiny quay and a pebble beach. The idyllic surroundings of the village tend to soothe away the normal healthy respect for the open sea, but a local lifeboat station that has saved 350 lives is a sobering reminder that the tranquillity is not permanent. The village, discovered by holidaymakers in the mid-19th century, is popular with artists and enjoys a climate as mild as that of the south Devon coast. Local gardens bloom well beyond their normal season. An attractive 2-mile walk leads west from the harbour to a magnificent range of 400ft cliffs.

Return along the B3237, then in 1¼ miles turn left on to the A39 'Bideford' road to reach Buck's Cross. An unclassified road to the left leads through a wooded glen to Buck's Mills.

BUCK'S MILL, Devon

This unspoilt fishing village of thatched cottages lies at the bottom of a wooded valley, on a section of coast noted for its picturesque cliff scenery.

Continue along the A39 and in 5½ miles at a roundabout take 1st exit on to an unclassified road to reach Abbotsham.

ABBOTSHAM, Devon

Abbotsham Church features a good 15th-century barrel roof bearing trade emblems and coats of arms, and preserves carved bench-ends and a Norman font.

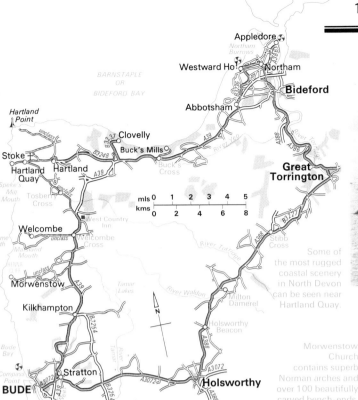

Appledore
Northam
Burrows
Westward Ho!
Northam
Bideford
Abbotsham

BARNSTAPLE
OR
BIDEFORD BAY

Hartland
Point

Clovelly
Buck's Mills
Buck's
Cross

Stoke
Hartland
Quay
Hartland

Great
Torrington

River Yeo

River Torridge

Speke's
Mill
Mouth

Tosbery
Cross

West Country
Inn

mls 0 1 2 3 4 5
kms 0 2 4 6 8

Welcombe
Welcombe
Cross

River Torridge

Stibb
Cross

Some of
the most rugged
coastal scenery
in North Devon
can be seen near
Hartland Quay.

Morwenstow

Kilkhampton

Tamar
Lakes

River Waldon

Milton
Damerel

Holsworthy
Beacon

Morwenstow
Church
contains superb
Norman arches and
over 100 beautifully
carved bench-ends.

Stratton

Holsworthy

BUDE

Bude
Bay

Compass
Point

Continue and in 1¼ miles turn left on to the B3236 to reach Westward Ho!

WESTWARD HO!, Devon
Named after the famous novel by Charles Kingsley, this seaside resort offers a well-known golf course and 3 miles of sandy beach. West of the town the sands merge into rocks scattered with teeming pools, ideal ground for the infant naturalist. North-east is the 650-acre expanse of Northam Burrows, which now includes a country park and is protected from the Atlantic by a remarkable pebble ridge.

Follow signs Bideford and continue to Northam.

NORTHAM, Devon
Northam village lies close to the attractive Torridge Estuary. An inscribed stone at Bloody Corner recalls King Alfred's successful last battle againt Hubba the Dane in the 9th century.

A detour can be made to Appledore by turning left on to the A386.

APPLEDORE, Devon
Cobbled streets leading to a quay and a sandy beach contribute to the great charm of this village, which has several attractive Georgian houses and cottages. Its tranquility is somehow maintained despite the establishment in 1970 of one of Europe's largest covered shipbuilding docks, on the Torridge estuary. A maritime museum displays North Devon's shipping history.

Follow the main route on the A386 and drive to Bideford crossing the approach to the new by-pass bridge over the Torridge.

BIDEFORD, Devon
Between c1550 and 1750 this town was the principal port of north Devon and the home of a renowned

ship-building industry. Sir Richard Grenville, who obtained a charter for the town from Queen Elizabeth I, crewed his ship *Revenge* entirely with Bideford men. That brave little vessel will always be famous for its stand against 15 Spanish ships in the Azores. The mile-long, tree-lined quay remains lively, and the estuary is popular with yachtsmen and small-boat sailors. Bridgeland Road preserves evidence of a once prosperous past in the shape of 17th-century merchants' houses. Pre-dating these is the bridge over the River Torridge, a 15th-century structure unusual in that none of its 24 arches is of the same width. It has been considerably renovated and widened to take the burden of 20th-century traffic. The Royal Hotel, across the river, was originally a merchant's house and dates from 1688. It was here that Charles Kingsley wrote part of *Westward Ho!*

Leave Bideford following SP 'Torrington' and drive beside the River Torridge to reach Great Torrington.

GREAT TORRINGTON, Devon
The church in this hilltop market town was rebuilt in 1651, 6 years after it and 200 Royalist soldiers imprisoned inside were blown up by gunpowder. The tragedy was caused by Roundhead troops using the church as a gunpowder store as well as a prison. A fine 17th-century pulpit can be seen inside the building. The well-known Dartington glass is made in the town, and visitors to the factory can watch the highly skilled glassblowers at work. About 1 mile south-east of Great Torrington is Rosemoor Garden (open), where hybrid rhododendrons, eucalyptus, roses, and ornamental trees and shrubs can be seen. Within easy reach are two magnificent vantage points. The castle mound by the town centre stands on a steep hillside high above the Torridge and 1 mile north-west across a ravine the crag of Furzebeam Hill juts out above the meandering river.

From the Bideford end of the town follow SP 'Holsworthy, Bude' B3277 and cross the river into Taddiport. After 6 miles enter Stibb Cross, then forward on to the A388 for Holsworthy.

HOLSWORTHY, Devon
This bustling market town has a dubious claim to fame as the last place in England where a man was punished by being sent to the stocks. The mainly 13th-century church here has a pinnacled 15th-century tower and a carillion which plays one of a number of tunes on the hour.

Leave Holsworthy on the A3072 SP 'Bude'. Later cross the River Tamar into Cornwall and 4 miles further on reach Stratton.

STRATTON, Cornwall
An ancient town that was probably founded by the Romans, Stratton is made up of old and sometimes thatched buildings lining a steep main street. The Tree Inn was once a manor, and in 1643 it served as the home and headquarters of Sir Bevil Grenville before he led the Royalists to victory at the battle of Stamford Hill, ½ mile north-west. Features of the local church include a pinnacled 15th-century tower, a barrel roof with carved bosses, a fine 16th-century brass, and a window by the talented artist and designer Burne-Jones.

Follow SP 'Bude' on the A3072 for the return to Bude.

Clovelly is one of the most popular of Devon's picturesque fishing villages.

CHELTENHAM SPA, Glos

Cheltenham started life as a typical Cotswold village, but in 1715 a mineral spring was discovered here. A pump room was built in 1738, George III gave the place his personal approval, and within half a century architects were commissioned to design a new town. The result attracted many people of education and means, who came as much for Cheltenham's fashionable elegance and taste as for its water's vaunted medicinal properties. The architect Papworth was responsible for much that is best in Cheltenham, and Forbes built the famous Pittville Pump Room. Schools flourished too, including the Cheltenham College for Boys of 1841, and the Cheltenham Ladies' College of 1853. Composer Gustav Holst was a pupil at the town's grammar school. Each March Prestbury Park is host to the Cheltenham Gold Cup horse race.

GOLD IN THE COTSWOLD COUNTRYSIDE

Here is a mature countryside, first civilized by the Romans, later smoothed by the wealth of medieval clothiers, and finally polished by Regency high fashion. Everywhere is the honey colour of Cotswold stone, giving the name of Gloucestershire's rich Golden Valley another meaning.

Turn right on to the B4070, then turn left. After ¾ mile branch right on to the unclassified 'Painswick' road. In 2¾ miles meet a T-junction and turn left on to the A46. Continue to Painswick.

PAINSWICK, Glos

Years ago Painswick was an important centre of the cloth industry. This prosperity is evident in

Follow SP 'Cirencester A419' passing the wide expanse of Rodborough Common.

RODBOROUGH COMMON, Glos

Rodborough Common (NT) lies 1 mile south of Stroud. Its 240-acre site includes part of an early agricultural enclosure.

The 19th-century lines of Sudeley Castle are complemented by beautiful formal gardens.

An Ionic temple was the inspiration for Cheltenham Spa's 19th-century Pump Room.

Follow SP 'Stroud A46' then SP 'Birdlip B4070' to leave Cheltenham, then climb Leckhampton Hill. At the top meet the main road and turn right, then enter a roundabout and leave by the 1st exit on to the A417. The 2nd exit leads to delightful Crickley Hill and can be taken as a diversion from the main tour.

CRICKLEY HILL, Glos

This Country Park (part NT) comprises 36½ acres of beautiful Cotswold escarpment and an interesting Iron Age promontory fort.

Continue along the A417, with magnificent views across the Severn Valley to the Malvern Hills, and enter Birdlip.

BIRDLIP, Glos

Birdlip stands on the edge of the Cotswolds, at an altitude of 900ft. Several mosaic pavements and a well-preserved hypocaust system have been uncovered at the site of a Roman villa to the west.

its many old houses and inns, amongst which are the tall-chimneyed Court House (associated with Charles I) and 18th-century Painswick House. One of the country's few original bowling greens has been preserved at the Falcon Hotel, and a few old cloth mills have survived south of the town. St Mary's Churchyard boasts almost a hundred yews that are kept tidy in a traditional annual clipping ceremony.

Follow the Painswick Valley to Stroud.

STROUD, Glos

Situated on the modest River Frome and the Stroudwater Canal, this town was once reckoned to produce the finest broadcloth in the country. It still makes most of the baize for the world's billiard tables, and has an excellent reputation for its scarlet dyes. A number of 18th-century mills and typical Cotswold cottages have survived. The District (Cowle) Museum contains exhibits of local interest.

Painswick's carefully clipped churchyard yews were planted at the end of the 18th century.

After Rodborough Common continue along the A419 and enter Brimscombe.

BRIMSCOMBE, Glos

Most of the key buildings in Brimscombe are of relatively recent date. Holy Trinity Church was built in 1840, and both Hope Mill and Port Mill are of 19th-century origin. A few earlier buildings survive at Bourne Mill.

Continue along the pleasant Golden Valley to Chalford.

CHALFORD, Glos

Views from Chalford's steep and narrow streets encompass the fertile Golden Valley, the River Frome, and stretches of the disused Stroud Canal. An old round house which originally served as a lock-keeper's cottage now houses an interesting museum of canal relics. Thoughts of past prosperity are woken by the local mills and wool masters' houses.

THE GOLDEN VALLEY, Glos
The original Golden Valley runs from Dorstone to Pontrilas in Herefordshire. The Gloucestershire Golden Valley cradles the River Frome and, like its namesake, is known for peaceful villages and unspoilt countryside.

After 2 miles (from Chalford) reach the White Horse Inn and turn left on to an unclassified road for Frampton Mansell.

FRAMPTON MANSELL, Glos
Important buildings in this village follow Cotswold tradition by dating mainly from the years of wool prosperity. Manor Farmhouse is of the late 17th century, and St Luke's Church was built in 1844.

Continue to Sapperton.

SAPPERTON, Glos
Views from the local churchyard extend along the length of the Golden Valley. Cotswold-stone cottages in the area date back to the 17th century, and Daneway House (1 mile north-west) can claim even greater antiquity, with parts dating at least from the 13th century. The Thames and Severn Canal ran through here via a 2½-mile tunnel through which 18th- and 19th-century bargees propelled their craft by lying on their backs and pushing against the walls or roof with their feet. This was commonly known as 'legging it'.

Turn right, then meet a T-junction and turn left. After 1 mile turn right to Daglingworth.

DAGLINGWORTH, Glos
Saxon work has survived in the local church in spite of major 19th-century rebuilding.

Continue, and ⅔ mile beyond the village turn right on to the A417 for Cirencester.

CIRENCESTER, Glos
In Roman times Cirencester was *Corinium Dobunorum*, the second largest town in England and the focus of several major highways. When the Romans withdrew the town declined, but wool later boosted it and wool money paid for its Church of St John the Baptist, one of the largest of its kind in the country. The town's Corinium Museum contains one of the country's most comprehensive collections of Roman remains, which includes mosaic floors and Romano-British sculpture.

Follow SP 'Burford A433' to leave Cirencester. Drive to Barnsley.

BARNSLEY, Glos
The church at Barnsley was restored in the 19th century, but its 16th-century tower and two ancient carved tables survived. Sir Isaac Newton's library was discovered at Barnsley Park after it had been removed from Thame Park.

Continue to Bibury.

BIBURY, Glos
William Morris thought Bibury 'the most beautiful village in England'. Most of its stone-built houses have gardens that run down to the River Coln, and the Arlington Row (NT) of river-fronted cottages is famous. Near Arlington Mill, which houses a museum, is a bird sanctuary. Bibury Court Hotel is of Jacobean origin, and The Swan – at the end of the street – is a pleasant coaching inn.

Drive to the Swan Inn and take an unclassified road through the Coln Valley to Ablington.

ABLINGTON, Glos
This lovely River Coln community has a late 16th-century manor house with an impressive barn. There is a prehistoric long barrow near by.

After Ablington turn left to cross a river bridge over the Coln. Later turn right and continue to Winson.

WINSON, Glos
Winson Manor dates from 1740, but Manor Farm is of slightly earlier origin. Most of the village cottages are of 17th- or 18th-century date, and the church is early-Norman.

Drive through the village and turn right for Coln Rogers.

COLN ROGERS, Glos
The nave and chancel of local St Andrew's Church are Saxon. Both the Old Rectory, at the south end of the village, and Lower Farm, belong to the 17th century.

Proceed to Coln St Dennis.

COLN ST DENNIS, Glos
Coln St Dennis has a Norman church and a 19th-century rectory. The hotel at Fosse Bridge, a ¼ mile to the north-west, is also of 19th-century date. Colnpen is a 300ft long barrow near by.

Turn left for Fossebridge, left again on to the A429, then right on to an unclassified road. Follow SP 'Chedworth Roman Villa'.

CLEPWORTH ROMAN VILLA, Glos
Chedworth Roman Villa (NT) dates from the 2nd to 4th centuries, and was rediscovered in 1864. It has various rooms and two bath suites laid out around two courtyards. The site has an excellent museum.

Return for 1½ miles into Yanworth.

YANWORTH, Glos
Traces of wall paintings, fragments of medieval glass, and a Norman font can be seen in Yanworth's 12th-century church.

Continue for 2 miles to the main road. Turn left on to the A429 and drive to the outskirts of Northleach.

NORTHLEACH, Glos
Northleach stands on high ground, east of the Roman Fosse Way, between the Coln and Windrush valleys. Its attractive stone-built

cottages and almshouses are dominated by a magnificent church. Nearby is the Cotswold Countryside Collection.

Continue to roundabout, turn left on to the A40 'Cheltenham' road, then after 2¾ miles pass the Puesdown Inn. After a further ¾ mile meet crossroads and turn right on to the unclassified 'Brockhampton' road. Proceed for 2¼ miles and cross the main road for Brockhampton. After ¼ mile meet crossroads and turn right SP 'Charlton Abbots'. Drive to the next crossroads, turn right SP 'Guiting Power'. Ascend and, at next crossroads, turn left along Roel Hill, passing Sudeley Castle.

SUDELEY CASTLE, Glos
Catherine Parr, the last of Henry VIII's wives, lived in this medieval castle (open). In 1858 it was reconstructed by Sir Gilbert Scott, who also designed Catherine's tomb to replace one destroyed during the Civil War.

Continue into Winchcombe.

WINCHCOMBE, Glos
Ancient Winchcombe was once capital of the Kingdom of Mercia. The site of its abbey, founded in 797 and destroyed by Henry VIII, is being excavated. Within the town hall is a Folk and Police Museum.

Mellow stone houses nestle amongst rolling Cotswold scenery at Bibury.

Follow the A46 'Cheltenham' road. After ⅓ mile reach an unclassified left turn leading to prehistoric Belas Knap.

BELAS KNAP, Glos
About 2 miles south-south-west of Winchcombe is the 180ft-long Belas Knap long barrow (AM). This was restored in 1930 and is considered one of the finest of its type extant.

Return and continue along the A46, with extensive views from the highest area in the Cotswolds.

CLEEVE HILL, Glos
Early 20th-century St Peter's Church shares Cleeve Hill with 17th-century Cockbury Court and 18th-century Hayes. The area is dominated by lofty Cleeve Cloud.

CLEEVE CLOUD, Glos
Overshadowing Cleeve Hill is the massive 1,031ft bulk of Cleeve Cloud, one of the highest points in the Cotswolds. Magnificent views can be enjoyed from its summit.

Continue the descent through Prestbury to Cheltenham, passing the racecourse and airfield on the way.

Several architectural styles are incorporated to glorious effect in Cirencester's parish church.

REGENCY TOWNS AND COTSWOLD VILLAGES

Cheltenham has become a byword for refinement, elegance and gentility, qualities it has managed to preserve, with its tree-lined walks, exclusive shops and graceful architecture. More rural but scarcely less elegant is Pershore in the Vale of Evesham, while Tewkesbury is a rare survival of a medieval town.

CHELTENHAM, Glos

The architects of Regency Cheltenham created a supremely elegant town where houses are arranged in patterns of leafy squares, crescents and avenues. The material used was either cream-coloured ashlar from Leckhampton quarry, or brick faced with stucco of the same delicate shade. Balconies of finely wrought iron adorn many of the buildings, adding a Continental atmosphere to the streets and squares. Cheltenham became fashionable as a spa town in the 18th century after the discovery of what is now called the Royal Old Well, and, like Bath, the whole town was designed and rebuilt during the 18th and early-19th centuries. The atmosphere is best appreciated in Lansdown Place, the Promenade, Suffolk Square,

Montpellier Walk and Montpellier Parade. The Pittville Pump Room (OACT), with its colonnaded façade, portico and beautiful interior, is a masterpiece of the Greek Revival style. South of the High Street, is Cheltenham Ladies' College, one of the oldest and most famous girls' public schools in Britain.

Leave Cheltenham on the A46, SP 'Broadway', and continue to Prestbury.

PRESTBURY, Glos

Prestbury Park, the famous steeplechase course where the prestigious Gold Cup takes place every spring, is situated just outside the village, now a residential suburb of Cheltenham. Prestbury lies at the foot of Cleeve Hill, the highest (1,082ft) point of the Cotswold Hills; from the summit the views are superb.

At the end of Prestbury turn left and climb on to Cleeve Hill, then descend to Winchcombe.

WINCHCOMBE, Glos

Many pretty gardens in the main street slope down to the River Isbourne which flows by Winchcombe. Buildings of Cotswold stone, with uneven stone roofs, preserve the charm and character of the town, once the seat of a great Benedictine Abbey, which was so thoroughly destroyed by Lord Seymour of Sudeley Castle at the time of the Reformation, that no trace of it survives. The Railway Museum (OACT) has a fine collection of relics of the steam age. Overlooking the village is Sudeley Castle, (OACT) the home of Catherine Parr — one of Henry VIII's wives who married her lover, Seymour, after the king's death. She is buried in the chapel having died a year later during childbirth. Interesting art collections, costume and furniture exhibitions can be seen in the house, which was restored in the 19th century after suffering severe damage during the Civil War. The parkland surrounding the house has an ornamental lake with a colourful assortment of wildfowl.

Continue on the A46 and after 2 miles (right) a short detour leads to the remains of Hailes Abbey.

HAILES ABBEY, Glos

The romantic ruins of the great Cistercian abbey (AM, NT), founded in 1246, stir the imagination to reconstruct the austere monastic life of medieval

times, when pilgrims came to revere the 'Blood of Hailes', a sacred phial said to contain the blood of Christ. The small museum on the site displays fragments of sculpture from the abbey.

The main tour continues on the A46. At the Toddington roundabout take the B4077, SP 'Stow-on-the-Wold'. ¾ mile farther, at a crossroads, turn left, SP 'Stanway'. Continue on this unclassified road, and in 1¼ miles keep right for Stanton.

STANTON, Glos

Beautiful villages abound in the Cotswolds, where the local golden stone blends so well with the wooded hills, but Stanton, thanks to the restoration of the 17th-century houses that line both sides of its main street, is exceptionally attractive. Village cross, church, manor house and cottages are all in harmony with the gentle countryside around.

Follow SP 'Broadway' and in ¾ mile turn right on to the A46. In 1 mile turn left for Aston Somerville, then at the T-junction turn right, SP 'Evesham'. In another mile, turn left on to the A435, SP 'Cheltenham', to reach the edge of Sedgeberrow. In 1¼ miles turn right for Ashton-under-Hill, then turn right and continue to Elmley Castle. Turn right through the village, then left, SP 'Pershore', for Little Comberton. At the crossroads turn right, SP 'Wick', and after 1½ miles turn right on to the A44, SP 'Evesham'. In 2 miles turn left on to an unclassified road for Cropthorne.

Bredon Hill — 961ft high

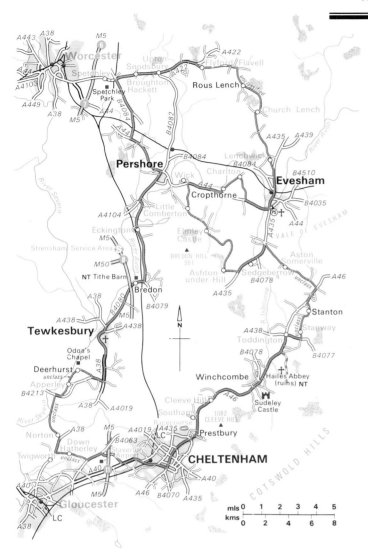

SPETCHLEY PARK, Herefs & Worcs
The house, home of the Berkeley family, is not open, but the beautiful wooded grounds (OACT) around the ornamental lake, and the garden centre, can be visited. Red and fallow deer roam the park which extends on both sides of the main road, and is linked by a graceful iron footbridge.

The main tour turns left on to the B4084, SP 'Pershore'. In 2 miles bear right, then in another 1½ miles turn left on to the A44 to reach the edge of Pershore.

PERSHORE, Herefs & Worcs
The River Avon flows past the end of the High Street of this enchanting market town in the Vale of Evesham. The land round about is celebrated for Pershore plums, which come in 2 varieties, purple and yellow. Pershore's architecture is classical Georgian, most of the elegant houses being faced in stone or stucco. The great abbey church was only partially destroyed at the Reformation, and what remains, the tower, crossing and transepts, is extremely fine.

At the edge of Pershore turn right on to the A4104, SP 'Upton', then in 2 miles turn left on to the B4080, SP 'Tewkesbury'. Cross the River Avon by a 16th-century bridge to reach Eckington. In 3 miles turn right into Bredon.

BREDON, Herefs & Worcs
Bredon, standing high above the River Avon, is a remarkably pretty village, with an impressive Norman church whose slender spire soars 160ft above the countryside around. A fine stone rectory and 2 large private residences, one Jacobean, the other Georgian, set off the church. Bredon tithe barn (NT) is a magnificent limestone structure with a steep-pitched, stone shingled roof, and dates from the 14th century.

3¼ miles beyond Bredon join the A38 to enter Tewkesbury.

TEWKESBURY, Glos
Almost all the buildings in Tewkesbury are old, timber-framed structures of considerable charm. Shortage of space in the multitude of narrow winding alleys leading off the main street has meant that the houses are tightly packed, producing a pleasing jumble of styles. It is a fascinating town to explore and Tewkesbury Abbey is one of the finest Norman buildings in the country. The interior is magnificent, particularly in the presbytery, where the roof is supported by superb vaulting. Several medieval stained-glass windows have survived, depicting the Last Judgment and the Coronation of the Virgin.

Leave Tewkesbury on the A38, SP 'Gloucester'. In 3 miles turn right on to the B4213, SP 'Ledbury', then in ½ mile bear right for Deerhurst.

DEERHURST, Glos
The village has the distinction of possessing 2 Saxon churches. St Mary's was built in the 9th and 10th centuries, while Odda's Chapel, an outstanding Saxon survival, was dedicated in 1056, as an inscribed stone, now in the Ashmolean Museum at Oxford, proves. The chapel was 'lost' for centuries, as it had been incorporated in a half-timbered farmhouse, until found in 1965.

Continue to Apperley and in 1 mile turn right on to the B4213 then take the next turning left, SP 'Norton'. Continue to Norton, and at the T-junction, turn right, then right again on to the A38, SP 'Gloucester'. In 1 mile turn left on to an unclassified road for Down Hatherley, then in another mile turn left on to the B4063, SP 'Cheltenham'. At the next roundabout join the A40 for the return to Cheltenham.

CROPTHORNE, Herefs & Worcs
Black and white cottages set in pretty gardens characterise this charming village overlooking the River Avon. In the church are monuments to the Dingley family, whose descendants became mayors of Evesham but lost respectability in the 18th century when Samuel Dingley murdered his brother in cold blood after years of quarrels and bitter rivalry.

Continue through Cropthorne to Charlton. Turn right, then in 1½ miles turn left to rejoin the A44. In 1¼ miles, turn left on to the A435 to enter Evesham.

EVESHAM, Herefs & Worcs
The town stands in a bend of the River Avon, the hub of a fertile region of orchards in the Vale of Evesham. In the centre of the market place is the charming half-timbered Round House (Booth Hall) with overhanging upper storeys and gabled attics. It was not a market hall originally, despite its position, but one of the many attractive old inns that Evesham has preserved in its pleasant streets. From the market place an old gateway leads to the abbey gardens where there is a splendid 16th-century bell tower, once a part of the ruined abbey. Flanking the bell tower are the 2

churches of St Nicholas and All Saints.

Leave Evesham on the A435, SP 'Birmingham', and in 1½ miles turn left for Lenchwick. At the T-junction, turn left, and continue to Church Lench. Here turn right then left for Rous Lench.

ROUS LENCH, Herefs & Worcs
There are 5 little villages, all within a stone's throw of each other, that bear the name Lench. Rous Lench is the largest and prettiest of the villages. It takes its name from the Rouses, a local family, one of whom, in the late 19th century, built most of the attractive houses that stand around the shady village green. The old manor house (not open) is famous for its topiary yew garden, which dates back 300 years, and can be glimpsed from the main road.

Continue through Rous Lench and in 1 mile, at a T-junction, turn left for Flyford Flavell. In ½ mile join the A422 and continue through Upton Snodsbury to Broughton Hackett. In 1¼ miles a detour can be taken by continuing on the A422 for ¾ mile to Spetchley Park.

The ornate Neptune Fountain in Cheltenham's Promenade is based on the famous Trevi Fountain in Rome

CHIPPENHAM, Wilts

Chippenham has been a market community since Saxon days when King Alfred stayed here and hunted in the neighbouring forests, and despite housing and industrial developments its character is essentially the same. The centre of this stone-built town is Market Place and the oldest building is the 15th century town hall.

Leave Chippenham on the A4, SP, 'Bath'. In 3½ miles turn left on to an unclassified road for Corsham.

CORSHAM, Wilts

The mellow, stone buildings of the old village centre are among the best in Wiltshire. Corsham was a weaving village in medieval times and the gabled weavers' cottages still stand in their cobbled street, as does the gabled block of the Hungerford Almshouses and School, dating from the same period. The school has kept its original seating arrangements and the master's old-fashioned pulpit desk. Near the church stands Corsham Court (OACT) — an Elizabethan stone manor house first built by 'Customer Smythe', a wealthy haberdasher from London. The present E-shaped design and pinnacled gables are a result of Paul Methuen's ownership from 1745.

Leave on the B3353, SP 'Melksham'. At Gastard, branch left by the Harp and Crown PH, SP 'Lacock', and continue to the A350 and turn right. Take the next turning left into Lacock.

LACOCK, Wilts

Lacock (NT) could stand as the pattern of the perfect English village with its twisting streets, packed with attractive buildings from the 15th to 18th centuries. Half-timbered, grey-stone, redbrick and whitewashed façades crowd together and above eye-level, uneven upper storeys, gabled ends and stone roofs blend with charming ease. Of all the outstanding buildings in the village, Lacock Abbey (NT) on the outskirts is the most beautiful. It began as an Augustinian nunnery in 1232, but after the Reformation Sir William Sharington used the remains to build a Tudor mansion, preserving the cloisters, sacristy and nuns' chapter house, and adding an octagonal tower, a large courtyard and twisted chimney stacks. It was here that W. H. Fox Talbot conducted his pioneer photographic experiments.

Turn right in Lacock, SP 'Bowden Hill', and shortly pass the entrance to Lacock Abbey. After crossing the River Avon ascend Bowden Hill, with fine views to the right. After 2 miles the tour reaches the A342. From here a detour can be made by turning left to Bowood.

BETWEEN THE COTSWOLD HILLS AND THE MARLBOROUGH DOWNS

Golden manor houses stud the countryside in the lee of the chalky heights of the Marlborough Downs and the gentler slopes of the Cotswold Hills. Between them glorious open vistas are broken only by wool towns and villages with their market crosses and stone church spires.

Silbury Hill, built c2500BC, would have taken 700 men 10 years to complete then

BOWOOD, Wilts

The magnificent Georgian house of Bowood is brilliantly complemented by its extensive gardens. The park was laid out by Capability Brown between 1762-1768 and is considered by many as the finest park in England, centring on a long narrow lake. The development of the formal gardens immediately surrounding the house and the establishment of the pleasure gardens, which cover almost a hundred acres, evolved between 1820-1850. The planting in the pleasure grounds, which began in 1820, now forms one of the great collections of trees and shrubs in England. It includes the tallest Cedar of Lebanon and poplar in the country. The whole area is mown. At the outfall from the lake are cascades and grottos, which give a sense of mystery and excitement. During May and June, a separate woodland garden is open which covers over 50 acres. The garden surrounds the family mausoleum, built in 1761 by Robert Adam. Interlinking paths wind beneath tall oaks, through banks of rhododendrons and azaleas. The house itself contains superb collections of paintings, sculpture, costumes and Victoriana. The fine library was designed by Robert Adam, and also on view is the laboratory where Dr Joseph Priestley discovered oxygen gas in 1774.

The main tour turns right, SP 'Devizes', into the village of Sandy Lane. Continue through Rowde to Devizes.

DEVIZES, Wilts

New shopping developments at Devizes have enhanced, rather than detracted from, its busy country town atmosphere. Market Square is the most attractive area and in the centre of this is the market cross, surrounded by 18th-century buildings, including the Black Swan and the Bear Hotel. Devizes, sited on the edge of Salisbury Plain, is a good centre for exploring this area rich in traces of prehistoric man.

Leave Devizes on the A361, SP 'Swindon'. In 2¼ miles turn right, SP 'Bishop's Cannings'. In ½ mile turn right SP 'Florton', into Bishop's Cannings.

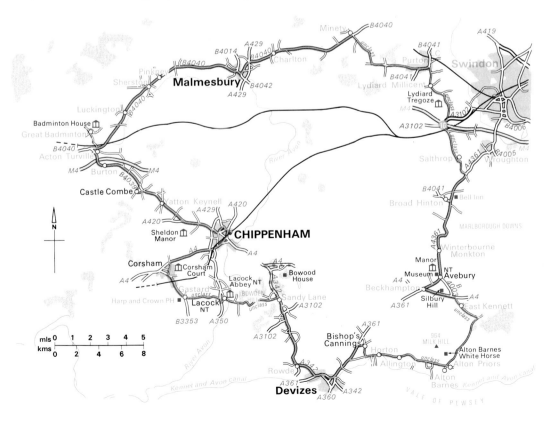

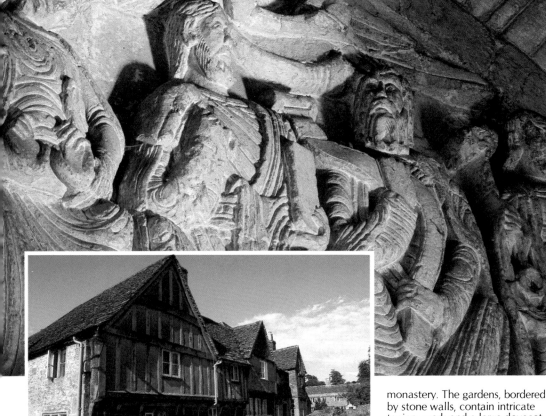

Lacock was built with the wealth brought by the wool trade and has remained intact since the 18th century

BISHOP'S CANNINGS, Wilts
Thatched cottages lie in the shadow of St Mary's Church which was built as a parish church on the Bishop of Salisbury's estate during the 13th century. There is a curious confessional chair inside, on which an enormous hand is painted together with a number of gloomy Latin inscriptions about death and sin, such as 'The hour of death is uncertain'.

In another ½ mile, at the T-junction, turn left, SP 'Alton Priors', then cross the Kennet and Avon Canal and continue to the outskirts of Allington. After 2 miles there are views to the left of the Alton Barnes White Horse.

ALTON BARNES WHITE HORSE, Wilts
Above the twin villages of Alton Barnes and Alton Priors is a white horse carved in chalk. An unlikely local story says a man called Jack the Painter was paid £20 to cut it, but he fled with the money instead. Rough justice was later done when Jack was caught and hanged, and someone else carved the horse in 1812.

At the T-junction turn left, SP 'Marlborough'. In 2 miles turn left, SP 'East and West Kennet'. Continue through East Kennet then at the A4 turn left, SP 'Chippenham'. Later pass the prehistoric mound of Silbury Hill to the right.

SILBURY HILL, Wilts
No-one knows why this huge, mysterious conical hill (AM) was created. One fanciful theory is that the devil made it and buried beneath is a mounted warrior in gold armour. At about 130ft high, it is the highest artificial mound in Europe and covers 5½ acres.

At the Beckhampton roundabout take the A4361, SP 'Swindon', and in 1 mile keep left for Avebury.

AVEBURY, Wilts
Avebury village stands inside the outer ditch of a huge prehistoric monument — Avebury stone circle (AM). Little is known about the purpose of these famous ancient standing stones, spread over about 28 acres, but the largest ring has 100 sarsen stones left now, and what are actually the remains of 2 inner circles are scattered, seemingly at random, about the village. Avebury Manor (NT) is an Elizabethan manor house standing on the site of a small Benedictine monastery. The gardens, bordered by stone walls, contain intricate topiary work and a large dovecot.

Continue on the Swindon road with views of the Marlborough Downs to the right. After 3½ miles pass the Bell Inn, then in another 1½ miles turn left, SP 'Wootton Bassett'. Follow this for 3¼ miles to the motorway roundabout and take the A3102, SP 'Swindon'. In ½ mile, at the next roundabout, turn left, SP 'Lydiard Millicent'. In 1 mile, to the left, lies the Lydiard Tregoze Estate.

LYDIARD TREGOZE, Wilts
Sir John St John was chiefly responsible for the spectacular monuments and decorations inside Lydiard Tregoze church which includes a splendid folding screen dedicated to his parents and an elaborate white marble monument for himself, his 2 wives and their 13 children.
The church stands in the park attached to the manor house of Lydiard Tregoze (OACT) in which the St John family lived for 4 centuries. It has been extensively restored and is mainly Georgian in appearance and interior furnishing.

Continue on the unclassified road and in ½ mile turn left, SP 'Purton', for Lydiard Millicent. At the far end of the village turn right and continue to Purton. Turn left in to the main street (B4041) and at the end of the village turn right on to an unclassified road (no SP). In 1¼ miles go over the crossroads, SP 'Minety', then ½ mile farther branch right. At the edge of Minety turn left on to the B4040, for Malmesbury.

MALMESBURY, Wilts
A tall, slender spire soars up above Malmesbury which, in turn, sits up on an isolated hill amid the surrounding water meadows. The spire belongs to the town's majestic abbey which has stood here since the 7th century. Look particularly at the splendid south porch covered in carvings and sculptures: it is one of England's best examples of Romanesque art.

Leave on the B4040, SP 'Bristol', and continue through Pinkney, Sherston and Luckington to Acton Turville. 1¼ miles to the north is Great Badminton and Badminton House.

BADMINTON HOUSE, Avon
The exciting 3-day event horse trials held annually at Badminton House have made the estate famous. Both the stables' and hunt kennels' magnificence reflect Badminton's long association with horses and hunting. At the heart of the great park is the Palladian mansion, remodelled by William Kent in about 1740. It has been the home of the Dukes of Beaufort since the 17th century. The entrance hall, hung with hunting scenes, was where the game of badminton evolved.

The main tour turns left, SP 'Chippenham'. At the Fox and Hounds PH turn left again on to the B4039. Cross the M4 and pass through Burton, then in 2½ miles turn right on to an unclassified road to Castle Combe.

CASTLE COMBE, Wilts
This village, portrayed on many a poster and picture-postcard as a haven of beauty and tranquility, well deserves its fame. A river, Bye Brook, flows through the streets under stone foot-bridges, and honey-coloured cottages — their roofs grown uneven with the passage of time — surround the market cross.

Return to the B4039, SP 'Chippenham', and turn right for Yatton Keynell. In 1¼ miles turn left on to the A420. In 1 mile, on the right, is the turning for Sheldon Manor.

SHELDON MANOR, Wilts
Terraced gardens, rose beds, water gardens and ancient yew trees encircle the Plantaganet manor house (OACT). The oldest part of the house is its 13th-century porch, still with its original stone water cistern which was fed from pipes in the roof. Within the grounds is a 15th-century detached chapel belonging to the house.

Continue on the A420 for the return to Chippenham.

COTSWOLD VALLEYS AT THE SOURCE OF THE THAMES

Stretching northwards from the infant Thames, the deep valley of the River Churn and the broader valleys of the Coln and the Leach bore into the wooded Cotswold Hills. The towns and villages of the Thames stand out amid the flat water meadows while the Cotswold valleys protect their own dreamy villages.

CIRENCESTER, Glos
This 'capital' of the Cotswolds is the epitome of an old market town, with its beautiful Tudor church dominating the busy market place. The church, built from the riches of the wool trade, has a magnificent 3-storeyed south porch with delicate fan vaulting and many interesting brasses. Around the attractive Georgian market place are a number of old streets where the stone-built houses of the wealthy Elizabethan wool merchants still stand. Cirencester stands at the meeting point of 3 Roman roads — the Fosse Way, Akeman Street, and one of the 2 Ermine Streets. Roman remains, including some fine mosaic pavements, are housed in the Corinium Museum. Cirencester Park (house not open) stands in lovely woodland and has a superb 5-mile-long avenue of chestnut trees. The 17th-century poet Alexander Pope was a frequent visitor to the house, and a rustic seat at the edge of the tree-lined avenues called the Seven Rides is named after him.

Leave on the A429, SP 'The South West' and 'Chippenham'. In 1½ miles go forward on to the A433, SP 'Bristol'. After another mile, in the meadow to the right, is the reputed source of the River Thames. Pass under a railway bridge and turn left on to an unclassified road for Kemble. Cross the main road into the village, then go over the staggered crossroads, SP 'Ewen', follow SP 'South Cerney'.

SOUTH CERNEY, Glos
Just outside South Cerney, old gravel pits have been transformed into lakes which form part of the Cotswold Water Park; the marina here is gay with sailing dinghies and motor boats on summer weekends. The village stands on the River Churn and has several attractive old streets, including one with the extraordinary name of Bow Wow.

Turn right at the war memorial into Broadway Lane. In ¾ mile pass the Costwold Water Park and in ½ mile turn right, SP 'Ashton Keynes'. In 1¼ miles turn left and shortly branch left to Ashton Keynes.

ASHTON KEYNES, Wilts
Small bridges spanning the little stream of the infant Thames lead up to the doors of several of the cottages at one end of Ashton Keynes, and at the other, a group of old stone houses form a picturesque scene with an old watermill. Just outside the village, the church and manor house look out over peaceful countryside.

At the end of the village turn left on to the Cricklade road then bear right. In 2 miles turn left on to the B4040, and in another 1½ miles turn left again to enter Cricklade. At the clock tower turn right and follow SP 'Swindon' then in ¾ mile join the A419. In 1 mile turn left on to an unclassified road for Castle Eaton. Continue on the Highworth road through Hannington and in 1¼ miles turn left on to the B4019 for Highworth. Turn left on to the A361 Stow road and after 4 miles pass a riverside park before reaching Lechlade.

LECHLADE, Glos
Just outside Lechlade, a pleasant riverside park extends along the banks of the Thames, locally referred to (as at Oxford) as the Isis. Halfpenny Bridge leads across the river and into the Georgian market place. A delightful characteristic of the village are the many gazebos in the trim gardens of the older houses. The poet Shelley, journeying upriver from Windsor, was inspired by the calm of the river and the churchyard to write the poem *Stanzas in a Summer Evening Churchyard* while staying at the local inn. By St John's Bridge 3 shires meet — Gloucestershire, Oxfordshire and Wiltshire — and the nearby lock is an ideal picnic spot.

Leave on the A417 Faringdon road and in ¾ mile cross St John's Bridge. In 2 miles pass the grounds of Buscot Park.

BUSCOT PARK, Oxon
The Classical mansion (NT), built the Edward Loveden Townsend in 1780, is the home of a notable collection of European paintings spanning several centuries, from the Italian Renaissance to the pre-Raphaelites and 20th-century works. 18th-century paintings include a Gainsborough landscape.

The collection was begun in the 19th century by Alexander Henderson, Lord Faringdon, and continued by his descendants. The most famous portrait is by Rembrandt of Clement de Jongh. The house also contains lovely furniture of rosewood and satinwood.

Continue to Faringdon.

FARINGDON, Oxon
A traditional market town famous for its dairy produce and fine bacon, Faringdon has many interesting old inns and an 18th-century Market Hall. Faringdon House (not open) was owned by Lord Barners and the folly in the grounds was built by him during the Depression of the 1930s to relieve local unemployment. The 14th-century Radcot Bridge between Faringdon and Clanfield is said to be the oldest of the Thames bridges.

From the market square branch left on to the A4095, and after passing the church turn left. In 2½ miles cross the historic Radcot Bridge. At Clanfield go forward on to the B4020 for Alvescot. In ¼ mile turn left on to an unclassified road to Kencot and 1¼ miles beyond the village turn right into Filkins.

FILKINS, Oxon
Wistaria and clematis, for which the Cotswold villages are so famous, clamber over the pale stone of houses, barns and garden walls. Chestnut trees, laden with flower in spring, spread over the quiet main street of Filkins.

In the village turn right and after 1 mile turn right on to the A361, SP 'Stow'. In 2 miles, at the crossroads, turn left, SP 'Wildlife Park', and pass the entrance to the Cotswold Wildlife Park.

COTSWOLD WILDLIFE PARK, Oxon
In 1969, 120 acres of wooded parkland were chosen to house the animal collection of the Cotswold Wildlife Park. They have taken as their emblem one of their most attractive creatures, the chestnut-coloured Red panda, a smaller relative of the Giant panda, whose natural habitat is the high forests of the Himalayas and western China. There are

Most Roman villas had mosaic flooring such as this which can be seen at the Corinium Museum, Cirencester

many African and South American mammals, an interesting Reptile House, with crocodiles, alligators and poisonous snakes, and numerous spacious aviaries of exotic birds, including a Tropical House where sunbirds, brilliant humming birds and bluebirds hover among the blossoms of hibiscus and bougainvillea.

Continue on the unclassified road, and in ½ mile go over the crossroads, SP 'Eastleach Martin', then ½ mile later branch left and follow a narrow byroad to the twin Eastleaches.

EASTLEACH, Glos
The village consists of 2 charming Cotswold hamlets, Eastleach Martin and Eastleach Turville, standing on opposite banks of the River Leach. An old stone clapper bridge leads from one to the other, named after John Keble (founder of Keble College, Oxford), whose family were lords of the manor of Turville. The 2 old village churches were built within sight of each other; that of Eastleach Martin has 5 old sundials; that of its neighbour, a fine Norman arched doorway with a carving of Christ in Glory.

At Eastleach Turville keep right through the village on the Hatherop road. At the T-junction turn left, then in ½ mile turn right, and 2 miles farther turn right again into Hatherop. Turn left for Coln St Aldwyn. Turn left, SP 'Fairford', then cross the River Coln and ascend to Quenington.

QUENINGTON, Glos
A number of lovingly-restored 17th-century stone houses grace the village street, but it is the 12th-century village church, with its 2 beautifully carved Norman doorways that attracts visitors from miles around. The north doorway depicts in vivid detail the Harrowing of Hell and the south doorway shows Christ placing a crown on the head of the Virgin Mary.

At the green, turn left then at the end of the village recross the Coln and continue to Fairford.

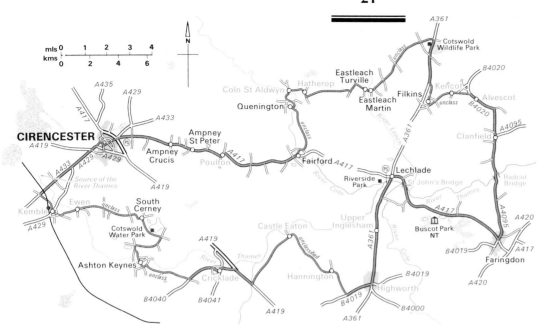

FAIRFORD, Glos

All the prosperity of the medieval wool trade is exemplified in the Church of St Mary at Fairford. The wool merchants, John Tame and his son Sir Edmund, paid for it to be built at the end of the 15th century and by a miracle the glorious stained-glass windows have been preserved almost intact. The church stands beside the river, overlooking the village square where houses of soft grey Cotswold stone have stood, their appearance virtually unaltered, for more than 200 years. A stroll around the streets leading off from the market place reveals old houses of all periods and, at the edge of the manor park, a picturesque stone watermill. The American air-base near Fairford was used for trials of *Concorde*.

Leave on the A417 and pass through Poulton to the villages of Ampney St Peter and Ampney Crucis.

THE AMPNEYS, Glos

Four villages all bearing the name Ampney. Ampney St Peter is generally thought to be the prettiest of them, with its village green bordered by old cottages. Ampney Crucis nearby, a pleasing blend of old and new, stands on the Ampney Brook. It takes the second part of its name from the ancient cross in the churchyard. At Down Ampney, some distance away, the composer Ralph Vaughan Williams was born.

Continue on the A417 for the return to Cirencester.

Fairford's 17th-century mill house stands beside the River Coln. St Mary's Church nearby marks the centre of the village

DARTMOUTH, Devon

Naval tradition in Dartmouth goes back to medieval times when the port was one of the busiest in England. The ships of the 2nd and 3rd Crusades anchored here on their way to the Holy Land, and in peacetime Dartmouth grew rich on the proceeds of the wine trade with France. In wartime, the town's formidable 15th-century castle could rake the estuary with cannon shot and close off the river mouth with a massive chain running across to Kingwear Castle on the opposite shore. Today the town is dominated by the Royal Naval College, designed by Sir Aston Webb and opened in 1905. Dartmouth's streets, climbing the steep wooded slope of the Dart Estuary, are intriguing to explore. Of the many ancient buildings scattered throughout the town, 14th-century Agincourt House contains a small museum, and there is another museum with a fine collection of model ships in the Butterwalk, a picturesque 17th-century market arcade. In the gardens on the quay stands what may be the world's oldest steam pumping engine, designed in 1725 by Thomas Newcomen, a native of Dartmouth. The 14th-century church of St Saviour, whose building was mainly financed by Sir John Hawley, 7 times mayor of the town, is worth a visit. The interior is richly decorated and contains an elaborate brass to Hawley and his 2 wives. Although the church door bears the date 1631, the ironwork depicting prancing leopards on the branches of a great tree belongs to the 14th century. Dartmouth has a carnival every year in July and its famous regatta is held on the Dart during late August.

Leave Dartmouth on the A379, SP 'Kingsbridge', and climb past the grounds of the Naval College. At the top turn left, SP 'Stoke Fleming' and 'Strete', and continue with occasional coastal views to Stoke Fleming.

STOKE FLEMING, Devon

Perched on the cliffs 300ft above the sea, the pretty streets of Stoke Fleming overlook a Mediterranean seascape; the white shingle of Blackpool Sands sweeping away to the south, framed by shelving headlands wooded with dark green pines. The tower of the 14th-century church served for centuries as a daymark for shipping; inside are two brasses, one, almost lifesize, to John Corp and his little grandaughter Elyenor, and one to Elias Newcomen, a 17th-century rector and ancestor of the Dartmouth born inventor, Thomas Newcomen. From the cliff path there is a fine view over Redlap Cove to the awesome Dancing Beggar rocks.

The tour skirts the cove of Blackpool Sands before ascending to Strete.

DARTMOUTH AND THE SOUTH HAMS

The scenery of the South Hams is a landscape of rounded hills and quiet valleys, of greens and browns. In contrast are the greys and blues of the slate cliffs and the rocky outline of the coast and it is the lure of the sea which leaves the working countryside free from bustling tourism.

The sheltered naval town of Dartmouth

STRETE, Devon

Old stone houses set in a pleasant sheltered valley stand in peaceful contrast to the wild slate cliffs of Pilchard's Cove. Down in this cove once lived a community of fishermen, but now only the placename survives; the houses long since destroyed by the sea.

Continue on the A379 and later descend to reach Slapton Sands.

SLAPTON SANDS & SLAPTON LEY, Devon

The simple obelisk on the edge of Slapton Sands was erected to commemorate the United States troops who used this area in World War II as a training ground to practise for the Normandy landings in 1944. The long stretch of shingle beach is a good hunting ground for collectors of shells and pretty pebbles, but bathing can sometimes be dangerous. A 3-mile sandbar, carrying the road, protects the freshwater lagoon of Slapton Ley from contamination by the sea. The lake and its surrounding reedbeds are now a nature reserve for birdlife, particularly waterfowl and reed warblers.

From Slapton Sands a turning to the right may be taken to Slapton.

SLAPTON, Devon

The village lies inland from the coast road, along the steep side of the valley. Many houses in its twisting streets have had their

walls rendered to hide shell damage. During the last war, villagers had to evacuate their homes when the US Army took the place over for manoeuvres. The ruined tower is all that remains of a 14th-century collegiate chantry founded by Sir Guy de Brien, one of the first Knights of the Garter and Standardbearer to Edward III.

The main tour continues with the coast road to Torcross.

TORCROSS, Devon

Pleasant old houses line the seafront along Start Bay at Torcross. Until the pilchard shoals disappeared from the south-west coast, Torcross was the most easterly fishing village to engage in this trade. The fishermen kept Newfoundland dogs who were trained to swim out to the returning boats and carry back ropes to those waiting on the shore, who hauled the laden craft to safety.

From Torcross bear right and continue inland to Stokenham.

STOKENHAM, Devon

In earlier centuries it was the duty of the inhabitants of this large hillside village to maintain a watch on the coast for shoals of fish. The fishing industry has declined, but the local fishermen still put out their pots for lobster and crab.

Turn left at Stokenham and at the next crossroads, turn left again, SP 'Start Point'. In ½ mile bear right and in just over another ½ mile pass the turning on the left to Beesands. Continue for nearly ¾ mile then bear left, and in 1 mile pass the road which leads to North Hallsands.

BEESANDS & NORTH HALLSANDS, Devon

Steep, narrow lanes lead to the two little hamlets of Beesands and North Hallsands at the southern end of Start Bay. The fierce and treacherous storms that periodically assault this part of the coast have, in the past, brought tragedy in their wake. In 1917 a former village of Hallsands, sited to the south of the present one, was completely destroyed in a storm because the Admiralty had allowed the excavation of its shingle bank. Remains of some of its houses still stand as an eerie memorial.

The main tour continues to Start Point.

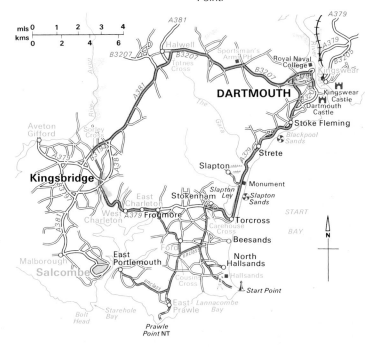

START POINT, Devon

The jagged ridge of Start Point overlooks the whole sweep of the South Hams coast and is an excellent vantage point for birdwatchers. Early migrants from the Continent alight here, and there are many native breeding colonies of seabirds. More seriously, the clifftop lighthouse warns of the Blackstone Rock on which many a ship has foundered. In 1581, a pirate was hanged in chains here as a warning to other outlaws of the ocean.

Return towards Stokenham and after 2¼ miles turn sharp left, SP 'East Prawle' and 'East Portlemouth'. In 1 mile at Cousin's Cross, bear left, then in 1¾ miles turn right. Alternatively, keep forward for the village of East Prawle and the road to Prawle Point.

PRAWLE POINT, Devon

Prawle Point (NT) is the extreme southern tip of Devon, looking west towards the Eddystone Lighthouse and east across Lannacombe Bay to Start Point. 'Prawle' comes from an old English word meaning 'look-out hill', and no name could better fit the lonely, sombre cliffs of this immemorial watching place.

The main tour continues to East Portlemouth.

Above: lobster-pots at Beesands

Right: The freshwater lagoon of Slapton Ley is separated from the sea by a shingle bar.

EAST PORTLEMOUTH, Devon

This small clifftop village looks across the Kingsbridge estuary to the lovely town of Salcombe, where pines, cypresses and palms flourish in almost Mediterranean profusion. Magnolia and fuchsia thrive here and there is an astonishing variety of wild flowers. The estuary is so sheltered that most plants bloom early and fruit ripens early. There are fine views up the many-branched estuary to Kingsbridge and beyond to the bleak expanse of Dartmoor. To the south, paths along the cliffs (NT) lead past sandy coves and weathered rocks as far as Prawle Point.

Return along the unclassified road, SP 'Kingsbridge'. In 2½ miles, at the T-junction, turn left, then in 1¾ miles go over the crossroads, SP 'Frogmore' and 'Kingsbridge'. In ½ mile descend to the hamlet of Ford and turn sharp left and in ¾ mile, at the T-junction, turn right. At the head of Frogmore Creek bear left across the bridge, then turn left on to the A379 for Frogmore.

FROGMORE, Devon

All over the South Hams district slate was used for building, both for important structures such as Dartmouth Castle and for farms and cottages. There were quarries at Frogmore and the nearby village of Molescombe, and traces of old workings, some dating back to medieval times, can be seen along Frogmore Creek.

Continue on the A379 and pass through East and West Charleton before reaching Kingsbridge.

KINGSBRIDGE, Devon

Kingsbridge, an attractive little place at the head of the estuary, offers a sheltered harbour for yachting and is also the market centre for the area. Its town hall boasts an unusual, slate hung ball clock of 1875 and the 16th-century market arcade, the Shambles, restored in the 18th century, is particularly appealing. The miniature railway on the quay carries passengers on a ½ mile trip, and the Cookworthy Museum in Fore Street commemorates William Cookworthy. Born here in 1705, he discovered china clay in Cornwall and made the first true English porcelain.

Leave by the unclassified road SP 'Totnes'. At Sorley Green Cross turn right on to the B3194 and in just over 1 mile turn left on to the A381. After 4¼ miles turn right on to the B3207, SP 'Dartmouth'. In another 4 miles, at the Sportsman's Arms PH, bear right and continue with the B3207 which later joins the A379 for Dartmouth.

DEVON'S ANCIENT CAPITAL AND THE SOUTHERN COAST

From Exeter, 2,000-year-old capital of Devon, the tour follows the contours of the southern coastline from Starcross down to colourful, Italianate Torquay. Turning inland to the wooded slopes of the Haldon Hills, it finally descends to a chequerboard farmland and back to Exeter.

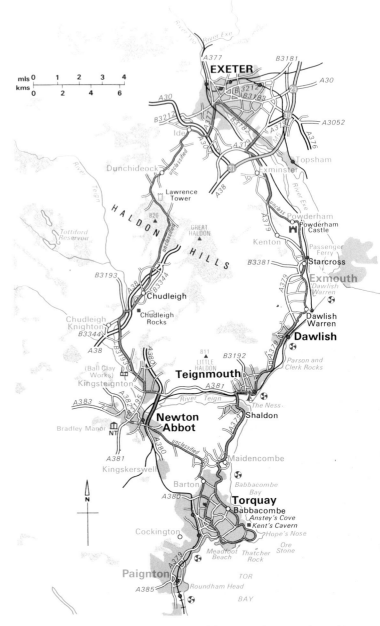

EXETER, Devon

Parts of the massive red walls of the old Roman city can still be seen, but, sadly, much of medieval Exeter was destroyed in World War II. The cathedral, with its 300ft nave, the longest span of Gothic vaulting in the world, was spared, as were the attractive old houses round the Close. The Guildhall in the High Street claims to be the oldest municipal building in England; inside, the hall is roofed with gilded beams supported by figures of bears holding staves. In Princesshay stands the entrance to a network of underground tunnels (OACT), constructed in the 13th century to carry fresh spring water around the city. Exeter's maritime traditions are well represented in the marvellous Maritime Museum on the quay which contains over 100 historic ships, from Arab dhows and Fijian outriggers to Portuguese craft and early steamships. Some are afloat on the canal and several can be boarded and explored. The handsome museum buildings have featured in the BBC television series 'The Onedin Line'.

Follow SP 'Exmouth' (A376) and at the Countess Wear roundabout, take the 3rd exit, SP 'Plymouth' (A38). Shortly cross the River Exe and the Exeter Canal, and at the next roundabout take the 1st exit on the A379, SP 'Dawlish'. Bypass Exminster and after 2½ miles turn left, SP 'Powderham Castle', and continue with views of the Exe estuary to the entrance to Powderham Castle.

POWDERHAM CASTLE, Devon

The castle (OACT), seat of the Earls of Devon, is a grand medieval fortified mansion, extended and altered in the 18th and 19th centuries but with a core some 400 years older. The somewhat flamboyantly decorated rooms are beautifully furnished and well worth a visit. Powderham sits in a magnificent deer park divided by grand avenues of cedar and ilex trees.

At the castle entrance turn left, then at the church turn right. After 1¼ miles turn left on to the A379 and continue to Starcross.

STARCROSS, Devon

Starcross, with its pretty little harbour, has kept much of its quiet village character. In the red tower of an old pumping house it preserves a relic of Brunel's short-lived atmospheric railway which ran through the village just before 1820. The engines were designed to work on the vacuum principle, using atmospheric pressure to drive the pistons, but the leather valves (there was no rubber then) leaked, and so, although trains between Exeter and Newton Abbot reached an incredible 70 mph for short stretches, the experiment failed.

Remain on the A379 for ½ mile then at the crossroads turn left on to an unclassified road, then turn left again for Dawlish Warren.

Teignmouth, seen from Shaldon across the busy estuary that separates them

DAWLISH WARREN, Devon

This promontory of sand and dune was created when a breakwater was built to protect the railway line. It has a fine golf course. On a spithead, the Warren Nature Reserve protects the vegetation, animal and birdlife in an area of just over 500 acres. It is the site of one of the estuary's high-tide wader roosts, which can be viewed from a large hide looking back up the estuary. The most exciting time for birds here is winter.

Turn right at the T-junction. In ½ mile turn left then in ¾ mile turn left again to rejoin the A379 for Dawlish.

DAWLISH, Devon

A charming 18th-century resort, Dawlish has a sandy beach framed by rocky cliffs and the main railway line from London to Penzance runs right along the sands. Through the centre of the town runs Dawlish Water, on whose banks the Lawn, a lovely miniature garden complete with cascading waterfalls and decorative black Australian swans, was created in the 19th century.

Follow SP 'Teignmouth'.

TEIGNMOUTH, Devon

A golfcourse overlooking the town from a height of 800ft, a safe sandy beach with a sheltered harbour and a pleasant promenade, combine to make Teignmouth a perennially popular resort. To the north the bay is guarded by the Parson and Clerk stack rocks, and to the south by a small lonely lighthouse. A number of twisty old lanes wind down to New Quay, built in the 19th century for the purpose of shipping Dartmoor granite to London to rebuild London Bridge — itself replaced in 1968 and shipped to the USA. A ferry runs across the estuary to Shaldon.

Follow SP 'Torbay' and in ¾ mile, at the traffic signals, turn left and cross the River Teign for Shaldon.

Two tiers of kings, queens, saints and angels are carved into the west front of Exeter Cathedral. Inset: the nave

SHALDON, Devon

The French set fire to Shaldon in 1690 and burned about 100 houses and its pretty streets now are lined with Regency buildings. Narrow lanes and alleys converge at Crown Square, the old centre, and among them the traditional Devon cottages of whitewashed cob (clay mixed with chopped straw) and thatch can be seen. Shaldon has 2 beaches; one, otherwise cut off at high tide, is reached by a 'smugglers' tunnel.

Turn right with the main road and continue with some good coastal views. In 4 miles, at the Palk Arms PH, turn left into Hartop Road (one-way), SP 'Babbacombe' and 'St Marychurch'. At the end turn left then at the mini-roundabout turn right. At the next traffic signals turn left into Babbacombe.

BABBACOMBE, Devon

A model village, set in 4 acres of perfectly landscaped miniature gardens, is the main attraction at Babbacombe. There are over 400 model buildings, each beautifully made and detailed, and over 1,200ft of model railway track. Babbacombe also has a pleasant pebbly beach.

Continue along Babbacombe Road and in just over ¾ mile turn left, SP 'Anstey's Cove', into a narrow, one-way road. Shortly pass the car park for Anstey's Cove.

ANSTEY'S COVE & KENT'S CAVERN, Devon

On the heights above Anstey's Cove is Kent's Cavern (AM), a Palaeolithic cave dwelling. There are 2 main caves, containing stalagmites and stalactites and numerous flint and bone implements and weapons, such as harpoons, have been found in them, as well as traces of prehistoric animals including the mammoth and woolly rhinoceros.

From the car park descend to Ilsham Road. (From here turn right to visit Kent's Cavern.) The main tour turns left and almost immediately left again into Ilsham Marine Drive. At the foot of the hill turn sharp left, SP 'The Town'. In ¾ mile, at the crossroads, turn left into Parkhill Road and continue to Torquay.

TORQUAY, Devon

Its white-painted villas, sub-tropical plants and shady gardens set among the limestone crags of the hillside overlooking the bay, have earned Torquay its title of queen of the Devon coast. From Marine Drive, which skirts the headland, there are superb views out across Tor Bay and inland to the town. Torquay is the creation of Sir Robert Palk, a governor of Madras, who made his own fortune in India and was left another by a friend, General Stinger Lawrence, which included the hamlet of Tor Quay. He appreciated the beauty of the site and exploited it during the Napoleonic Wars when the Continent was closed to holidaymakers: Torquay has never looked back. Among its attractions are Aqualand on Beacon Quay, the largest aquarium in the West Country, specialising in tropical marine fish; Torre Abbey Gardens, and the Torquay Museum in Babbacombe Road exhibits finds from Kent's Cavern and other south Devon caves.

Follow SP 'Teignmouth' A379 and at the mini-roundabout turn left into Hele Road. At the next roundabout take the 3rd exit into Barton Hill Road, SP 'Barton'. Ascend through Barton and near the top bear right, SP 'Newton'. Continue with views of Dartmoor ahead and at the T-junction turn left. At the next roundabout take the 3rd exit on to the A380, SP 'Exeter'. Alternatively, take the 2nd exit for Newton Abbot.

NEWTON ABBOT, Devon

A railway town with extensive marshalling yards, Newton Abbot's steep streets are lined with stepped terraces of workmen's cottages. All that remains of its church is the 14th-century tower at the town centre. Charles I once stayed at Forde House and so, later, did William of Orange after he had landed at Torbay when he came to rule England with Mary II. Wednesday is market day, when the town springs to life as people crowd in from the surrounding region. South-west of Newton Abbot, set in the deep valley of the River Lemon, lies Bradley Manor (NT), a charming 15th-century house with a gabled front and pleasingly irregular windows. It is considered to be one of the best examples of a medieval Gothic house in the West Country.

The main tour following the bypass crosses the River Teign then branch left SP 'Kingsteignton', and at the roundabout take the B3193 to Kingsteignton. Here at the Kings Arms PH, turn right, SP 'Exeter', then in just over ¼ mile turn left on to the B3193 SP 'Chudleigh'. In 3 miles cross the A38 and the River Teign. Shortly bear right to join the B3344, then ½ mile farther bear right again and continue to Chudleigh.

CHUDLEIGH, Devon

This pleasant little hillside town is much visited for the sake of its Rocks, a picturesque and romantic limestone outcrop just south of the village. There is a pretty waterfall here and a cavern called the Pixie's Hole. This has a distinctive stalagmite called the Pope's Head. On the walls, among countless less famous initials, are carved those of the poet Samuel Taylor Coleridge and his brother.

At the war memorial in Chudleigh branch left into Old Exeter Street. In 1 mile go forward, SP 'Exeter', and climb on to the Haldon Hills.

THE HALDON HILLS, Devon

The moorland slopes and woods of the Haldon Hills mark the start of the switchback landscapes of east Devon, where hill and valley alternate in a constant upheaval. From the tops of the hills there are wide views of the rich red farmland around Exeter and the patchwork effect of the small fields and hedges so typical of Devon. A landmark on the hills is Lawrence Tower, built by Sir Robert Palk in 1788 in memory of General Stringer Lawrence (see Torquay).

At the crossroads turn left, SP 'Dunchideock' and 'Ide', to follow a high ridge. After a mile, on the right, is Lawrence Tower and in ½ mile bear right. A long descent then leads to Ide. At the T-junction at the end of the village turn right, SP 'Exeter'. At the next roundabout, take the A377 for Exeter.

THE HILLS OF EAST DEVON

East Devon is a mild, well-rounded collection of contrasts. Gracious Regency coastal resorts rub shoulders with simple picturesque villages, sub-tropical gardens grow alongside native woodlands, and little stone farms fringe the parkland estates of grand country houses

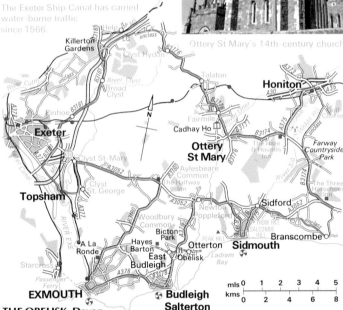

Ottery St Mary's 14th-century church.

HAYES BARTON, Devon
1 mile west of East Budleigh is the thatched 16th-century house of Hayes Barton (not open), birthplace of the famous adventurer Sir Walter Raleigh in 1552.

At the church turn right and shortly rejoin the A376. Proceed to the next crossroads, where there is an obelisk.

EXMOUTH, Devon
Situated on the estuary of the River Exe, this pleasant town and small port is the oldest and one of the largest seaside resorts in Devon. Most of its sandy beaches offer safe and sheltered bathing, and there are extensive coastal views. Local tourist facilities include swimming pools, the town museum and the Country Life museum. Good Georgian houses can be seen in The Beacon, and a picturesque group near by includes quaint almshouses and a tiny chapel. A passenger ferry makes frequent estuary crossings between Exmouth and Starcross.

A LA RONDE, Devon
This unusual circular house (open) stands east of the Exeter road and was built in 1798 by a Miss Jane Parminter. Its rooms are arranged around an octagonal hall, and the curious Shell Gallery is imaginatively decorated with shells, feathers, and fascinating pictures made from a variety of natural objects.

Leave Exmouth on the Budleigh Salterton road A376 and pass through attractive woodland scenery to Budleigh Salterton.

BUDLEIGH SALTERTON, Devon
During the 13th century this Ottermouth town was a salt-panning community supplying the local priory. At the mouth of the river is a shingle beach backed by red sandstone cliffs, and less than a mile away are the challenging fairways of

the best golf course in east Devon. Several Georgian houses can be seen in the town, and a small but interesting museum called the Fairlynch Arts Centre is in an 18th-century thatched house.

Keep forward through the town and then ascend and turn left. In 2 miles at crossroads turn left into East Budleigh.

EAST BUDLEIGH, Devon
Typical of many Devon communities, this charming little village has delightful thatched cottages and seems hardly to have been touched by time.

A miniature railway provides a mobile viewpoint from which to enjoy the varied scenery of Bicton Gardens.

THE OBELISK, Devon
This curious and rather attractive brick and stone cross is dated 1743 and carries route directions couched in biblical terms and phrases.

A possible detour leads 1 mile to the right, across the River Otter, to Otterton.

OTTERTON, Devon
Fine thatched cottages and a handsome chestnut grove combine to make this one of the most picturesque villages in the area. Restored Otterton Watermill is now an interesting craft centre.

Keep forward on the A376 and after ½ mile reach the entrance to Bicton Park on the left.

BICTON PARK, Devon
The gardens here are among the most beautiful in Britain. Le Nôtre, the designer of the superb gardens of Versailles in France, laid out the fine lawns of the Italian Garden in 1735 and there is an extensive pinetum. Other features include a narrow-gauge woodland railway, countryside and transport museums, the World of Tomorrow and World of Yesterday entertainment themes, and a large adventure playground.

After 1½ miles turn right on to the A3052 and enter Newton Poppleford. Cross the River Otter and ascend alongside Harpford Wood. Shortly turn right on to the B3176 SP 'Sidmouth' and skirt Bulverton Hill on the right before descending into Sidmouth.

SIDMOUTH, Devon
Created as a resort from almost nothing in the 18th century, Sidmouth has a shingle beach backed by spectacular red cliffs and is still a popular holiday town. Rows of Regency terraces are reminders of the prosperous recent past, while elsewhere are the more ancient Old Chancel and Manor House. The former incorporates medieval parts of the old parish church, and the latter now houses a museum. On either side of the town are Peak Hill to the west and Salcombe Hill to the east, both of which offer exceptional views of the coastline. Peak Hill shelters the Royal Glen, a former residence of Queen Victoria. Every August the town is a host to a well-known International Folk Song and Dance Festival.

Follow SP 'Honiton' B3175 and drive to Sidford.

SIDFORD, Devon
Although rebuilt and widened in 1930, Sidford's bridge still displays the pleasing lines of the old high-backed packhorse bridge that stood here from c1100. Porch House, which dates from the 16th century, is said to have hidden Charles II after the Battle of Worcester.

Turn right on to the A3052 and climb Trow Hill, which offers magnificent views across the Sid Valley. Shortly beyond the summit bear left then after ¼ mile turn right on to an unclassifed road for Branscombe.

BRANSCOMBE, Devon

It is difficult to find the centre of this village, which sprawls along steep lanes in a wooded valley, but its situation makes it one of the loveliest in Devon. Features of the upper village include thatched roofs, an old smithy, and a Norman to later church. Some 300 acres of the beautiful Branscombe Estate is owned by the National Trust.

Pass the Mason's Arms PH then follow SP 'Beer', reach to the top of an ascent, and turn left SP 'Honiton'. Continue for 1 mile then turn left on to the A3052. After ¾ mile pass the Three Horseshoes Inn before turning right on to the B3174. After 2½ miles pass the road to the Farway Countryside Park on the right.

FARWAY COUNTRYSIDE PARK, Devon

Much of this 189-acre park is preserved in its natural state, though one or two places have been prepared as picnic sites. Attractions include pony rides, nature trails and a rare breeds farm.

In ¾ mile bear right on to an unclassified road SP 'Farway' and cross Farway Hill, with fine views into the Coly Valley on the right. After ¾ mile keep forward on the 'Honiton' road. Reach a golf course and turn left, then descend into Honiton.

HONITON, Devon

This town gave its name to Honiton lace, a material which is now produced in neighbouring villages and can still be bought in some local shops. Examples can be seen in a small museum housed in the old chapel beside the towered church. Marwood House, Honiton's oldest building, dates from 1619 and contains one of many antique shops that thrive in this acknowledged centre of the trade. A 17th-century black marble tomb to Thomas Marwood, physician to Queen Elizabeth I, can be seen in the parish church above the town. Visitors to the local pottery can watch work being thrown on the wheel and hand painted. An unusual building known as Copper Castle stands by the side of old toll gates on the eastern outskirts.

Turn left into Honiton High Street (the Exeter road), and in ¾ mile turn left on to the A375 SP 'Sidmouth'. Ascend Gittisham Hill and continue to crossroads at the Hare and Hounds Inn. Turn right on to the B3174 SP 'Ottery' and descend into Ottery St Mary.

OTTERY ST MARY, Devon

Various literary figures are associated with this pleasant River Otter town. The poet Samual Taylor Coleridge was born here in 1772, and satirist William Thackeray set his novel *Pendennis* here (though he changed the name to Clavering St Mary). The magnificent collegiate church was modelled on Exeter Cathedral by Bishop Grandisson, and dates largely from 1337. Notable features include twin 14th-

Branscombe Mouth is an unspoilt beach protected by the National Trust.

century stalls and a curious Elizabethan clock. An annual carnival is held in the town on November 5.

Go forward through the town and at the end turn right onto the B3176 SP 'Fairmile'. Cross the river to reach Cadhay House.

CADHAY HOUSE, Devon

This fine Tudor and Georgian courtyard manor house dates mainly from 1550 and is open during the summer.

Continue to Fairmile, cross the A30, and follow SP 'Clyst Hydon'. Continue through farming country to Clyst Hydon and at the end of the village turn right SP 'Cullompton'. In ¾ mile turn left on to an unclassified road. SP 'Hele' then after a further 2 miles meet a junction with the B3185 and turn left then immediately right for Hele. Pass under the M5 motorway, drive over a level crossing and the River Culm, to enter Hele

Portuguese fishing boats are displayed along with many other vessels at Exeter's Maritime Museum.

then turn left. SP 'Silverton'. In ½ mile turn left then in 1¼ miles at crossroads go forward onto the B3185 SP 'Broad Clyst' and recross the River Culm near paper mills. Skirt Killerton Gardens on the right.

KILLERTON GARDENS, Devon

The Georgian Killerton House containing a fine collection of period costumes stands in magnificent 300-acre grounds covering a hilltop. There are many ancient beech trees and a fine 15-acre garden of rare trees and shrubs.

Follow SP 'Poltimore' then 'Exeter' and descend into the city of Exeter.

EXETER, Devon

With a population of 96,000 is the county town, and administrative and commercial centre of Devon. Founded by the Romans at the lowest crossing point of the River Exe, it is one of the oldest cities in England. The cathedral, with unusual Norman twin transeptal

towers, is mainly 14th-century, and the ancient guildhall has an elaborate late 16th-century facade. The modern university is on a hilltop site on the north side of the city and, despite the depredation of wartime bombing, attractive Georgian and earlier houses may still be found in many streets. The maritime museum at the head of the Exeter Canal on the south side of the city is of great interest, as are the Royal Albert Memorial Museum, the Devonshire Regiment Museum, 15th-century Tucker's Hall, St Nicholas's Priory (AM), Rougemont House Museum, and the underground passages. Part of the Norman Rougemont Castle has survived, and stretches of the ancient city walls can still be seen.

Recross the M5 and turn right onto the B3181 SP 'Exeter'. Proceed through Broad Clyst to Pinhoe. Keep forward SP 'Ring Road' and in 1 mile at traffic signals bear left (Exeter City Centre is to the right) and at the next roundabout take 2nd exit SP 'Torbay, Plymouth'. Keep forward to reach Countess Wear Roundabout then take 1st exit unclassified SP 'Topsham'. In 1¼ miles pass under the M5 Exe Estuary viaduct and shortly enter Topsham.

TOPSHAM, Devon

Once an important seaport, Topsham stands on the Exe estuary and features 17th- and 18th-century Dutch-gabled houses. These fine buildings, mainly in the Strand, are reminders of a flourishing trade with Holland. One of them contains a local history museum in its sail loft.

Turn left, (for town centre keep forward) go over a level-crossing then bear right. Shortly cross the River Clyst then at the George Dragon PH turn left on to the A376 and continue to reach a roundabout at Clyst St Mary, and take the 3rd exit on to the A3052 'Lyme Regis' road. In 4¾ miles reach the Halfway Inn and turn right on to the B3180 for the return over Woodbury Common to Exmouth.

COAST TO COAST

From Falmouth and the gentle southern coast where land and sea interlace in a maze of wooded waterways; inland to Redruth, onetime centre of tin mining and still Cornwall's industrial pulse; then northwards to jagged cliffs constantly struggling with the fierce Atlantic.

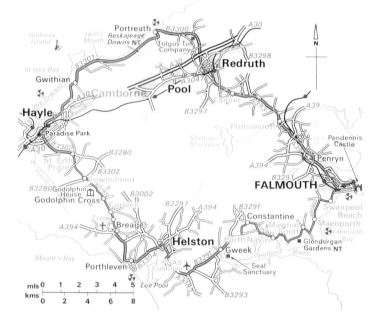

FALMOUTH, Cornwall

Falmouth has 2 distinct roles — holiday resort and port — and although tourism is more prosperous now than shipping, the harbour and docks remain busy. The town stands at the entrance to the Carrick Roads, a beautiful stretch of water formed by the merging of 7 river estuaries, and has a huge natural harbour on one side and sandy beaches and gardens on the other. The port really began to develop in the 17th century when Falmouth was made a Mail Packet Station, reaching its heyday in the 19th century. At this time it served as the hub of communications for the British Empire, and 39 ships were despatching letters all over the world. Unfortunately for Falmouth the packet service was later transferred to Southampton and prosperity declined. However, Falmouth's second role as a resort developed rapidly when the railway reached Cornwall and the exceptionally mild climate assured it year-round popularity. The long main street of the town runs beside the River Fal up from the harbour and here the older, more attractive, buildings are to be found. The twin castles of Pendennis (OACT) and St Mawes (opposite Falmouth) once stood stern guard over the entrance to the Carrick Roads. They were built by Henry VIII and Pendennis was the last Royalist stronghold to fall during the Civil War, having valiantly withstood Cromwellian armies for 5 months.

Follow SP 'Beaches' and 'Helford Passage', then 'Maenporth' and 'Mawnan'. Pass Swanpool Beach and in ½ mile at the T-junction turn left to Maenporth. In 1¼ miles turn right for Mawnan Smith. At the Red Lion Inn turn left, SP 'Helford Passage', and in ¾ mile pass (left) Glendurgan Gardens.

GLENDURGAN GARDENS, Cornwall

A small, almost secret valley descending to the Helford Passage has been turned into an oasis of exotic trees, flowers and shrubs. The gardens (NT), including a laurel maze, were originally planted on these slopes in 1833 by Alfred Fox. Three successive generations continued to cultivate the gardens which thrive in southern Cornwall's almost subtropical climate.

Continue for nearly ½ mile then turn right, SP 'Constantine'. After 1¼ miles turn left across a bridge, continue to Porth Navas, and in 1½ miles turn left to Constantine.

CONSTANTINE, Cornwall

The village of Constantine climbs up a long, winding street and its cottages, built of locally quarried stone, are nearly all fronted with neat, pretty gardens. Just to the north, opposite Trewardrera Manor, is an underground passage imaginatively called Piskie Hall (not open). It was part of a prehistoric fortified enclosure and is known as a fogou, the Cornish word for cave.

Continue through the village and turn left, SP 'Gweek'. In 1 mile turn right, then ½ mile farther join the B3291 to reach Gweek.

GWEEK, Cornwall

The tranquil banks of the Helford River at Gweek have become a sanctuary (OACT) for seals and birds that have been washed up around the Cornish coastline. Five large open-air pools house the animals in varying stages of recovery and the seals in particular are very appealing.

Cross the Helford River and in 1¾ miles turn right on to the B3293, then in ½ mile turn right again to join the A3083, pass the Culdrose Royal Naval Air Station and, in another 1¾ miles turn left, SP 'Penzance', for Helston.

Seals well on their way to recovery at Gweek Seal Sanctuary after being rescued from Cornish beaches where they were found orphaned or injured

HELSTON, Cornwall

At one time Helston, like most of its neighbours, was a port. However, when the Cober River silted up in the 13th century the town became landlocked and its sea trading days ended. It was not until the 18th century that Helston gained importance once more, this time as one of Cornwall's 4 official stannary towns, to which all the smelted tin in the area had to be taken for quality testing and taxing. A stannary was a mining district in Devon and Cornwall at that time. Now this pleasant market town is probably most famous for its annual festival called the Furry Dance, or Floral Dance. In early May there is continual dancing in the streets and many people dress up in top hats for the occasion. Folklore claims the dance is a celebration of the fact that no harm was done when a dragon dropped a boulder down on the town. Whatever its origins, the custom certainly stretches back thousands of years. Among Helston's hilly streets and grey stone houses is the Old Butter Market, now serving as the town museum. The small but interesting collection here covers all aspects of local history and includes an old cider mill. Also of interest is the Cornwall Aero Park and Flambards Victorian Village, an all weather family leisure park. South-west of Helston is Loe Pool, which, with a circumference of 7 miles, is Cornwall's largest lake. It was formed about 600 years ago when the Loe Bar cut the Cober off from the sea. It is possible to walk right round the lake (NT), but the less energetic might content themselves with a stroll through the beautiful woodlands on the lake's west side.

Leave Helston on the A394 Penzance Road and then turn left on to the B3304, SP 'Porthleven'.

PORTHLEVEN, Cornwall
The sweep of Mount's Bay lies at the foot of this small rocky village perched above its harbour, which at one time sheltered many sea-going vessels. Now, ship-building yards are the mainstay of the village's economy.

At the harbour turn right then right again, SP 'Penzance'. In 1¼ miles turn left on to the A394 and 1 mile farther turn right, SP 'Carleen and Godolphin', to enter Breage.

BREAGE, Cornwall
Breage's church of St Breaca is of unusual interest. Built entirely of granite and dating originally from the 15th century, it contains wall paintings on the north wall depicting, amongst others, St Christopher and the Warning to the Sabbath-Breakers. Although as old as the church itself, these were not discovered until 1891. The churchyard has a sandstone 4-holed wheel cross with Saxon decoration.

At the T-junction in Breage turn left and continue through Trew and Carleen to Godolphin Cross.

GODOLPHIN CROSS, Cornwall
A Cornish family of diverse interests gave this tiny hamlet its name, and they occupied Godolphin House (OACT) from the 15th to late 18th century. Francis Godolphin was one of the first local landowners to finance tin mining; Sidney Godolphin was Queen Anne's 1st Minister for 7 years; and the 2nd Earl of Godolphin owned one of the 3 imported Arab stallions from which all British thoroughbred horses descend. The house itself is mainly 16th century and looks most impressive from the north side with its heavy colonnade. Of particular interest inside are the

A creek of the Helford Passage

Jacobean range with its fireplace and a painting of the famous Godolphin Arabian stallion.

At Godolphin Cross go over the crossroads and after ¾ mile pass Godolphin House on the left. In ½ mile bear right over the bridge and at Townshead cross the main road, SP 'Hayle'. In another 1¾ miles turn left on to the B3302 for St Erth Praze. Before entering Hayle a side road (left) may be taken to Paradise Park.

PARADISE PARK, Cornwall
Aviaries full of richly-coloured foreign birds such as the Hyacinthine Macaw and Great African Wattled Crane are the main attractions of this complex; others include a zoo for children, a miniature steam railway and a craft village.

Continue into Hayle.

HAYLE, Cornwall
During the 18th century, Cornish copper miners had to send ore to South Wales for smelting and Hayle developed as a port for this trade. Now it is mainly a light industrial town but there is a good bathing beach beyond the nearby sand dunes called The Towans.

At Hayle join the B3301 Redruth road, then in 1½ miles turn left SP 'Portreath'. Pass grass-covered sand dunes and continue to Gwithian.

GWITHIAN, Cornwall
There is no visible evidence of it in sea-facing Gwithian, but buried beneath the sands lies a small chapel, possibly dating back to Celtic Christianity when nearby Hayle was an arrival point for Irish saints. The chapel was uncovered during excavations in the last century but has sunk into oblivion once again through neglect. The present church was built in 1886.

From Gwithian the B3301 runs parallel with the coast to Portreath. There are several good viewpoints to the left within short walking distance of the road.

PORTREATH, Cornwall
At the bottom of bleak windswept cliffs nestles the small port and holiday resort of Portreath, consisting of a cluster of tiny harbour cottages around an 18th-century pier. The views from Reskajeage Downs (NT) above are spectacular.

From Portreath follow the B3300 Redruth road. After 2 miles, on the right, is the Tolgus Tin Company.

TOLGUS TIN COMPANY, Cornwall
A small part of 18th-century industrial Cornwall can still be seen at the Tolgus Tin Mill where the ancient practice of streaming — a process which involves washing the deposits of tin from the stream bed — has been carried out for generations. The

machinery which sifts and washes the extracted deposits includes the only Cornish stamps in commercial use. These heavy stamps, powered by the water mill, crush the ore so the tin can be separated from the waste. A small shop and visitor centre are open to the public.

Continue into Redruth.

REDRUTH, Cornwall
Camborne and Redruth have practically merged into one town and between them support the largest concentration of population in Cornwall. Redruth has always been at the centre of the mining industry and the town has remained primarily an industrial centre. Probably the most interesting aspects of this tradition are the engines displayed at nearby Pool. One of these is an 1887 winding engine which used to wind men as well as materials several hundred feet up and down copper and tin mine shafts. The other is an 1892 pumping engine, with a 52-ton beam used to pump water.

In Redruth turn left with the one-way traffic, then turn right and follow SP 'Falmouth' on the A393. Continue through Lanner to Ponsanooth, then in 1¾ miles go forward on to the A39 and skirt Penryn.

PENRYN, Cornwall
Almost everything that could be is built of granite here, and huge blocks of it from the Penryn quarries lie on the docks waiting to be shipped out of Cornwall. Penryn lies around the headland from Falmouth on another finger of the Carrick Roads, enjoying the same mild climate and luxuriant vegetation.

Return to Falmouth on the A39.

Hundreds of ships, including the *Nile* that cost many lives, were wrecked before Godrevy Lighthouse was built off Godrevy Point in 1859

WOOL, WEAVING AND WATER

The old wool towns and villages of Somerset and Wiltshire stud the valleys of the Rivers Frome and Avon. Blending harmoniously with the landscape is the warm-toned stone that takes its name from Bath, where it was used so effectively in the Georgian streets and squares that characterise the town.

FROME, Somerset
See page 63 for a description of this ancient wool town.

Leave Frome on the A361 Trowbridge road and continue to Beckington. Here join the A36, SP 'Bath', and continue to Woolverton. Beyond the Red Lion Inn, turn right and after ½ mile pass the Rode Tropical Bird Gardens.

RODE TROPICAL BIRD GARDENS, Somerset
Seventeen acres of trees, shrubs and lakes provide a setting for over 180 species of exotic birds. These include flamingoes, pelicans, cranes, vultures and cockatoos.

Continue and shortly pass the edge of Rode. At the crossroads turn right on to the B3109, SP Beckington, and in ¼ mile turn right again on to the A361. Pass Rode church and in just over ¼ mile turn left, SP 'Rudge' and 'Brokerswood'. In ½ mile at the T-junction, turn left. At the Full Moon PH in Rudge turn left and shortly turn left again. In ¼ mile, at the crossroads, turn right, SP 'Dilton' and 'Westbury'. Alternatively, continue with the North Bradley road to visit the Woodland Heritage Museum and Woodland Park.

WOODLAND HERITAGE MUSEUM AND WOODLAND PARK, Wilts
A lake alive with wildfowl lies in natural woodland which has been well laid out with nature walks. The natural history museum here, which includes a good forestry exhibition, provides interesting information about the park.

The main tour continues on the Westbury road and after 2 miles turn left on to the B3099, and shortly left again on to the A3098 for Westbury. Leave Westbury on the B3098, SP 'Bratton'. To the right is the Westbury White Horse.

WESTBURY WHITE HORSE, Wilts
Gleaming white on its hillside, the famous horse, carved into the chalk of Westbury Hill, dominates the landscape between Westbury and Bratton. The oldest of several in Wiltshire, this one is thought to commemorate King Alfred's victory over the Danes in AD 878. The elegant shape we see today, however, is an 18th-century remodelling of the original figure.

On the approach to Bratton turn left on to the unclassified Steeple Ashton road. After a mile, go over the crossroads and in a further ½ mile, at the T-junction, turn left and continue to Steeple Ashton.

STEEPLE ASHTON, Wilts
In medieval times, the village once had an important cloth market, and its name was originally Staple Ashton — taken from the wool staple (fibre). The market cross on the green stands next to an octagonal lock-up, where offenders were temporarily detained in the 18th and 19th centuries.

1 mile beyond the village turn left, SP 'Trowbridge', and later cross the A350 for Hilperton. Here turn left on to the A361, then take the next turning right on to the B3105. In 1¼ miles bear right and cross the Kennet and Avon Canal. Beyond Staverton turn left on to the B3107 for Bradford-on-Avon.

BRADFORD-ON-AVON, Wilts
Old houses of honey-coloured Bath stone line Bradford's steep, winding streets. The buildings range in style from late medieval to the elegant Georgian mansions erected by the wealthy cloth merchants. On the arched stone Town Bridge stands a chapel that for generations served as the town lock-up and near the river, in Barton Farm Country Park, stands a monumental 14th-century tithe barn (AM).

From Bradford follow SP 'Frome', across the River Avon, then turn right on to the B3109. Cross the Kennet and Avon Canal, then in ½ mile branch right, SP 'Westwood'. In another ½ mile turn right to reach the edge of Westwood. At the New Inn PH turn left and to the right is Westwood Manor.

WESTWOOD MANOR, Wilts
Thomas Horton, a wealthy clothier, built the attractive stone manor house (NT) at the edge of the village in the 15th century. It contains a medieval great hall and the aptly named King's Room, whose panels are decorated with the portraits of 22 sovereigns up to Charles I. The outstanding feature of the gardens is the topiary work; one of the bushes is shaped like a cottage, and even has a doorway.

The White Horse of Westbury

Continue along this narrow byroad for 1 mile, then turn right on to the A366, SP 'Frome', and continue to Farleigh Castle.

FARLEIGH CASTLE, Somerset
Only ruins remain of the castle (AM) built by Sir Thomas Hungerford in 1370. A later descendant, it is said, cruelly incarcerated his wife in the tower for 4 years and was himself executed for treason and 'unnatural vice' in 1540. A collection of armour and weapons is displayed in the chapel, including about 100 painted shields, a crusader's sword, and a scimitar.

Continue along the A366 and after 1 mile turn left then immediately right, SP 'Radstock', to reach Norton St Phillip.

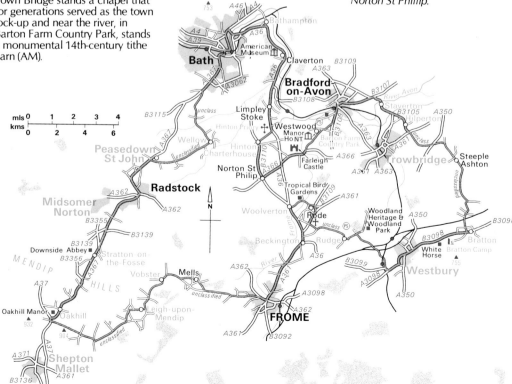

During the 19th century it was a custom in rural America for a group of friends of a bride-to-be to weave a quilt for her trousseau. This one at Claverton Manor was made in Baltimore in 1845

NORTON ST PHILIP, Somerset
The George is one of the best preserved medieval inns in the country. Founded in the 13th century as a guesthouse for Hinton Priory, its half-timbered upper storey was added in the 15th century. The ruined priory nearby, founded in 1232, is the second oldest Carthusian house in England. Among the famous guests were the diarist Samuel Pepys, the rebel Duke of Monmouth and 'hanging' Judge Jeffreys who sentenced so many of the Duke of Monmouth's followers to death in the Bloody Assize of 1685.

At the George Inn turn on to the B3110 Bath road, and continue to Hinton Charterhouse. Here, at the 2nd crossroads, turn right (no sign). In ¾ mile, at the T-junction, turn left on to the A36 and continue to Limpley Stoke.

LIMPLEY STOKE, Wilts
The impressive arches of John Rennie's Dundas Aqueduct carry the Kennet and Avon canal across the river at Limpley Stoke. Rennie designed the canal and many of its bridges and aqueducts in the early 19th century.

Remain on the A36 and after 2 miles pass, on the left, the turning for Claverton.

CLAVERTON, Somerset
Claverton Manor (OACT), built in 1820, now houses an American museum. Period rooms and furnishings give a convincing picture of American domestic life from the 17th to the 19th century, and other exhibits include Shaker and Red Indian art.

The main tour continues along the valley of the River Avon to Bath.

BATH, Avon
Aquae Sulis to the Romans, Bath's warm, healing waters have been famous for more than 2,000 years. Parts of the original Roman baths can still be seen and the nearby museum displays a fascinating collection of Roman remains. The splendid abbey dates from the 15th century, but there has been a church here since Saxon times. Bath's heyday came in the 18th century when the dandy Beau Nash made the place fashionable. Wealthy citizens flocked to take the waters at the Pump Room and attend evening parties at the Assembly Rooms. From this period date the elegant squares, crescents and terraces that have made Bath the finest Georgian city in the country. Ralph Allen, who owned the quarries at Combe Down which provided the warm-toned Bath stone, commissioned a father and son, both named John Wood, to design Queen Square, the Circus and Royal Crescent. Later architects, including Robert Adam, who built Pulteney Bridge, completed the transformation of the city. No. 1 Royal Crescent, furnished in period, is open to the public. The Costume Museum in the Assembly Rooms displays an unrivalled collection and the Holburne of Menstrie Museum in Sydney Gardens has fine examples of china and glass.

Leave Bath on the A367, SP 'Exeter', and begin a long climb out of the city. At the roundabout at the top take the 2nd exit. In ½ mile turn left onto an unclassified road SP 'Wellow' and continue to Wellow. Turn right into the main street, SP 'Radstock', and after 3 miles turn left on to the A367 and later reach Radstock.

RADSTOCK, Somerset
This small, industrial town on a hilly site was a centre of coal-mining from the 18th to the early 20th century; the last pit closed in 1973. All that now remains of the industry are the neat rows of miners' cottages, and traces of disused railway lines and canals.

Leave on the A367 Shepton Mallet road and continue to Stratton-on-Fosse passing, on the right, Downside Abbey.

DOWNSIDE ABBEY, Somerset
The abbey was a Benedictine foundation and is now one of the leading Roman Catholic boys' public schools in England. A group of English monks, who had settled in France but were driven out during the French Revolution, founded it in 1814.

Continue on the Shepton Mallet/ Yeovil road to Oakhill passing on the right Oakhill Manor.

OAKHILL MANOR, Somerset
Eight acres of attractive gardens, nestling in the Mendip Hills around Oakhill Manor (OACT), provide the setting for a magnificent miniature railway that covers ¾ mile. There is a museum here as well with numerous models of various modes of transport, all well displayed in an imaginative setting.

Remain on the A367 and in just over ½ mile turn left on to the A37, then almost immediately turn left again, SP 'Frome'. After 2 miles turn right then immediately left. In another 2 miles turn left again, SP 'Leigh-upon-Mendip. In ½ mile, at the T-junction, turn right for Leigh-upon-Mendip. Here, bear left with the Coleford/Radstock road, then keep forward, SP 'Vobster'. Enter Vobster and turn right on to the Mells road and follow SP 'Mells'.

MELLS, Somerset
Mells, with its well-kept cottage gardens, ranks as one of the prettiest villages in Somerset. The Elizabethan manor house (not open) once belonged to Abbot Selwood of Glastonbury, who, hoping to save the abbey from the Dissolution, sent the title deeds of the manor, concealed in a pie, to Henry VIII. John Horner is said to have stolen them and thus has been identified with Jack Horner of nursery-rhyme fame.

Follow SP 'Frome' and in 1¾ miles turn left. In 1 mile turn right on to the A362 for the return to the town centre.

Pulteney Bridge, Bath

GLOUCESTER, Glos

The Romans, the first to build here, created a fortified port as a springboard for their invasion of Wales, and the town later became one of the 4 *coloniae* from which Rome ruled Britain. Today Gloucester is still an inland port; a canal, opened in 1837, connects the city's docks with the River Severn and can accommodate ships of up to 1,000 tons. After the Romans left the Saxons occupied the town, and made it a *burgh,* but it was not until the Normans arrived that tangible evidence of occupation was left, for they brought with them the will and knowledge to create Gloucester Cathedral. Their church remains at the heart of the cathedral, and, as later generations added without destroying what had gone before, Gloucester preserves an unparalleled display of ecclesiastical architecture through the ages. Within the church the tomb of murdered Edward II and the glorious east window, which commemorates the Battle of Crecy in 1346, are renowned for their quality and beauty. The city retains as its main streets the 4 Roman roads which meet at the cross in the town centre. Along these ancient routes survive some old houses from Gloucester's past. A little square of medieval England remains in Northgate Street as the outer galleried courtyard of the timbered New Inn. In 1555, Bishop John Hooper spent his last night before being burnt at the stake in the house which now bears his name in Westgate Street. This splendid 16th-century building houses a superb folk museum, where trades and crafts of the past are displayed, along with numerous items of historical interest connected with the city and the county.

Leave the city centre on the A430, SP 'Bristol (A38)'. In 2¼ miles, at the roundabout, take the B4008, SP 'Quedgeley'. In ½ mile, turn right, SP 'Elmore'. After ¾ mile, at the River Severn, the famous Severn Bore can be seen during the spring and autumn high tides, when the bore waves force their way up the narrow estuary. In 1¼ miles, at the T-junction, turn right for Elmore.

ELMORE, Glos

Tucked away in the Vale of Gloucester is Elmore village, a gathering of cruck-framed barns and timbered, thatched cottages clustered about a church and a churchyard renowned for its 18th-century table tombs. Acanthus and hart's tongue fern decorate the wrought iron gates of Elmore Court (not open), a mostly Elizabethan manor with a Georgian wing. Built on ground which the Guise family has owned since the 13th century, the house is delightfully situated in a loop of the Severn.

THE VALE OF BERKELEY AND THE SEVERN VALLEY

Along the Vale of Berkeley, beside the River Severn, are flat fertile lands where cattle grew fat and lords built great houses. Higher up, on the Cotswolds, the land changes and becomes a chequerboard of stone-walled fields beneath limitless skies.

A Whooper swan taking off — just one of the 2,500-odd birds kept at the Severn Wildfowl Trust

In 1¼ miles turn left and continue to Longney. Here turn right, SP 'Saul and Frampton', then in ¾ mile, at the T-junction, turn right again for Epney. At Saul join the B4071 and in ¾ mile turn left across the swing bridge, then in ½ mile, at the crossroads, turn right to Frampton-on-Severn.

FRAMPTON-ON-SEVERN, Glos

The road splits a 22-acre village green bordered by Georgian brick houses. On the left lies 18th-century Frampton Court (not open) home of the Clifford family. In the grounds, beyond the chestnut trees which partly screen the house from the road, a delightful Gothic orangery by William Halfpenny overlooks a rectangular canal sunk in landscaped surroundings. The green ends past the duck pond and thatched and gabled houses converge towards the heart of the village. Here is the spacious church, and closeby is the Berkeley-Gloucester canal, and a canal keeper's house with a pedimented portico.

VALE OF BERKELEY, Glos

Some 700ft below the Cotswold escarpment lies the Vale of Berkeley, a great expanse of flat land beneath huge skies bounded by distant horizons: a rich area of fat cattle, orchards and old timber-framed dairy-farms. The thick deposit of clay, in places over 700ft deep, is a prime raw material for the manufacture of bricks and tiles.

Return to the B4071 and turn right, then in 1½ miles, turn right on to the A38, SP 'Bristol', and continue to Cambridge. In ¾ mile, turn right for Slimbridge. 1 mile beyond the village, cross the canal bridge for the Severn Wildfowl Trust.

SEVERN WILDFOWL TRUST, Glos

An area of flat marshland between the Gloucester and Sharpness canal and the River Severn has been reserved solely for birds. Their host is a Wildfowl Trust, founded in 1964 by Sir Peter Scott to study and preserve wildfowl throughout the world. This is one of the finest collections in the world, where some 180 species are kept out of the known 247. The Trust caters admirably for the visitor, and its real work of preservation and research has an unparalleled record which is well documented in the main hall. One example of the value of the work is the story of the Hawaiian goose. Only 42 birds were known to be alive in 1952, but since then, from 3 birds procured by Sir Peter Scott, more than 800 have been bred and either distributed to zoos or returned to their natural habitat in the wild.

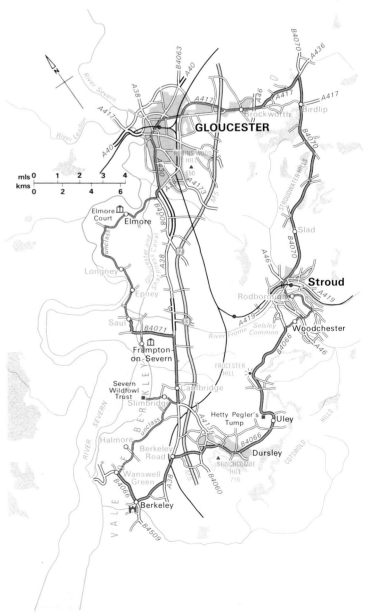

Return to Slimbridge and beyond the church turn right, SP 'Halmore', then in 1 mile, at the T-junction, turn right again. Follow a narrow byroad across flat countryside and after 2¼ miles turn left and immediately right for Wanswell Green. Here turn left on to the B4066 for Berkeley.

BERKELEY, Glos

A quiet Georgian town, Berkeley is dominated by 2 giants, Berkeley Castle from the past and an Atomic Power Station of the future. The castle (OACT) is a rugged sentinel of 900 years of English history, built in 1153 by permission of Henry I and home of the Berkeley family for centuries. It is still more a fortress than a stately home, and is best remembered for an act of violence. In 1327, Edward II was kept prisoner here and brutally murdered in the guardroom at the instigation of his wife and the Earl of Mortimer.

Follow SP 'Bristol' then keep forward, SP 'Gloucester', and in 1½ mile bear left to join the A38. At Berkeley Road turn right on to the B4066, SP 'Dursley'. In 2¼ miles turn right on to the A4135 for Dursley.

DURSLEY, Glos

Dursley's Market Hall of 1738, raised up on 12 arches of stone and graced by a statue of Queen Anne, keeps company with some elegant Georgian homes in a town which in recent years has experienced a flurry of new buildings and an influx of industry which has revitalised the community. The church has a 15th-century chapel, built of Tufa stone by a rich wool merchant, and a Gothic tower of the 1700s.

In Dursley turn left (one-way) and follow SP 'Stroud'. At the end of the town turn left on to the B4066 for Uley.

ULEY, Glos

Spilling down a hillside, distinguished houses of the 17th and 18th centuries are a legacy of Uley's success as a weaving community. Broadcloths, Spanish cloths and a blue dye of excellent quality were made here.

From Uley climb on to the Cotswolds. After 1½ miles, (left) is Hetty Pegler's Tump.

HETTY PEGLERS TUMP, Glos

Hetty Pegler's Tump (AM), is a Neolithic long barrow measuring 180ft by 90ft, where 28 people were buried in the stone-walled burial chamber. There are fine views over the Severn to the Welsh Mountains from the top.

Continue along a ridge, with good views, particularly at the Frocester Hill Viewpoint (NT). In 2¾ miles, turn right on to an unclassified road to Woodchester.

WOODCHESTER, Glos

One of the largest Roman villas found in England stood here, and in the churchyard a remarkable mosaic of Orpheus is occasionally on display, though it is mostly kept covered. The Industrial Revolution shaped the Woodchester of today and left it many fine clothiers houses, such as Southfield Mill House, and the Victorian mills which brought them prosperity.

Turn right on to the A46, then take the 1st turning left, SP 'Rodborough Common'. By the Bear Inn PH, turn left then left again, SP 'Rodborough', to cross the lofty Rodborough Common (NT). Descend through Rodborough before rejoining the A46 to enter Stroud.

STROUD, Glos

The River Frome and its tributaries powered 150 cloth mills here by 1824, and with the advent of steam, a canal was built to bring coal from the Midlands for the new machinery which brought Stroud into the forefront of England's broadcloth industry. The town still supplies most of the world's demand for greenbaize billiard table cloth. Stroud is also famous for its scarlet dyes, which were used to give the 'Redcoats' of the military their characteristic hue. Some of the old mills remain in this hilly town of narrow streets, though few of the wealthy clothiers houses have survived. The museum at Lansdown illustrates old methods of cloth weaving, many local crafts and past industries of the town. The Archaeological Room displays finds from barrows at nearby Rodborough and Nymphsfield.

Leave Stroud on the B4070, SP 'Birdlip', and gradually climb up to the Stroudwater Hills to Slad. Continue, to Birdlip. Turn right into the village then turn left on to the A417, SP 'Gloucester'. Magnificent views can be seen across the Severn Vale to the distant Malvern Hills. At the next roundabout take the 1st exit and return to Gloucester.

Above: a detail of the painting that decorates the inside of a wooden chest which belonged to Sir Francis Drake and is now kept at Berkeley Castle

Below: the cloisters of Gloucester Cathedral were built between 1351 and 1377

COVES OF THE LIZARD

Wreckers once used the jagged reefs and towering cliffs of the Lizard to cripple their prey. All round the peninsula's coast are stern little villages in rocky bays, towering stacks and pinnacles of multi-hued serpentine, and the constant boom of waves crashing into hidden caves.

HELSTON, Cornwall
In Elizabethan times Helston was one of Cornwall's 4 stannary or coinage towns, where all the smelted tin mined in the area was brought to be tested for quality and taxed. Even earlier it had been a busy port, until the Loe Bar formed across the mouth of the Cober River in the 13th century. Well-preserved Regency houses can be seen along Cross Street, and behind the early Victorian Guildhall is an interesting museum with many old implements, including a cider press. Local people would say that May 8 is the best day to visit the town, for that is the time of the Furry, or Floral Dance. From early in the morning the inhabitants dance through the winding streets and in and out of houses to celebrate the time a dragon dropped a rock on the town without causing any damage. About 1¼ miles south west of Helston, on the B3304, is a footpath leading left to Loe Pool.

CORNWALL AERO PARK & FLAMBARDS VICTORIAN VILLAGE, Cornwall
This is an award winning all-weather family leisure park with a large exhibition hall set in beautiful landscaped gardens. Flambards is an authentic life-size Victorian village. A special display covers Britain in the Blitz. The Aero Park has historic aircraft, vehicles, helicopters, Battle of Britain gallery, Concorde flight deck and an SR2 simulator.

Leave Helston on the A3083 SP 'Lizard'. Pass Culdrose Airfield and turn left on to the B3293, SP 'St Keverne'. The road to the viewing area is on the left in ½ mile.

CULDROSE ROYAL NAVAL AIR STATION, Cornwall
Navy search aircraft operate over a wide area of sea around Cornwall from this helicopter base. The public are only admitted to an aircraft viewing area.

Continue to the Mawgan Cross war memorial and branch left over crossroads on to an unclassifed road to Mawgan. Continue on the 'Manaccan, Helford' road, through St Martin's Green to Newtown. Keep left, then in 250yds turn left again. After another 1½ miles meet crossroads and go forward, then in ¾ mile turn left and descend to Helford.

HELFORD, Cornwall
This lovely little village on the wooded banks of the Helford River is a favourite haunt of anglers and yachtsmen. The river is dotted with small villages and creeks, and a passenger ferry sails from here to Helford Passage – where there is a bright, attractive inn.

Leave Helford and return along the same road for ¾ mile. Turn left for St Anthony.

The sheltered waters and hidden creeks of Helford River once made ideal bases for the secret activities of smugglers.

ST ANTHONY, Cornwall
The church of St Anthony in Meneage stands only 30yds from the creek. Its chancel and parts of the south wall are Norman, and tradition holds that it was built by shipwrecked Norman sailors as a thank-offering to St Anthony for saving them from drowning. The tranquil scenery of Gillan Creek presents a charming, timeless picture of Cornish maritime life.

Leaving St Anthony drive alongside the creek and after 1 mile turn left, SP 'St Keverne'. Climb to the edge of Gillan, keep right and follow signs for St Keverne.

A fisherman's cottage in Cadgwith.

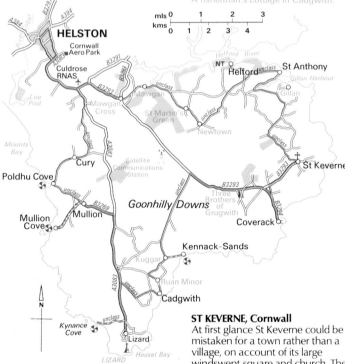

ST KEVERNE, Cornwall
At first glance St Keverne could be mistaken for a town rather than a village, on account of its large windswept square and church. The latter dates from the 15th century and carries an unusual octagonal spire which has been a welcome landmark for sailors for hundreds of years. Just 1 mile offshore are the treacherous Manacle Rocks, which have made shipwrecks a gruesome part of the village's history. Over 400 victims are buried at the church, including 126 people who died when the *Primrose* was wrecked in 1809. Two miles south-west is a Bronze-Age burial chamber known as the Three Brothers of Grugwith.

Leave St Keverne on the B3293 'Coverack and Helston' road. After 1¼ miles turn left on to an unclassified road and later join the B3294. From here descend into Coverack.

COVERACK, Cornwall
Smugglers once frequented this small fishing village, and wreckers lured unsuspecting vessels on to the Manacle Rocks to plunder their cargoes. Coverack formerly had a lifeboat station that was established after a particularly bad series of disasters. The harbour is overlooked by thatched cottages.

Climb out of Coverack on the B3294 'Helston' road, then join the B3293, and in 2½ miles at crossroads turn left on to an unclassified road SP 'Cadgwith'. Views to the right take in Goonhilly Downs Satellite Communications Station.

GOONHILLY DOWNS, Cornwall

Goonhilly Downs, a small windswept moor only about 7 square miles in area, was once covered by oak forests. Nowadays there is nothing here but a bleak stretch of gorse and heather dominated by the huge radio aerials of the Satellite Communications Station.

Drive over Goonhilly Downs for 3 miles and at Kuggar meet a T-junction. A detour from the main route leads left to Kennack Sands.

Goonhilly Downs Satellite Communications Station receives signals from all over the world.

KENNACK SANDS, Cornwall

Wide firm sands, wave-ribbed and dotted with large shallow pools at low tide, make this a perfect beach for families with children.

Turn right and in ¾ mile at crossroads, turn left for Ruan Minor. At the village turn right and make descent (1 in 4) to Cadgwith.

CADGWITH, Cornwall

Cadgwith's attractive thatched cottages overlook a stone strand dotted with beached boats and the paraphernalia of a working fishing community. All along the coast are sandy coves, and to the south is the great tidal chasm the Devil's Frying Pan. This was formed when a vast sea cave collapsed, and is at its scenic best in stormy weather.

Leave Cadgwith, continue with an unclassified road SP 'Lizard', and ascend. In ¾ mile turn right, then after another ¾ mile turn left on to the A3083 for Lizard.

LIZARD, Cornwall

A mile from Lizard is the headland of Lizard Point, the southernmost tip of a lovely peninsula that has become famous for its outstanding natural beauty (NT). In the heather and bogs of the interior rivulets and streams rise to chatter down to the beach through small valleys and, occasionally, as miniature falls over the edge of the cliffs. Many rare plants grow here, and some of the

area is leased to the Cornwall Naturalists' Trust. Splendid walks extend along the clifftops of the Point. To the east the countryside is sheltered from the full force of Atlantic gales and is lush and green, but round the Point to the west everything becomes wilder and more desolate. Much of the land on this side is pitted with holes left by people digging for the mineral serpentine, a lovely stone prized for the rich shades of greens, reds and purple released by cutting and polishing. Magnificent views from Lizard Point extend many miles along the Cornish coast to Rame Head, (near Plymouth), and when ideal conditions prevail, as far as Bolt Head in the South Hams district of Devon. This superb vantage point forms an ideal site for the Lizard Lighthouse.

Leave Lizard by returning along the A3083 SP 'Helston'. After ½ mile a detour can be made from the main route along a toll road to breathtaking Kynance Cove.

KYNANCE COVE, Cornwall

Serpentine is seen at its very best in Kynance Cove, where spectacular formations of the mineral rise in pillars, stacks, and pyramids from a flat surface of firm sand. An infinity of shades from red through to green, blue and purple lace exposed rock surfaces and ornament the insides of sea-bored caves. High above the surrealistic beach is a stark promontory that affords wonderful views along the coast. Slightly inland is a softer landscape of grass and flowers alongside small streams that eventually trickle from the cliff edge to the beach far below.

Continue with the main tour route on the A3083, and after 3½ miles turn left on to the B3296 for Mullion. From Mullion a possible detour from the main route leads left along the B3296 to lovely Mullion Cove.

Sea, rocks, and sand combine to create a spectacular seascape at Kynance Cove.

MULLION COVE, Cornwall

Almost as dramatic as Kynance, this superb cove is fringed by steep, cave-pocked cliffs that form a splendid counterpoint to rocky Mullion Island, just offshore. The small harbour (NT) here is used by local fishermen and visiting skin divers.

MULLION, Cornwall

Here the local rock changes from the colourful serpentine to greenstone, a very hard mineral that will spark when struck with steel. The village itself is large, with several shops, and boasts a fine 15th-century church. Notable bench ends inside the latter date from the 16th-century and depict a jester, a monk, Instruments of the Passion, and a few profiles.

At Mullion keep left (one-way) then turn right down an unclassified road for Poldhu Cove.

Mullion Cove is protected from Atlantic breakers by its sturdy harbour walls.

POLDHU COVE, Cornwall

A pleasant beach fringes the sheltered waters of this inlet. On top of the cliffs, which are composed of an unstable slate and clay mixture known as killas, the Marconi Memorial commemorates the first successful transatlantic radio signal in 1901. Some 22 years later this same spot was used for the testing of a short-wave beam system. At the beginning of the century the headland was covered in masts, aerials, wire, and sheds. All that remains now is the simple stone memorial and a few foundations.

Continue from Poldhu Cove, cross a bridge, and ascend to Cury.

CURY, Cornwall

The village church of St Corentin is set in a high windy churchyard and probably dates back to Norman times. It has since been added to.

Continue through the village and in ½ mile turn left, SP 'Helston'. In 1¾ miles turn left again to rejoin the A3083. Return to Helston.

36

CORNWALL'S INTERIOR

Wild moorland once ridden over by highwaymen and trodden by smugglers: a landscape interrupted only by the ruins of an ancient past and lonely, forgotten mine workings: a landscape sometimes as savage or as moody as the better known coast.

LISKEARD, Cornwall
This small, busy town with several Georgian and Victorian buildings is well placed in east Cornwall as an agricultural and industrial centre. See page 39.

Leave Liskeard on the A390, SP 'Tavistock', and continue through Merrymeet to St Ive.

ST IVE, Cornwall
Eight centuries ago the Knights Templar built a hostel in St Ive and Trebeigh manor house (not open) now marks the site. They also founded the church, although the present building dates mainly from the 14th century.

Continue on the A390 then in 2¾ miles cross the River Lynher and continue to Callington. In 1½ miles pass the turning on the left to Kit Hill (toll).

KIT HILL, Cornwall
To the north of Callington is a magnificent 1,094ft viewpoint called Kit Hill. Its summit is marked by a modern radio mast and, in contrast, the old chimney stack of a derelict tin mine. Spread out below in a breathtaking panorama is the valley of the Tamar and the waters of Plymouth Sound.

There are more fine views from the A390 before reaching St Ann's Chapel. From here an unclassified road on the right leads to Cotehele House.

COTEHELE HOUSE, Cornwall
Cotehele (NT) is all a romantic, medieval house should be, and it seems suspended in that distant time. Its grey, granite walls surrounding 3 courtyards have scarcely changed since they were built between 1485 and 1627 by the Edgcumbes, nor have the furniture, tapestries and armour which grace the rooms altered. Colourful gardens of terraces, ponds and walls slope gently down to the Tamar and merge with the thick natural woodland of the valley. Cotehele Mill, the manorial water mill used for grinding corn, is here in full working order and Cotehele Quay on the banks of the river has some attractive 18th-and 19th-century boathouses.

Continue into Gunnislake. Beyond the town cross the River Tamar into Devon and climb out of the valley. In 1½ miles turn right on to an unclassified road and follow SP 'Morwellham'.

MORWELLHAM, Devon
At one time Morwellham was the busiest inland port west of Exeter and its active life spanning 900 years continued until the beginning of this century. The quays and docks on the River Tamar handled copper from nearby mines, which was then shipped to Tavistock. Now the area is preserved as an open-air industrial musuem (OACT) and an underground canal built to reach the ancient productive copper mine is just one of the fascinating things to see here amid lime kilns, waterwheels, riverside and woodland walks.

Return along the unclassified road and follow SP 'Tavistock'. On reaching the A390 turn right and continue to Tavistock.

TAVISTOCK, Devon
Tavistock's long industrial history began in the 14th century and today light industrial and timber firms keep the tradition going. Before the Dissolution, Tavistock's 10th-century Benedictine abbey was one of the richest in Devon, but little remains as evidence of this now. The town was granted to the Russell family (Dukes of Bedford), and they owned it until 1911. Of its 3 phases of industry — tin, cloth and copper — the latter had the most impact on Tavistock, although the 15th-century church was built with Devon serge profits. During the 19th-century boom the Dukes of Bedford virtually rebuilt the castellated town centre around Bedford Square and the result was a pleasant combination of architecture. With its weekly cattle and pannier market Tavistock is an attractive market town which makes an ideal touring base. Sir Francis Drake was born south of the town and a statue (of which a replica stands on Plymouth Hoe) commemorates him.

Leave Tavistock on the A384, SP 'Liskeard', and later pass the edge of Lamerton.

LAMERTON, Devon
A shady avenue of trees leads to the village church, the priest's house and the vicarage. The original church was practically destroyed by fire and the priest's house, now the church hall, was rebuilt in the 15th century. Two impressive monuments were saved from the church; one to the Tremaynes and one to the Fortescues. The Tremayne's home was Collacombe Manor (not open) — a lovely Elizabethan farmhouse just off the Launceston Road.

Continue to Milton Abbot.

The ancient borough of Liskeard is well-known for its monthly cattle fair

Strange outcrops of granite, such as this one on Rough Tor, are scattered all over Bodmin Moor's bleak face

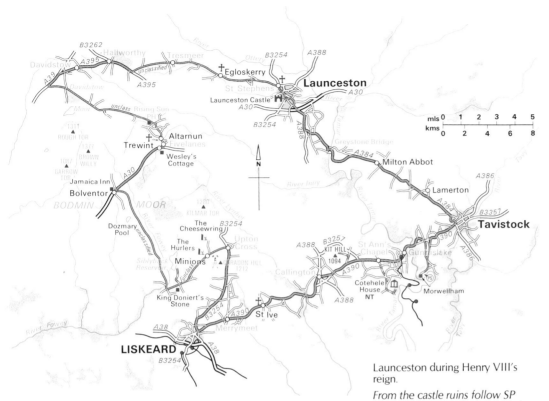

Continue to Fivelanes then turn right, SP 'Bodmin', and join the A30 to skirt the hamlet of Trewint.

TREWINT, Cornwall

John Wesley, founder of Methodism, spent some time in a small cottage here between 1744 and 1762. The cottage, restored in 1950, has been turned into a shrine to his memory and a Wesley Day Service is held here annually.

Remain on the A30 to Bolventor.

BOLVENTOR, Cornwall

On the outskirts of this tiny hamlet lies the inn made famous by Daphne du Maurier's novel *Jamaica Inn.* The lonely hostelry on the main highway across Bodmin Moor provided an ideal meeting point for smugglers in Cornwall's lawless past.

DOZMARY POOL, Cornwall

High up on Bodmin Moor, Dozmary Pool lends itself well to the many romantic legends associated with it. One of the most famous says that Sir Bedivere threw King Arthur's sword, Excalibur, into the pool at the King's request.

By the nearside of Jamaica Inn at Bolventor, turn left SP 'St Cleer'. Follow the Fowey River for 6½ miles then, at the crossroads, turn left. In ½ mile pass, on the right, King Doniert's Stone.

KING DONIERT'S STONE, Cornwall

A cross standing just off the main road bears a Latin inscription stating that 'Doniert ordered this cross for the good of his soul'. This may have been Dungarth, King of Cornwall in 875. Another Saxon cross stands next to it.

Continue on the unclassified road then in ¾ mile bear left to the village of Minions.

MINIONS, Cornwall

Near Minions, 3 stone circles make up a prehistoric monument (AM) known as the Hurlers. In the 15th century local people thought the stones were men who had been turned to stone as a punishment for hurling a ball on the Sabbath. Whatever their mysterious origin and purpose, the tops of the stones apparently needed to be on the same level. They were placed in pits of varying depths to achieve this and held in place with small granite boulders. Not more than a mile from the Hurlers on Stowe's Hill is a natural phenomenon called the Cheesewring. Encircling the summit of this strange stack of rocks is a stone rampart which once formed part of a fort — possibly Bronze Age.

Beyond Minions the tour passes a TV transmitting mast on Caradon Hill before descending to Upton Cross. Here turn right on to the B3254 for the return to Liskeard.

MILTON ABBOT, Cornwall

Tavistock Abbey used to own the village, but, like Tavistock, Milton Abbot was granted to the Russell family after the Dissolution. Similarities to the 19th-century architecture of Tavistock can be seen in the village which reflects the Russell's prosperity from copper and lead mining. Milton Green (just south) in particular has several attractive Gothic buildings, notably a Poor School and Schoolmaster's House which was a freehouse for the estate labourers' children. Endsleigh Cottage above the Tamar (now a hotel) is the romantically ornate house built in 1810 for the Dowager Duchess of Bedford.

Remain on the A384 and cross the River Tamar at Greystone Bridge to re-enter Cornwall. In 2 miles, turn right on to the A388. After crossing the Launceston Bypass go forward over the crossroads and enter Launceston.

13th-century ruins of Launceston Castle

LAUNCESTON, Cornwall

Arguably Cornwall's most appealing town, Launceston was the county capital until 1838. There was early settlement here because of the advantages offered by this elevated site, and the castle ruins (AM) show it to have been a Norman stronghold. The castle, erstwhile seat of William the Conqueror's brother, still has its huge round keep and from its walls great tracts of Cornish and Devonshire landscape can be surveyed. The grass below was a public execution site until 1821. Ancient, narrow streets surround the town's main square and among the many interesting Georgian buildings is Lawrence House (NT) in Castle Street. The rooms have been turned into a museum of local history now, but at one time the house was a well-known rendezvous for French prisoners on parole during the Napoleonic Wars. Narrow South Gate is the only evidence left of the town walls which encircled

Launceston during Henry VIII's reign.

From the castle ruins follow SP 'Bude (B3254)'. At the bottom of the hill cross the river bridge and at the mini-roundabout go forward. At St Stephen's Church turn left SP 'Egloskerry'.

EGLOSKERRY, Cornwall

Cottages cluster around the little church which has been the village centre since Norman times. Much of the building has since been rebuilt, but the font has survived intact. On the walls hang memorials to the Specott family who lived a mile away at the large manor house called Penheale (not open) during the 17th century.

Continue along the unclassified road to Tresmeer and go forward with the Hallworthy road. In 2 miles turn right on to the A395 to reach the hamlet of Hallworthy. In 2¾ miles turn left on to the A39, then in another mile turn left again, SP 'Altarnun'. This byroad crosses Davidstow Moor with occasional views of Bodmin Moor to the right. In 5 miles, at the Rising Sun PH, bear left, then take the next turning right for Altarnun.

ALTARNUN, Cornwall

This, Cornwall's second largest parish, lies in a hollow on the edge of Bodmin Moor. Two little streams, crossed by a ford and a narrow bridge, flow through the village past the uneven stone walls of Altarnun's cottages. The church, nicknamed Cathedral of the Cornish Moors because of its size, is mainly 15th century. One of its best features is the collection of 16th-century carved bench ends depicting Tudor men and women, a piper, a jester, dancers, sheep and sheaves of corn.

LOOE, Cornwall

Now one resort, until 1883 West and East Looe were separate towns facing each other over the Looe River. Large beaches provide good bathing, surfing and angling, and Looe is Cornwall's main centre for shark fishing. The British International Sea Angling Festival is held here every autumn, and the captured sharks are subsequently chopped up and used as crab and lobster bait. West Looe has an attractive quay, and its focal point is the 19th-century church of St Nicholas, which was built mainly from the timber of wrecked ships. The tower of the church was effectively used at one time as a cage for scolding women. Nearby a 16th-century inn is renowned as a onetime haunt of smugglers. East Looe's museum is housed on the upper floor of the 16th-century guildhall (once used as a gaol), and downstairs the old town stocks and pillory can be seen. The narrow winding main street has little alleys and courts on one side leading to the quays. Near the Victorian warehouses is an aquarium which also has a stuffed shark and an old boat-building shed.

Leave on the A387 SP 'Plymouth via Torpoint'. In ½ mile branch right on to the B3253. In 3¾ miles rejoin the A387 and at Hessenford turn right on to the B3247, SP 'Seaton'. From Seaton an unclassified road on the right may be taken to the Woolly Monkey Sanctuary at Murrayton.

WOOLLY MONKEY SANCTUARY, Cornwall

South American woolly monkeys, Chinese geese, donkeys and rabbits live in this haven where there are no cages. Part of the wooded valley at Murrayton has been turned into a free-roaming sanctuary where visitors can observe these animals at close quarters (OACT).

From Seaton the main tour continues through Downderry and in 1¼ miles bears right. At Crafthole continue on the Millbrook road then in 2 miles turn right SP 'Whitsand Bay'. After 3 miles veer inland to reach the outskirts of Cawsand and Kingsand.

CAWSAND AND KINGSAND, Cornwall

As the streets of these twin villages run into each other it is hard to distinguish between them. Before the Plymouth breakwater was built, Cawsand Bay was an ideal place for the Royal Naval fleet to anchor in the 18th century and the wealth that they bought accounts for the many fine houses in the villages. The pubs too date from these prosperous times and Lord Nelson and Lady Hamilton used to stay at the Ship Inn.

SOUTH-EASTERN CORNWALL

Between Bodmin Moor and the Channel lies the high tableland of south-east Cornwall, its surface cut by deep wooded valleys branching into the sea. Two former capitals of the ancient royal Duchy lie within this peaceful region: the tiny cathedral 'city' of St Germans and the old stannary town of Lostwithiel.

Keep left and in ½ mile turn left, SP 'Millbrook'. At the top of the ascent turn left again on to the B3247. Alternatively, turn right to visit Mount Edgcumbe House and Country Park.

View from the long-distance coastal path, near Polperro

MOUNT EDGCUMBE HOUSE AND COUNTRY PARK, Cornwall

Facing Plymouth across the Sound is Mount Edgcumbe House. First built in the 16th century, it was a victim of the 1941 Plymouth Blitz and afterwards was restored as a Tudor mansion. The house, home of the Earl of Mount Edgcumbe, has fine Hepplewhite furniture, much of which came from the Edgcumbe family's original home, Cotehele. Most of the large estate has been turned into a country park and it provides scenic walks along 10 miles of beautiful coastline.

The main tour continues to Millbrook. Here turn left, SP 'Torpoint', then bear right. In 2¼ miles turn right and later descend to Antony. From here another detour can be made by turning right on to the A374 Torpoint road to Antony House.

ANTONY HOUSE, Cornwall

This dignified, silvery-grey Queen Anne mansion (NT) overlooks the Lynher River Estuary just over the water from Plymouth. The house is well known for its associations with the Cornish Carew family who played an active and often dangerous part in political affairs. Richard Carew wrote *Survey of Cornwall* in 1602, and it provides a unique record of the county during those days. The house is currently lived in by the Carew descendants and with its small, panelled rooms has more the air of a country home than a showplace.

From Antony follow the A374 Liskeard road, and continue through Sheviock to Polbathic. Here turn right on to the B3249, SP 'St Germans'. In 1 mile bear left, SP 'Saltash', to enter St Germans.

ST GERMANS, Cornwall

Until 1043 when the Cornish Bishopric merged with Exeter, this little village was Cornwall's cathedral 'city'. During the following century St Germans was recognised as an Augustinian priory and the existing church was consecrated in 1261. Much of this building has survived and stands as one of Cornwall's best examples of Norman architecture. The turreted house (not open) quite separate from the church, has been the home of the Earls of St Germans, the Eliots, since 1655. It was rebuilt about 1804 although the grounds were laid out 10 years

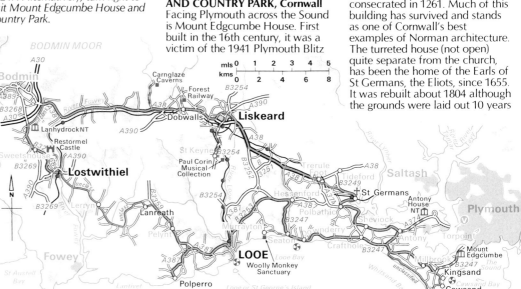

One of the Forest Railway's locos

DOBWALLS, Cornwall
Just north of the village run 2 miles of elaborate miniature railway line. This is the Forest Railway and it is based on the steam era of the American railroad and the corresponding landscape includes lakes, forests, tunnels and canyons. In addition, the Park has an indoor railway museum, a railway walk, and play and picnic areas. Next door, in a large converted barn, is a different source of interest — the Thorburn Museum and Gallery. Here are the works of Archibald Thorburn, one of Britain's greatest bird painters (1860-1935), as well as sketches, books, letters and photographs which make up a permanent memorial exhibition to the artist.

Remain on the Bodmin road and descend into the Fowey valley. After crossing the River Fowey a road on the right, SP 'St Neot', leads to Carnglaze Slate Caverns.

CARNGLAZE SLATE CAVERNS, Cornwall
Slate has been quarried from these caves (OACT) since the 14th century and it has been traditionally used as a roofing material; now it is used more widely for all types of building. One of the caverns is 300ft high and the original tramway built to haul the stone to the surface can be seen here. Deeper into the quarry is a clear greenish-blue underground lake and lichen on the surrounding rocks reflects the light.

Continue on the A38 for 5 miles before recrossing the River Fowey. After 1½ miles, at the crossroads, turn left, SP 'Lostwithiel. In another 1½ miles turn left again on to the B3268 passing, on the left, the entrance to Lanhydrock.

LANHYDROCK, Cornwall
Lanhydrock (NT) suffered badly from a fire in 1881 so there is little of the original building left, although the house was rebuilt to the same plan. However, the charming 2-storeyed gatehouse and north wing did survive and the long gallery, 116ft long, in the latter is particularly splendid with its ceiling of intricately carved plasterwork depicting biblical scenes. The estate is approached down a long avenue of beech and sycamore, some 4 centuries old. Formal gardens lie close to the house featuring rose-beds, yew hedges and some bronze vases by Ballin, goldsmith to Louis XIV.

Remain on the B3268 Lostwithiel road and at the hamlet of Sweetshouse keep left and continue to Lostwithiel.

LOSTWITHIEL, Cornwall
Lostwithiel, with Helston, Truro and Liskeard, is another of Cornwall's 4 stannary towns, and was also the county capital in the 13th century. The former stannary offices and county treasury in Quay Street occupied a great hall and there are still remains of this 13th-century building. Overlooking the Fowey valley a mile away is Restormel Castle (OACT), where Edmund, Earl of Cornwall, ruled the county. It has been a ruin since it was abandoned in the 16th century, having been used for a time by Parliamentarian forces.

From the centre of Lostwithiel turn right into Fore Street (one-way) and at the end turn right across the River Fowey and go over the level crossing. In ¼ mile, at the crossroads, turn right for Lerryn. At the Post Office keep left, then take the next turning left, 'SP 'Polperro'. In ¾ mile go over the crossroads and follow this narrow byroad for another 1½ miles where, at the T-junction, turn left. In 2 miles turn right to enter Lanreath.

LANREATH, Cornwall
There is an extremely interesting farm museum (OACT) in Lanreath featuring farm machinery from the past. Vintage tractors, engines and old farm implements, such as a turnip and cattle cake cutter and grappling irons, are just some of the things to see and sometimes there are demonstrations of traditional rural crafts including spinning and the making of corn dollies.

At the church keep left and then turn right on to the B3359 for Pelynt. In 1½ miles turn right, SP 'Polperro', then right again on to the A387 for Polperro.

POLPERRO, Cornwall
All Polperro's tiny streets and alleyways lead down to the harbour tucked into a fold in the cliffs, well protected by timber and masonry from the savage onslaught of Atlantic winter storms. Lime-washed cottages seem to grow out of the rock one on top of another, understandably attracting artists wishing to capture the true flavour of Cornwall. The Land of Legend and Model Village (OACT) gives a fascinating glimpse of old Cornwall all through the medium of animated models.

Return along the A387 to complete the tour at Looe.

earlier by the famous landscape gardener Humphry Repton. Of particular interest in the village itself are 6 gabled almshouses. The projecting gables stand on tall stone piers, forming a balcony which may be reached by an outside flight of steps.

At the far end of the village branch left, SP 'Liskeard'. In 1 mile go over the crossroads and in another ¾ mile turn right on to the A374. At the roundabout take the 2nd exit to join the A38. Follow this trunk road for 5½ miles before branching left on to the A390 to reach Liskeard.

LISKEARD, Cornwall
Liskeard's site across a valley accounts for its steep, narrow streets. It is a pleasant market town with a large monthly cattle fair and was one of Cornwall's 4 stannary towns. Among Liskeard's (pronounced Liscard) attractive buildings is Stuart House, where Charles I slept for a week during 1644. Well Lane is so named because a spring there, Pipe Well, was supposed to have healing properties in medieval days. Four pipes from an arched grotto produce a continual flow of water.

A 2½ mile diversion south of Liskeard leads to the Paul Corin Musical Collection at St Keyne Station. The best approach is via the B3254 and an unclassified road, SP 'St Keyne'.

PAUL CORIN MUSICAL COLLECTION, Cornwall
This fascinating collection of mechanical musical instruments founded by Paul Corin at St Keyne is housed in an old mill. Examples from all over Europe can be seen here, including fairground organs, cafe and street organs and pianos. The exhibits are all played daily, and there are European cafe orchestrations and piano performances of famous pianists to be heard.

From Liskeard the main tour follows SP 'Bodmin' and then rejoins the A38 to Dobwalls.

Polperro, smuggling haven during the 18th century

LYME REGIS, Dorset

Beautiful Lyme Regis, set in lovely scenery with the River Lym running swiftly through the town, was one of the first seaside towns on the south-west coast to become a popular resort in the 18th century. Its history as a port goes back much further, however, to medieval times when the picturesque old harbour round the Cobb was first built. Lyme Regis saw the first battle of the Armada in 1588 when local ships joined Drake's fleet in a skirmish with some of the Spanish galleons. Among the town's distinguished visitors in the 18th century was Jane Austen, who loved Lyme Regis and set part of her last novel, *Persuasion,* in the old port. Shingly Lyme Bay is sheltered by cliffs rising to the magnificent Golden Cap, the highest cliff on the south coast. The area is noted for fossils and there is a fine collection in Lyme Regis museum.

Leave on the A3070 Axminster road and ascend to Uplyme.

UPLYME, Devon

Old stone cottages set in a fold of the hills behind Lyme Regis form a pleasant village street overlooked by the church, built on a hilltop from where there are glorious views westwards of the Devon landscape. In the church, near the Jacobean pulpit, is an engraved glass memorial to 2 children by the modern artist Lawrence Whistler.

In 2¼ miles turn left on to the A35 and continue to Axminster.

AXMINSTER, Devon

Some of the finest British carpets come from this delightful, busy, market town which lies on a rise of ground above the River Axe. The Axminster carpet industry was founded in 1755 by Thomas Whitty, who had made a thorough study of Turkish craftsmanship and built his factory in the town centre. Many luxurious carpets were specially woven for the great stately homes of England and the business flourished for 80 years, rivalling Wilton for its superb creations. In 1835, however, the Axminster factory went bankrupt and was bought out by a Wilton weaver. Not until 1937 was the business revived in new premises, where visitors are welcome. Bow-fronted Georgian and early Victorian houses lend charm to Axminster's bustling streets leading up to a shady green where the church looks out over the attractive town centre with its many coaching inns.

Leave on the A358 Chard road and in 3¼ miles pass through Tytherleigh and ½ mile farther turn right on to the B3167, SP 'Crewkerne'. After another 1½ miles, at the end of Perry Street, an unclassified road on the right may be taken to visit Forde Abbey.

SOMERSET TOWNS AND DEVON VILLAGES

Where the south coast cliffs sweep down to the sea around Lyme Bay and the charming seaside resort of Lyme Regis, and the ever changing vista of hills and vales reveals a pageant of historic towns and delightful villages.

The harbour at Lyme Regis

FORDE ABBEY, Dorset

Cromwell's Attorney General Sir Edmund Prideaux acquired this lovely 12th-century Cistercian monastery in 1649 and transformed it into a country house. Among its many treasures are the 5 Mortlake tapestries woven in the early 18th century to fit the walls of the saloon. The tapestries represent Raphael cartoons now in the Victoria and Albert Museum in London. Water and rock gardens are a special feature of the extensive grounds.

The main tour continues on the B3167 and in 3 miles turns right on to the A30 for Cricket St Thomas.

CRICKET ST THOMAS, Somerset

Llamas, camels, bison and wallabies roam incongruously in the landscaped parkland of a Georgian mansion, set in a secluded valley sheltered beneath the aptly named Windwhistle Ridge. Gardens and terraces lead down to a sequence of 9 lakes where flamingoes wade and black swans glide gracefully among a colourful variety of waterfowl. Cricket St Thomas is the home of the National Heavy Horse Centre and a small zoo, aviary and dairy farm add to the interest of the estate, which once belonged to the Bridport family who were connected by marriage to Lord Nelson.

Remain on the A30 for 2½ miles, then turn left on to an unclassified road, SP 'Ilminster'. After 3¼ miles, at the hamlet of Kingstone, bear right. Alternatively keep forward, then take the next turning left to visit Dowlish Wake.

DOWLISH WAKE, Somerset

Standing in the middle of the village is a thatched 16th-century barn (OACT) which belongs to Perry Bros., the famous cider producers. Here the past is recalled by a collection of farm machinery, wagons, cider presses, etc., now, sadly, replaced by more modern equipment. Cider is made on the premises during the autumn after the harvest of locally grown apples and is traditionally matured in wooden barrels under a watchful expert eye. It is for sale in the shop, together with numerous interesting gift items such as stone cider jars, corn dollies and ovenware.

The main tour continues to Ilminster. Join the A303, then branch left for the town centre.

ILMINSTER, Somerset

From the top of Beacon Hill it is said that 30 church towers and spires can be seen. That of Ilminster church, modelled on the central tower of Wells Cathedral, must be among the loveliest. Ilminster, nestling at the foot of the Black Down Hills, hides its prettiest streets away from the main roads and thatched cottages lead to a square built around a pillared market house.

Leave on the A3037 Chard road, then in 2 miles turn left on to the A358. After 1¼ miles, on the right, is Hornsbury Mill Museum.

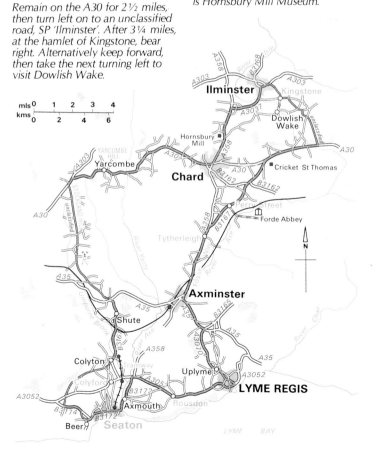

The 1,000-acre estate around Cricket House has been turned into a magnificent wildlife park

HORNSBURY MILL MUSEUM, Somerset
A splendid water wheel 18ft high dominates this 19th-century corn mill (OACT) which is kept in immaculate working order. The mill stands in attractive grounds and has a small museum of country bygones, a craft shop, and cream teas are available.

Continue on the A358 to Chard.

CHARD, Somerset
The long main street of Somerset's highest town is bordered by 2 streams, one flowing north to the Bristol Channel, the other south to the English Channel. The handsome Guildhall faces a charming Elizabethan building, once the town's manor house, where the old court room on the 1st floor can be visited. Here the infamous Judge Jeffries presided during the Bloody Assizes that followed the Duke of Monmouth's rebellion.

Leave on the A30, SP 'Exeter', and follow an undulating road to Yarcombe.

YARCOMBE, Devon
The lovely scenery of the Yarty Valley provides the setting for this graceful village. In the 15th-century church is a rare Breeches Bible (see Aylesham tour) and the carving on the bench ends is particularly fine. Almost within the churchyard, the charming village inn may well once have been the Church House.

Continue on the A30 and in 2 miles, at the A303 junction, keep left, then take the next turning left, SP 'Axminster'. Later pass the TV mast on Stockland Hill and at the A35 junction turn right, then immediately left on to the B3161 and continue to Shute.

SHUTE, Devon
A castellated 16th-century gatehouse forms the entrance to the medieval manor house of Shute Barton (NT) of which 2 wings remain. In the kitchen, the enormous hearth holds a spit large enough to roast 2 oxen. The house was once owned by Henry Grey, Duke of Suffolk and father of Lady Jane Grey, the tragic Nine Days Queen whose reign lasted from July 9 to 19 1553. She was condemned for treason and executed by order of Mary I in February 1554.

Continue on the B3161 to Colyton.

COLYTON, Devon
Pretty houses and cottages, mostly of the 17th and 18th centuries, line the narrow streets that wind up the slopes of the hillside where Colyton was founded by the Saxons in AD 700. The vicarage, the grammar school and the fine Great House, with its chequerboard frontage, all date from the Tudor period, when the manor of Colyton was bought by local inhabitants from Henry VIII. They called themselves the Chamber of Feoffees and this name has been preserved by the town authorities ever since.

At the town hall keep left, then turn right into Queen Street. Shortly turn left again on to the unclassified Sidmouth road. Nearly 3 miles farther (at Stafford Cross) go over the staggered crossroads, then at the next crossroads turn left on to the B3174, SP 'Beer', and continue to Beer.

BEER, Devon
Up on the slopes behind the seaside village of Beer runs Beer Heights Light Railway. This steam-operated passenger line travels through the Peco Modelrama park and fine views are to be had of the bay below along the way. There is even a full-size replica railway station with refreshments. Nine separate model railways are on permanent show around the house and gardens and there are souvenir and model shops to browse around.

The main tour turns left on to the B3172 to Seaton. On entering the town follow SP Sea Front. At the end of the Sea Front turn left, then turn right on to the B3172 and cross the River Axe. Follow the Axe estuary to Axmouth.

AXMOUTH, Devon
Thatched, colour-washed cottages and an old inn, grouped around the church, make up the unspoilt village scene at Axmouth. Once a busy port, situated at the point where the Roman Fosse Way crossed the river, Axmouth has seen the Axe estuary gradually silt up, today allowing passage for yachts and pleasure boats only. In 1877 the first concrete bridge in England was built across the Axe.

In 1 mile, at Boshill Cross, turn right on to the A3052 for the return to Lyme Regis.

Much of Forde Abbey's original medieval stonework can be identified in the present Tudor mansion

LYNTON, Devon

This pleasant and very popular resort is sited high on a cliff some 500ft above its sister village of Lynmouth. Tree-covered Summerhouse Hill shields it from the blustery sea gales, and a solid ring of hills protects it from the worst of Exmoor's rain. The Victorians were quick to recognize these attributes as being suited to seaside holidays, and since then the resort has attracted a constant stream of visitors. Victorian architecture predominates here, and a typical eccentricity of that era is the water-powered cliff lift. This was donated by a lawyer named George Newnes in 1890, and has been restored to working order. Newnes also built the Town Hall, behind which rise the flower-strewn slopes of viewpoint Hollerday Hill. Miles of coastline and the Exmoor hills can be seen from here. Other features of Lynton include a Catholic church containing rare and beautiful marble work, and the Lyn and Exmoor Museum in old St Vincent's Cottage. The local cliffs afford views across the Bristol Channel to Wales, and the magnificent Valley of the Rocks is accessible by footpath.

VALLEY OF THE ROCKS, Devon

The poet Robert Southey described this fantastic place of jagged tors and breathtaking coastal scenery with the words '. . . rock reeling upon rock, stone piled upon stone, a huge terrific reeling mass'.

Descend Lynmouth Hill (1 in 4) to Lynmouth and turn right on to the A39 'Barnstaple' road for Watersmeet.

WATERSMEET, Devon

As its name suggests, this National Trust beauty spot is the place where the tumbling waters of the East Lyn River converge with the Hoaroak Water, which cascades down a rocky bed in a series of waterfalls. It is best to leave the car and explore the cool beauty of this wooded gorge on foot.

Continue alongside the Hoaroak Water for ⅓ mile then turn left on to the B3223 SP 'Simonsbath'. Cross Hillsford Bridge, and in ¾ mile go round a hairpin bend and drive forward on to an unclassified road SP 'Brendon Valley'. Pass Brendon Church, with views of the tree-covered slopes that characterize this area, then descend through the oak-wooded valley of the East Lyn River for Brendon.

BRENDON, Devon

This picturesque village is situated on the banks of the East Lyn, which is spanned here by an attractive medieval packhorse bridge.

Continue alongside the East Lyn River to Malmsmead

MALMSMEAD, Devon

Ponies can be hired here for a 2½ - mile trek along the deep valley of Badgworthy Water, leading to the legendary Doone Country. The journey can just as easily be undertaken on foot.

INTO THE DOONE COUNTRY

Before they come here many people half believe Blackmore's romantic novel 'Lorna Doone' to be a true historical account. By the time they leave, the region's gorse and heather covered moors, wooded ravines, and exquisite little stone villages have convinced them of it.

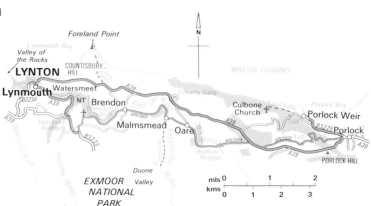

DOONE VALLEY, Devon & Somerset

R D Blackmore immortalized isolated and beautiful Hoccombe Combe as 'Doone Valley' in his famous novel *Lorna Doone*. Thanks to his brilliantly emotive style this has become one of the most romantic places in the country, and many visitors go away firmly believing that the whole tale was actually a true historical account. Tales of a villainous Doone family who terrorized the moorfolk have been told here since 1790. It appears that Blackmore seized on these as a handy base for his novel,

and although he did not concentrate on authentic landscape description, several features can be identified from his text. Lanke Combe enters the valley from the west and has miniature versions of features attributed to Doone Valley by the author, including the famous waterslide. Records show that the remains of several buildings in this area belonged to a medieval settlement, but the name Doone is not mentioned. With or without the legend, this is a beautiful area that should not be missed.

EXMOOR NATIONAL PARK (NORTH), Devon & Somerset

In its northern reaches this vast national park meets the sea with magnificent results. Rugged hogs-back cliffs stretch continuously from Lynton to Porlock, falling steeply to the waters of the Bristol Channel and affording views across to the coast of South Wales. Lush coombs wind deep into rambling moorland, scattered here and there with tiny hamlets and picturesque villages. The burgeoning life of the valleys makes a striking contrast with the remote and heather-clad wastelands through which they cut, but together these opposites form a landscape that could be nowhere else but Exmoor. Agriculture and forestry play a large part in the park's life, and the rich patchwork of farmland in areas like the Porlock Vale are sharp reminders that this is more than just a place of outstanding natural beauty. Wildlife abounds on Exmoor. The shy red deer that haunt its wooded coombs are unique in being direct descendants of the wild deer that once roamed prehistoric Britain. Common mammals thrive in a variety of habitats, and the park boasts many species of birds. Vestiges of prehistoric ages can be found in the form of earthworks, tumuli, standing stones, and barrows. Of particular note is the stone circle on Porlock Hill, but there are many other fascinating examples easily reached from Lynton.

From Malmsmead cross a river bridge into Somerset and continue to Oare.

OARE, Somerset

This tiny Oare Valley hamlet stands by the Oare Water and has strong connexions with the fiction of R D Blackmore. It was here that his heroine Lorna was married, and here that she almost met an untimely end. The village church is a lovely little 15th-century building well suited to the magical tale that has been woven around it. Inside are 19th-century boxpews and a curious piscina shaped like a man's head. Exceptionally fine coomb scenery with wooded valleys and steep screes surrounds the area.

Follow the road SP 'Oareford, Robber's Bridge' for 1½ miles. Cross the bridge and continue the steep ascent to join the A39. Proceed along a scenic moorland road, with fine views across the Bristol Channel, and reach Porlock Hill.

PORLOCK HILL, Somerset

The notorious incline of this hill as it rises from Porlock is one of the steepest in Britain, and the breathtaking view from its summit surpasses many. A prehistoric stone circle survives close by.

Make a steep and winding descent (1 in 4) into Porlock.

Rain and mist add extra dimensions of beauty and mystery to Northern Exmoor.

PORLOCK, Somerset

Saxon Kings chose the site of this enchanting coastal village as a base from which to hunt in Exmoor Forest, and nowadays it serves as an ideal touring centre. A famous riding school is established here, and it is difficult to venture far without meeting horses and riders. Notable buildings in Porlock include 15th-century Doverhay Manor House and a mainly 13th-century red-stone church containing the tomb of one John Harrington, who is said to have fought at Agincourt. This remarkable monument is topped by almost life-size effigies of Harrington and his wife. Like many of its neighbours Porlock attracted an artistic following bent on recording its delights in paint and verse. Robert Southey the poet was obviously disenchanted with the weather when he stayed at the Ship Inn and wrote: 'Porlock, I shall forget thee not, here by the unwelcome summer rain confined . . . .'

Leave the village on the B3225 and drive to Porlock Weir.

Lynmouth Bay is overlooked by the cliff mass of Blackhead and the ancient earthworks on Wind Hill.

Culbone Church occupies a delightfully wooded position beside a stream.

PORLOCK WEIR & CULBONE CHURCH, Somerset

In years gone by Porlock was a thriving port, but all that remains today is the miniature harbour of this unique little Porlock Bay hamlet. Pleasure craft make good use of its sheltered waters, and its shingle beach is backed by cliffs cloaked with thick woodland. A pleasant walk leads from here to Culbone, where can be seen the smallest English church still in regular use. The building displays Norman and later styles, and measures only 33 by 13½ft. Inside are old benches and a 14th-century screen, while all around are woods and pits once used by a charcoal-burning community.

Return to Porlock and take the 'Lynmouth' road, then branch right on to an unclassified road SP 'Alternative Route via Toll Road' and climb gradually to open moorland. Meet a main road and turn right on to the A39, re-entering Devon at County Gate with a picnic site to the left. After another 2¾ miles reach a footpath leading right to Foreland Point.

Out of season Porlock Weir once more becomes a quiet fishing hamlet.

FORELAND POINT AND LIGHTHOUSE, Devon

The footpath to this lighthouse runs through magnificent coastal scenery (NT) and affords extensive views of the Bristol Channel.

Continue to Countisbury Hill.

COUNTISBURY HILL, Devon

Stagecoach drivers had to change horses at the ancient inn on top of this exceptionally steep hill. West of the inn prehistoric earthworks (NT) overlook the sea and superb cliff walks can be made beyond the small local church.

Descend Countisbury Hill (1 in 4) to Lynmouth.

LYNMOUTH, Devon

In 1812 the poet Shelley and his 16-year-old bride were captivated by the beautiful little fishing village that stood here. Since then tourism and a rash of boarding houses have given it a new lease of commercial life, but the basic framework of towering cliffs and swirling river valleys remains. Disastrous floods that made national headlines in 1952 swept away part of the quay, a great deal of the resort, and a curious edifice known as the Rhenish Tower. Afterwards the East and West Lyn rivers were widened, and strong walls built to prevent a recurrence of the tragedy. This tidying up included the rebuilding of the tower, which is supposed to resemble a type found in Germany and was originally constructed to store salt water for indoor bathing. The picturesque lower town is a medley of colour-washed cottages clustered amid gardens bright with roses, fuchsias, and other shrubs.

Ascend Lynmouth Hill and return to Lynton.

HIGH DOWNS AND HOCKTIDE REVELS

The bare uplands of the Marlborough and Berkshire Downs overlook open, windswept country, while the lush lowlands are dotted with small villages and noted beauty spots. At Hungerford, Hocktide is celebrated with an annual ceremony that has its origins in the pagan rites of ancient Britons.

Wansdyke, seen between Marlborough and Oare, was a 50-mile defensive earthwork thought to be built in the 1st century

MARLBOROUGH, Wilts
Marlborough's broad Georgian High Street was once a great livestock market where thousands of downland sheep were herded. Today it is a pleasant shopping centre, with a number of interesting old passages and side streets branching off on both sides. By St Peter's Church an arched gateway leads to the town's famous public school, founded in 1843 around the site of the old castle.

Leave Marlborough on the A4 Chippenham road, then turn left on to the A345, SP 'Salisbury', and continue to Oare.

OARE, Wilts
Oare sits beneath the Marlborough Downs at the head of the Vale of Pewsey, a fertile valley that separates the arid downland from the flat expanse of Salisbury Plain. The 18th-century mansion house was enlarged in the 1920s by Clough Williams-Ellis, creator of the 'Italian' seaside village of Portmeirion. He also designed other houses in the village: a T-shaped, thatched house with the unwelcoming name of Cold Blow, and a terrace of whitewashed cottages with a central archway.

Continue on the A345 to Pewsey.

A perfect combination of roses and thatch in Longparish

PEWSEY, Wilts
King Alfred's statue gazes out from the market place of Pewsey, a pleasant town sheltered by Pewsey Hill whose slopes are distinguished by a chalk white horse. The parish church rests on great sarsen stones, similar to those used at Stonehenge.

Continue on the Amesbury road, cross the River Avon and turn left, SP 'Everleigh', then immediately turn right. The outline of the Pewsey White Horse can be seen before ascending Pewsey Hill. Continue to the edge of Everleigh. Here, turn left on to the A342, SP 'Andover'. In 2 miles at the T-junction turn left then immediately right for Ludgershall.

LUDGERSHALL, Wilts
After the modern housing developments on the outskirts, the old village centre, with its almshouses, ruined castle and rambling church, comes as something of a surprise. The ruins were once a royal castle where Queen Matilda fled from King Stephen after one of their 12th-century battles.

At the T-junction turn left SP 'Andover' and continue into Hampshire. In 4¼ miles at the roundabout turn right, SP 'Thruxton'. In ¼ mile turn left, SP 'Amport'. Shortly turn right then immediately turn left across the main road for Hawk Conservancy.

THE HAWK CONSERVANCY WEYHILL WILDLIFE PARK, Hants
Opened in 1965, the park specialises in European birds, including hawks, falcons, eagles, owls and vultures; the hawks and falcons are flown whenever weather permits. Among the other wildlife represented are many native British mammals such as polecats, squirrels, foxes and wildcats.

Continue to Amport, turn left for Monxton, then go over the crossroads and continue to Abbots Ann.

ABBOTTS ANN, Hants
The 18th-century church at Abbotts Ann contains numerous white paper garlands; more, it is said than any other village in the country. This reflects well on the morals of the inhabitants because

these used to be carried at the funerals of men and women who had died chaste and celibate.

At Abbotts Ann turn right, then left at the Eagle PH and shortly keep left then bear right. At the A343 turn left then take the next turning right SP 'The Clatfords', into Anna valley. Continue through Upper Clatford and on to Goodworth Clatford. Here, turn left, SP 'Andover', and cross the river bridge. At the A3057 junction turn right SP 'Stockbridge', then in ¼ mile turn left on to the B3420 for Wherwell (see tour 24). Keep left through the village and at the far end go forward on to the B3048, SP 'Longparish'. At the A303 turn right, then immediately left for Longparish.

LONGPARISH, Hants
As the name suggests, this village consists of a long main street along which are spaced a number of pretty, thatched cottages. It stands in the valley of the River Test, noted for its excellent trout fishing.

Continue along a winding road to Hurstbourne Priors. Here turn right then immediately left, SP 'Hurstbourne Tarrant', and follow the Bourne rivulet to St Mary Bourne.

ST MARY BOURNE, Hants
The Bourne valley is watered by a pretty rivulet which in a dry summer sometimes disappears, as do many of the chalk streams in this area. There is enough moisture, however, to feed the many dark green watercress beds that surround this attractive village. Its church contains a massive, carved, black marbled font from Tournai, similar to the one in Winchester Cathedral. The yew tree in the churchyard is one of the oldest in Hampshire.

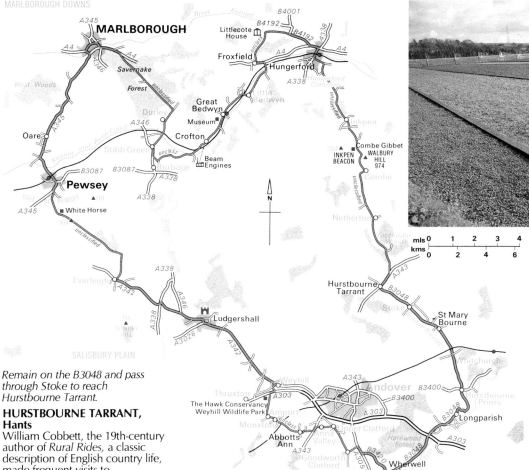

Remain on the B3048 and pass through Stoke to reach Hurstbourne Tarrant.

HURSTBOURNE TARRANT, Hants

William Cobbett, the 19th-century author of *Rural Rides*, a classic description of English country life, made frequent visits to Uphusband, as he called Hurstbourne Tarrant.

Turn right on to the A343, SP 'Newbury' then in ½ mile turn left, SP 'Netherton'. Follow this pleasant byroad for 3¼ miles, then keep forward, SP 'Combe' and Inkpen'. Later turn sharp right to reach the edge of Combe. Keep left and continue over the shoulder of Inkpen Hill and Walbury Hill.

INKPEN HILL & WALBURY HILL, Berks

Walbury Hill, at 974ft the highest point of the Berkshire Downs, is crowned by the forbidding banks of Walbury Camp, a massive Iron-Age hill fort. Almost opposite, Inkpen Beacon tops the barren, windswept upland of Inkpen Hill. Here Combe Gibbet stands as a sinister landmark. It was erected in 1676 for the hanging of 2 local villagers who had murdered 2 of their 3 young children. The gibbet was in use until the last century.

Descend and later go over the crossroads, SP 'Hungerford', to reach Inkpen. At the T-junction turn right, then take the first turning left. In 2½ miles bear right, then continue forward, SP 'Hungerford gated road', to cross Hungerford Common. At the next T-junction turn left for Hungerford.

HUNGERFORD, Berks

Hock Tuesday, the 2nd Tuesday after Easter, is the day to visit Hungerford, for the age-old

Hocktide Ceremony, at which the town officials are elected for the coming year, takes place. Hungerford has no Mayor and Corporation, but instead, a governing body of Feoffees is elected from among the townspeople. While the elections take place, Tuttimen bearing long staves decorated with bunches (tutti) of flowers roam through the town demanding a kiss or a penny from any girl or woman they meet. In return, the Orange Scrambler, who goes with them, gives an orange. Hungerford is an attractive old town at any time of the year, and the many antique shops in its main street are fascinating.

At Hungerford turn right on to the A338. Cross the Kennet and Avon Canal, then turn left on to the A4. In ¼ mile turn right on to the B4192 SP 'Swindon'. In 1 mile keep forward, SP 'Littlecote'. After ¾ mile pass the entrance to Littlecote House.

LITTLECOTE HOUSE, Wilts

An early Tudor manor house (OACT) contains beautiful furniture, paintings and a rare example of an intact Cromwellian chapel. The magnificent Littlecote armour restored by the Royal Armouries at the Tower of London is on display in the Great Hall. Wax figures designed to appear in realistic settings to

represent the domestic scene can be found in many rooms. A farm, self-sufficient in 17th-century manner, has had its original buildings restored and workers wear costumes of the period. Continuing the theme of original style and presentation, a company of six knights and their ladies are in residence and also wear costumes of the era. Excavations in the wooded grounds have revealed a large Roman mosaic, and a miniature railway system connects this to the house, gardens and play areas.

Continue to Froxfield.

FROXFIELD, Wilts

The centrepiece of this attractive village is the group of 50 redbrick almshouses, built around a peaceful courtyard in 1694 and later enlarged. They were originally endowed by the Duchess of Somerset as a refuge for poor widows.

Turn left on to the A4 and pass the Somerset almshouses on the left. In almost ½ mile turn right, SP 'Great Bedwyn'. Cross the bridges, then turn right again to follow the Kennet and Avon Canal. At Little Bedwyn continue on the Great Bedwyn road, recross the canal and railway bridge, then turn left.

GREAT BEDWYN, Wilts

Seven generations of stonemasons have lived and worked in Great Bedwyn. Their craftsmanship is commemorated in the Stone Museum, which contains monuments, gravestones, busts and sculpture going back to the 18th century.

At Great Bedwyn turn left, then right into Church Street, SP 'Crofton'. Shortly, on the right, is the Bedwyn Stone Museum. Continue to Crofton.

CROFTON, Wilts

Crofton stands at the highest point of the Kennet and Avon Canal, about 400ft above the River Kennet. Inside the early 19th-century pumping houses (OACT) in the village are 2 beam engines, designed by Boulton and Watt, which operate a massive cast-iron beam. They were used to pump water up to the canal and have now been restored; occasionally they are powered by steam and can be seen working.

Continue on the unclassified road then cross the canal and bear right, SP 'Burbage'. In 1¾ miles, at the T-junction, turn right, then at the A346 turn right again. In ½ mile, at Stibb Green, turn right by the Three Horseshoes PH, SP 'Savernake'. After 2 miles, opposite the gateway on the right, turn left (no SP) to enter Savernake Forest. (Forestry Commission road — rough surface in places).

SAVERNAKE FOREST, Wilts

This former royal hunting forest covers more than 2,000 acres. The walks and rides radiating from the superb Grand Avenue, a 3-mile drive lined by towering beech trees, are the handiwork of Capability Brown, who was commissioned by the Marquess of Ailesbury to landscape the natural woodland.

After 3 miles turn left on to the A4 for the return to Marlborough.

MINEHEAD, Somerset

The natural beauty of its surroundings combined with its delightful situation and mild climate have made this a popular seaside resort with holidaymakers from all over the country. The Esplanade commands a wide sweep of the bay, where the sands are good and bathing is safe. A prominent feature of the high ground behind the town is North Hill, which overlooks the quaint little harbour some hundreds of feet below and affords fine views across the Bristol Channel. On the landward slope is the parish church, where years ago a light burned constantly to guide travellers on the moor and lead ships to the harbour. During these times Minehead harbour was a busy Channel port second only to Bristol, but now it is just the pleasant holiday town it appears to be. Among its attractions are the beautifully-kept Blenheim Gardens, where there is a model town which is floodlit in the evening.

WEST SOMERSET RAILWAY, Somerset

Britain's longest private line, this railway was re-opened in 1976 and runs 20 miles from the coast at Minehead to Bishop's Lydeard. Steam and diesel trains provide a nostalgic way to enjoy the scenery. Refreshments and souvenirs are available at the Minehead terminus.

Leave Minehead on the A39 'Porlock' road and enter the Exmoor National Park area. In 2⅓ miles turn right on to an unclassified road and drive to Selworthy.

EXMOOR NATIONAL PARK (EAST), Somerset

East Exmoor and its associated area is a gentler landscape than the rugged central moor. Open moorland contrasts colourfully with the intensively farmed Brendon slopes, and both natural and planted forests lap occasional rocky summits that afford good all-round views. To the north is the beautiful Bristol Channel coast, while inland are National Trust villages that include some of the most picturesque communities in the entire west country.

SELWORTHY, Somerset

This charming village (NT) is one of the most frequented beauty spots in north Somerset, and is grouped round a walnut-shaped green attractively edged with flowers and overlooked by several old cottages. Also of note are the 15th-century almshouses and an old tithe barn, while over all is the sturdy square tower of the 16th-century church. This handsome building is renowned for the particularly fine wagon roof in its south aisle. Majestic Selworthy Beacon (NT) rises to 1,012ft north of the village and is a good viewpoint.

Return to the A39 'Porlock' road, turn right, and in ½ mile pass the edge of Allerford.

OVER THE BRENDON HILLS

Where Exmoor merges into the Brendon Hills the landscape changes from wild heathland to a tapestry of fields and forest. Wooded byways and patches of moor open on to panoramic seascapes fringed with busy resorts and unspoiled villages.

Beyond Luccombe well-tended countryside gives way to open moorland which rises to the summit of 1,705ft Dunkery Beacon.

ALLERFORD, Somerset

Quaint cottages and the remains of a manor house can be seen here; of particular note is Allerford's much-photographed double-arched packhorse bridge.

Continue on the A39 and in ½ mile turn left on to an unclassified road SP 'Luccombe'. Pass several packhorse bridges to the right and in ¾ mile at crossroads turn right SP 'Dunkery Beacon'. A detour to Luccombe village can be taken from the main route, by keeping straight ahead.

LUCCOMBE, Somerset

Access to this secluded little village (NT), whose name means 'closed-in combe', is by a narrow winding lane. The village church has a good tower, and the churchyard is entered through a charming lychgate.

On the main route, begin the long ascent of Dunkery Hill and bear left at the fork.

The packhorse bridge at Allerford.

HOLNICOTE ESTATE, Somerset

The rolling moorland and dense forest round Dunkery Hill are part of the Holnicote Estate (NT), which incorporates some of the loveliest scenery in the Exmoor National Park. About half its 12,443 acres fall within the Exmoor boundaries, and the whole forms a band 6 miles deep along the Bristol Channel coastline. Features include various prehistoric remains, 4 ancient packhorse bridges, and such notable villages as picturesque Selworthy and Luccombe (both NT).

Continue the ascent of Dunkery Hill through progressively wilder scenery and reach a road summit of 1,450ft. A footpath leads from the carpark here to the 1,705 ft viewpoint of Dunkery Beacon.

DUNKERY BEACON, Somerset

Dunkery Beacon (NT), the highest point on Exmoor, is surrounded by some of the most breathtaking scenery in the national park. It was once a link in a chain of fire-beacon sites across the west country. The top is nowadays shared by a cairn commemorating the gift of the hill to the National Trust, the remains of several tumuli, and an official AA viewpoint marker. The Cloutsham Nature Trail (open all year) starts from Webber's Post and covers some 3 miles of varied habitat.

Stay on the unclassified road and descend for 2½ miles, then go forward on to the B3224 to reach Wheddon Cross. Go forward with the B3224 SP 'Taunton' and ascend on to the Brendon Hills.

BRENDON HILLS, Somerset

Undulating slopes with a rich patchwork of forest and farmland are the distinctive characteristics of this gentle range. Farmers, and more recently the Forestry Commission, have transformed the landscape from moorland into a semi-cultivated countryside of symmetrical fields bordered by beech hedges and interspersed with acres of dark conifers. In earlier times small hillside mining villages sprang up to work local deposits of iron ore, but the last Brendon iron mine closed down in 1883. Vestiges of an even earlier age can be seen along the Ridgeway, which is studded with round barrows dating from the Bronze Age.

After 1¾ miles reach Heath Poult Cross and turn right on to an unclassified road. Continue for 5 miles, along a ridge above the Exe Valley then descend into the Valley and turn left on to the A396, SP 'Tiverton'. In 2½ miles at Exebridge turn left on to an unclassified road SP 'Morebath'. After 1½ miles turn left on to the B3190 'Watchet' road, and shortly pass Morebath; 3 miles beyond the village a car park for Wimbleball Lake lies to the left.

The packhorse bridge at Allerford.

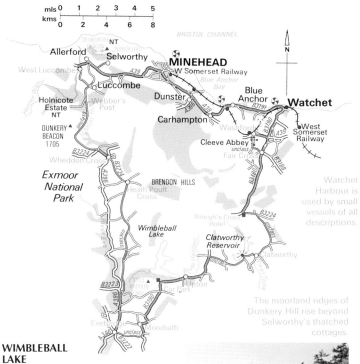

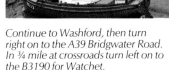

The moorland ridges of Dunkery Hill rise beyond Selworthy's thatched cottages.

Watchet Harbour is used by small vessels of all descriptions.

WIMBLEBALL LAKE
Somerset
Great care has been taken to blend this River Haddeo reservoir project with the countryside of south Exmoor. New plantations of trees native to the area have been established right down to the water's edge, and a small area of bank has been given over to leisure facilities for angling, small-boat sailing, and riding. Amenities include a carpark, a picnic area, and planned woodland walks.

Continue on the B3190 through Upton, then in 2 miles at crossroads turn right on to an unclassified road SP 'Wiveliscombe'. After a further 1 mile branch left and drive over crossroads to skirt Clatworthy Reservoir.

CLATWORTHY RESERVOIR,
Somerset
Like its close neighbour Wimbleball, this beautiful upland reservoir has been integrated with the local scenery and is a haven for all kinds of wildlife. A large carpark gives access to a 10-acre public viewing area with picnic facilities.

Continue, and on the descent turn left and shortly right before crossing the River Tone and reaching Clatworthy. Keep left through the village SP 'Brompton Ralph', and after 1 mile at crossroads, turn left SP 'Raleigh's Cross', then after a further 2 miles meet a T-junction and turn left on to the B3224. Reach Raleigh's Cross Hotel and turn right on to the B3190 SP 'Watchet'. There are excellent views of the Bristol Channel at first before the long descent to crossroads at Fair Cross. Here turn left on to an unclassified road SP 'Washford', and in 1 mile pass the entrance to Cleeve Abbey.

CLEEVE ABBEY, Somerset
Remains of this 13th-century Cistercian abbey (AM), founded in 1188, include a refectory with traceried windows, a timbered roof, and some fine wall paintings. The picturesque gatehouse and painted chamber are of particular note.

Continue to Washford, then turn right on to the A39 Bridgwater Road. In ¾ mile at crossroads turn left on to the B3190 for Watchet.

WATCHET, Somerset
Coleridge found the main character for his long, moralistic poem *The Rime of the Ancient Mariner* in this historic seaport, which now doubles as a popular resort. The Esplanade offers a grandstand view of the harbour, and the local beaches offer plenty of opportunities for the fossil hunter. Behind the town are the lofty heights of the Brendon and Quantock hill ranges.

Leave Watchet on the B3191 and continue, with views of the Bristol Channel, to Blue Anchor.

BLUE ANCHOR, Somerset
In front of this small hamlet is a clean white beach which sweeps round the alabaster rocks of Blue Anchor Bay in a brilliant arc. The area is well known for its fossils.

Continue on the B3191 to Carhampton.

The ancient village of Dunster is dominated by its romantic castle.

CARHAMPTON, Somerset
This little village dates back to 833, when it was the site of a Danish victory. Its restored church contains a magnificent painted screen which dates from the 15th century and stretches across the entire breadth of the building. Each January the villagers re-enact the old ceremony of Wassailing the Apple Trees, an ancient custom involving a toast to the largest apple tree in the cider orchards and a libation of cider thrown on its trunk. The whole procedure has more than a suggestion of ancient fertility rites. Close to the church lychgate is an old pub called the Butcher's Arms, which has the date 1638 worked in sheep's knuckle bones in the cobbled floor.

At Carhampton turn right on to the A39 'Minehead' road and after 1½ miles turn left on to the A396 SP 'Tiverton' to enter Dunster.

DUNSTER, Somerset
Dunster is a beautiful medieval village that has often been described as a 'perfect relic of feudal times'. Its unspoilt condition is largely due to its constant ownership by one family, the Luttrells, for some 600 years until 1950. The Norman castle (NT) was the family seat and is well worth visiting. Its oak-panelled halls display magnificent ceilings and fascinating relics. In the centre of the village is the octagonal Yarn Market, which was built in 1609, when Dunster was an important cloth centre. Not far away is the lovely Luttrell Arms, which is said to have stood for three centuries and was originally the house of the Abbot of Cleeve. Among its many features are an interesting 15th-century porch and a fine chamber displaying a wealth of carved oak. The parish church is by far the finest in this part of the country. Both it and its associated buildings are of particularly warm pink sandstone, and the whole harmonious group is set in a tranquil rural scene. Nearby the River Avill is spanned by the ancient Gallox packhorse bridge (AM).

Return along the A396 for ½ mile and turn left to rejoin the A39. Return to Minehead.

MORETON-IN-MARSH, Glos

Moreton-in-Marsh is a pleasant small market town under the edge of the north Cotswolds. Among many interesting old inns here are the White Hart, where Charles I slept in 1643, and the famous Redesdale Arms coaching stop. The town's curfew tower carries a 17th-century clock. Two miles north west, set in 50 acres, is the Batsford Arboretum.

Follow SP 'A44 Oxford' from Moreton-in-Marsh and continue to the Four Shire Stone, on the left of the road.

FOUR SHIRE STONE, Glos

About 2 miles east of Moreton-in-Marsh is the famous Four Shire Stone, where Gloucestershire met Oxfordshire, Warwickshire, and an isolated part of Worcestershire before the county reorganization of the 1970s.

Pass Four Shire Stone and in ¾ mile turn right on to an unclassified road for Chastleton.

CHASTLETON, Oxon

Chastleton House is of Cotswold stone and was built by wealthy wool merchant Walter Jones in 1603. His descendants are still in ownership. On the top floor of the house are state rooms and a long gallery, which contain many items of original furniture (open).

Go through Chastleton and after ¼ mile turn left. Cross a cattle grid and turn right on to the A44. Pass the Cross Hands (PH) and turn left on to an unclassified road. Proceed to the Rollright Stones.

ROLLRIGHT STONES, Oxon

This important bronze-age monument (AM) comprises two configurations of stones. The circle, nicknamed 'The King's Men', measures a full 100ft across and is close to 'The Whispering Knights' group and an isolated outlier called the 'King's Stone'.

After ¾ mile turn left on to the A34 and descend to Long Compton.

LONG COMPTON, Warwicks

A little thatched gatehouse tops the churchyard gate at Long Compton. The church itself is of Norman and later date and preserves an old stone figure of a lady in the porch.

Continue to Shipston-on-Stour

SHIPSTON-ON-STOUR, Warwicks

Situated on the edge of the Cotswolds in the Vale of Red Horse, this old wool town has attractive Georgian houses and inns complemented by a 19th-century church incorporating the 500-year-old tower of its predecessor.

Turn left on to the B4035 'Campden' road. Proceed for 1 ¾ miles, cross a main road. Continue for 1 ¼ miles then turn right on to an unclassified road through Charingworth to Ebrington.

EBRINGTON, Glos

Delightful cottages of stone and thatch enhance the undoubted appeal of this beautiful Cotswold village. Ebrington Manor shows a great deal of restoration to its basically 17th-century structure.

IN THE VALE OF RED HORSE

Relics of ancient man dot the North Cotswold Hills above vales of almost legendary richness, where English fruit and vegetables are raised round villages that grew fat on the profits of wool. Great men lived and died here; great rivers continue to flow.

Drive to the end of the village and keep right, then right again on to an unclassified road SP 'To the Hidcotes'. After 2 ¼ miles turn right for Hidcote Bartrim.

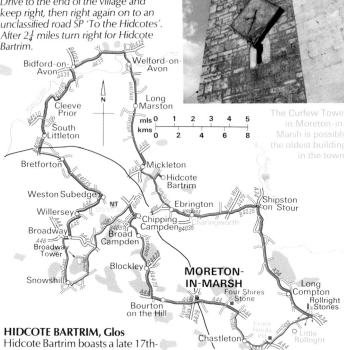

HIDCOTE BARTRIM, Glos

Hidcote Bartrim boasts a late 17th-century manor surrounded by lovely formal gardens (open) (NT).

Return to the T-junction and turn left, then take the next turning on the right SP 'Mickleton'. Meet the main road and turn right on to the A46 to enter Mickleton.

MICKLETON, Glos

Medford House is a superb example of Renaissance architecture, and the village itself preserves thatched and timber-framed buildings. Half a mile south east is Kingsgate Court Gardens magnificently situated, affording fine views. St Lawrence's Church dates from the 12th century.

Drive through the village and turn left. After ½ mile continue on to the unclassified road for Long Marston.

LONG MARSTON, Warwicks

King's Lodge in Long Marston has associations with King Charles II, who is said to have come here in disguise after the Battle of Worcester. The bell in the village church hangs in a turret built on great oak beams resting on the floor of the nave. The village itself is a delightful grouping of timber and thatch cottages in leafy country lanes. It has its own traditional morris dancing troupe.

Continue to Welford-on-Avon

WELFORD-ON-AVON, Warwicks

Welford-on-Avon's Norman church has an ancient lychgate and stands among charming timber-and-thatch cottages near a new maypole.

Go forward and later cross the River Avon, then turn left on to the A439 and drive to Bidford-on-Avon.

BIDFORD-ON-AVON, Warwicks
Traditionally this unspoilt village was the birthplace of playwright William Shakespeare. There is little doubt that Tudor Corner House was once the Falcon Inn beloved of both Shakespeare and his contemporary Ben Jonson. Latterly the inn has served as a workhouse and as a group of cottages. A fine 15th-century bridge spans the Avon.

Turn left on to the B4085 SP 'Broadway', and cross a bridge. After ½ mile turn right for Cleeve Prior.

CLEEVE PRIOR, Herefs & Worcs
The name of this village derives from the priors of Worcester, who were once lords of the manor here. Tall chimneys and a priest's hole that once hid Charles I's banker are features of the Jacobean manor house. Stone-built cottages overlook the triangular green, and the 15th-century King's Arms still offers comfort to the traveller.

Continue to South Littleton.

SOUTH LITTLETON, Herefs & Worcs
North, Middle, and South Littleton are a picturesque group of tiny Avon Valley villages. North Littleton has a manor house, a tithe barn, and dovecote, and a church that is considered to be of great architectural merit. South Littleton boasts a beautiful early 18th-century house.

Continue along the same road for a further 1 mile, then go over a level crossing and turn left on to the unclassified 'Bretforton' road. Continue to Bretforton.

BRETFORTON, Herefs & Worcs
Three tributaries of the Avon drain the lovely countryside round this ancient village. Of particular note here are the 600-year-old Fleece Inn (NT) and medieval Grange Farm. The latter, changed greatly from its original form by successive owners, gave shelter to Prince Rupert in 1645. The country's largest collection of dovecotes survives here, including several very old examples and one that has been made into a cottage.

Join the B4035 and continue to Weston-Sub-Edge.

WESTON-SUB-EDGE, Glos
Several appealing 17th-century houses preserved in the main street of this village include Latimer's, a particularly fine example associated with the historic bishop of that name. Bank House and Riknild are also of note. Slightly later than these is the Manor House, and the 'old' Rectory was built in the 19th century.

Meet a T-junction, turn right on to the A46, and pass through Willersey.

Chipping Campden's arched Market Hall was built in 1627.

WILLERSEY, Glos
The 6 bells of Willersey's Church of St Peter were re-cast from the original 3 in 1712 and rung the following year to celebrate the Treaty of Utrecht. Various medieval styles can be seen in the building itself. Willersey House was once a farmhouse in the village, but in 1912 was dismantled and rebuilt at the top of a hill in its present enlarged form and is now the Dormy House Hotel.

Later meet a T-junction and turn right on to the A44 into Broadway.

BROADWAY, Herefs & Worcs
Broadway's wide main street is lined with fine houses and pretty cottages built in Cotswold stone. St Eadburgha's Norman and later church is somewhat self-effacingly hidden away at one end of the community, and the 17th-century Lygon Arms coaching inn shows a narrow frontage to the street.

Drive to the end of the green and turn left on to an unclassified road to Snowshill. Ascend, then bear right into the village.

SNOWSHILL, Glos
Secluded Snowshill is a hillside village of ancient Cotswold cottages grouped round a handsome 19th-century church. Its manor house (NT) dates from the 16th century, but subsequent periods have left their marks in various alterations and additions. Inside are collections of clocks, toys, and musical instruments.

Continue to the church and turn left. Ascend to the top of the incline and meet crossroads. Go forward SP 'Chipping Campden, Broadway Tower'. After 1¾ miles turn left and proceed to Broadway Tower.

BROADWAY TOWER, Herefs & Worcs
Lady Coventry built this picturesque folly tower in the 18th century, and it now forms the nucleus of a 30-acre country park. Its lofty situation at over 1,000ft gives views over several counties, and in very clear weather it is possible to pick out such landmarks as Tewkesbury Abbey, Worcester Cathedral, and Warwick.

Continue for ½ mile, cross a main road with SP 'Mickleton', and after ¾ mile turn right. Continue for 2¼ miles and meet a T-junction. Turn right on to the B4081/B4035 for Chipping Campden.

Welford-on-Avon is a picturebook village set in a pastoral landscape.

CHIPPING CAMPDEN, Glos
Wool made Chipping Campden rich, and the handiwork of the merchants who prospered here can be seen in the fine gabled stone houses, the 14th-century Woolstaplers Hall, and the 15th-century wool church. Near the church are remains of the once-beautiful Campden House, whose owner burned it down in 1645 rather than see it fall into Parliamentarian hands.

Drive through the town and turn left with the B4081 SP 'Broad Campden'. After ¼ mile turn left again on to an unclassified road for Broad Campden.

BROAD CAMPDEN, Glos
Features of this village include an 18th-century Friends' Meeting House that has been restored and the much older Chapel House – a 12th-century chapel converted into a private dwelling.

Keep right through the village then bearing right before the climb to Blockley.

BLOCKLEY, Glos
Blockley's architecture follows the usual basic pattern for the area, with a high street of 18th- and 19th-century houses complementing a Norman church.

Turn left, continue for a short distance, then turn right on to the B4479. Proceed for 1¾ miles, meet a T-junction, and turn left on to the A44. Pass through Bourton-on-the-Hill.

BOURTON-ON-THE-HILL, Glos
A fine example of a Winchester bushel can be seen in Bourton's Norman and later church. The village itself stands on a hill and is made up of cottages standing in attractively-terraced gardens. Bourton House is of 18th-century date and has a superb 16th-century tithe barn.

Return to Moreton-in-Marsh.

NEWQUAY, Cornwall

Magnificent beaches, fine scenery, and a wide range of amenities for the holiday-maker have made Newquay one of the most popular seaside resorts in Cornwall. The original Iron-Age settlement was to the north east at Porth Island, where today's tourists admire the grand cliffs and splendid caves. Since the first train arrived here in 1875 tourism has been the main factor in Newquay's growth. The railway originally came to bring china clay and tin to the port, but the harbour proved too small and shallow for large cargo ships. Because of this the harbour has retained some of its original character and preserved a number of old structures. Another area of historic charm is St Columb Minor, once the mother parish of Newquay but now just a suburb. Amongst its old and attractive cottages is the church of St Columba, whose 115ft pinnacled and lichen-covered 15th-century tower is considered one of the finest in the country. Visitors can enjoy the amusement park in Trenance Garden, which also boasts the only zoo in Cornwall, and the mile-long main beach is close to the town. Between Newquay and the surfing beach at Fistral is the rock-strewn promontory of Towan Head, which affords magnificent views.

Leave Newquay on the A392 SP 'Bodmin' and continue to Quintrell Downs. Drive over a level crossing, then at roundabout SP 'St Austell' go forward on to the A3058. After ¾ mile turn right on to a narrow unclassified road SP 'Newlyn East'. Continue for 1 mile to Trerice Manor, on the right.

TRERICE MANOR, Cornwall

With its grey curving gables and E-shaped entrance front, Trerice Manor (NT) has hardly changed since it was first built by Sir John Arundell in 1573. Sir John, a member of an old and influential Cornish family, spent a great deal of time soldiering in the Low Countries. When he returned to his native Cornwall he did not entirely forget foreign parts, as the design of the house shows. Excellent plasterwork on the ceilings and fireplaces is acknowledged as the most outstanding feature of the interior.

Continue for 1 mile then at crossroads turn left. In ½ mile at a T-junction turn right. A detour can be taken from the main route by turning left and driving for ½ mile to the Lappa Valley Railway.

LAPPA VALLEY RAILWAY, Cornwall

This 15-inch gauge line built on part of the former Great Western route between Newquay and Chacewater runs through a 2-mile circuit of valley scenery. A stop is made at East Wheal Rose Halt, where passengers can disembark to explore a children's leisure park and the site of an old silver and lead mine.

Continue to St Newlyn East.

ATLANTIC SEASCAPES
Long, foam-capped rollers crash on to ideal surfing beaches between the craggy headlands and promontories of Cornwall's Atlantic coast. Away from the shore is the gentle rise and fall of downland, scored by deep lanes and scattered with the beautifully decayed remains of mine buildings.

The estuary of the River Gannel opens out to form Crantock Beach.

ST NEWLYN EAST, Cornwall

Known as St Newlyn East to distinguish it from the port of Newlyn near Penzance, this attractive village was probably the original settlement of Saint Newelina, the Cornish martyr to whom the parish church is dedicated. Beautiful examples of Norman and medieval carving can be seen inside the church, including particularly fine pieces of 14th-century work.

Follow signs 'Truro', and continue for 1 mile to Fiddler's Green. Turn left, then after 1¼ miles meet crossroads. Go forward SP 'Zelah' then turn right on to the A30. Go through Zelah and in ½ mile turn left on to an unclassified road SP 'Shortlanesend'. Continue for 2 miles to reach the Shortlanesend Inn, and join the B3284 for Truro.

TRURO, Cornwall

Cathedral city of Cornwall and the county's unofficial capital, Truro stands where the rivers Allen and Kenwyn join to form the large Fal-estuary inlet known as the Truro River. Until 1752 the town was one of Cornwall's 4 stannery or coinage towns, to which all smelted tin had to be brought to be tested for quality and taxed. During this time it developed into an important centre for the export of mineral ores, and in the 18th century it became a focus of social life to rival even Bath, the country's then most fashionable town. Among the fine Georgian structures surviving from the period is the outstanding Lemon Street, which was laid out c1795 and is complemented by Walsingham Place, a beautiful early 19th-century crescent just off Victoria Place. The former Assembly Rooms date from c1770 and were the main gathering place for 18th-century society. One of Cornwall's oldest and most famous potteries, Lake's, still works in Chapel Street, and is open to visitors. Edward VII, then the Prince of Wales, laid the cathedral's foundation stone in 1880. Various types of Cornish granite were used in the building's construction, and it stands on the site of the 16th-century church of St Mary. Part of the older building is retained in the east end. The Truro Museum, in River Street, is considered to be the finest in Cornwall and has a number of exhibits depicting the history of the local mineral industries.

Leave Truro following SP 'Redruth' on the A390. In 4 miles meet a roundabout and take the 2nd exit. Continue for a further 2¼ miles to another roundabout and take the 3rd exit on to the B3277 SP 'St Agnes'. Continue to St Agnes.

One of the Wheal Coates engine houses on the cliffs at Chapel Porth near St Agnes.

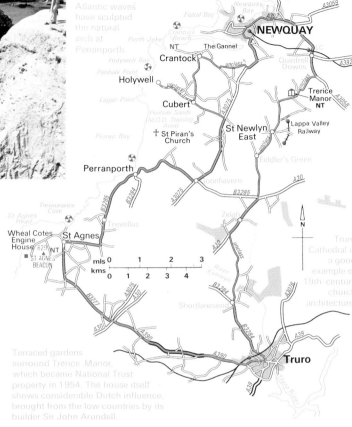

ST AGNES, Cornwall

St Agnes is one of those Cornish villages that has retained its charm and character despite the burden of two centuries of mining and one century of tourism. Decaying engine houses and wildflower-covered burrows bear silent witness to the mineral booms of years gone by, and ½ mile north is Trevaunance Cove – a lovely place with excellent sands. Many futile attempts have been made to build a harbour here, and remains of 18th-century piers from the last try can be seen from the western end of the cove. St Agnes itself fits snugly round the parish church, which was rebuilt in Cornish style during the mid-19th century but is unusual in having a slender spire. Among the pleasant streets and by-ways of the village is the quaint Stippy-Stappy, a steep and stepped row of slate-roofed cottages leading down Town Hill. The well-known beauty spot of St Agnes Beacon lies to the west. Also of interest are the St Agnes Leisure Park with five different themes, and the Little Puppet Theatre.

ST AGNES BEACON, Cornwall

It is said that 32 church towers and 23 miles of coast can be seen from 628ft St Agnes Beacon (NT), perhaps the most prominent landmark in the area. Much of the surrounding area (part NT) has been worked for minerals in times past, but the many mining scars and old buildings add a melancholy beauty rather than the sense of desecration that usually pervades industrial sites. Bolster's Dyke, a 2-mile earthwork on the Beacon, is named after a legendary giant who is supposed to have lived there in ancient times.

WHEAL COATES ENGINE HOUSE, Cornwall

One of the Wheal Coates engine houses, (NT) stands precariously on a forbidding cliff to the west of St Agnes Beacon. It contained a pumping engine for the Towanroath shaft and from a sea-cave below it is possible to look up one of the shafts beneath the pump-house.

Leave St Agnes on the B3285 Perranporth road and continue through Trevellas, then in 1 mile descend into Perranporth.

PERRANPORTH, Cornwall

Terraces of hotels and guesthouses rise from the sea-level centre of this popular resort which was formerly a mining centre. Even though it lacks the quaint cottages and blue-jerseyed fishermen the public expect of the west, visitors find a more than ample attraction in the magnificent bay that sweeps away to the north. This boasts a 3-mile stretch of smooth golden sand, and is reputed to be where surfing was introduced into Britain. Penhale Point offers spectacular rock scenery, and the sands at this end of the beach have been blown into large dunes. Near by, on the road to Goonhavern, is the 2,000-year old hilltop enclosure of St Piran's Round (AM).

ST PIRAN'S CHURCH, Cornwall

Perranporth is in the parish of *Perranzabuloe* which means 'St Piran in the Sand'. St Piran is thought to have come to Cornwall from Ireland in the 6th-century, and legend has it that he wasn't always sober. However, he is said to have taught the Cornish the art of smelting and was adopted as the patron saint of tinners. He built his church north of Perranporth on the Penhale Sands, but by the 11th century shifting dunes had closed in and completely enveloped the little building. It wasn't until the 19th century that it was excavated, and nowadays it is housed in a concrete shell to protect it from further damage. The mile-long walk over easy ground to see the church is well worth the effort.

Leave Perranporth on the B3285 SP 'Newquay' and in 2 miles at Goonhavern turn left on to the A3075. In 2½ miles turn left on to an unclassified road for Cubert.

CUBERT, Cornwall

High above the sandy landscape round Cubert is the spire of the church, a local landmark. Although restored in 1852 the interior of the church preserves fine Norman and 14th-century carvings and a font. In a café in the village centre are the granite remains of a 17th-century Cornish cider press.

A pleasant detour from the main route can be taken to Holywell, some 1¼ miles beyond Cubert.

HOLYWELL, Cornwall

The large beach at Holywell Bay is quieter than most on this coastline and offers good bathing except at low tide. At the north end is a freshwater spring that gave the place its name, one of the holy wells of Cornwall. It can only be reached at low tide via steps cut into the cliff. Magnificent views can be enjoyed from Penhale Point.

Leave Cubert by the Crantock road. Continue for 1½ miles to reach Crantock.

CRANTOCK, Cornwall

A plaque records that the old stocks in the churchyard here were last used in 1817 on a 'Smuggler's son and a vagabond'. This is not surprising since the village was once notorious for its involvement in contraband. The church itself is a showpiece of Edwardian restoration. Attractive countryside (NT) lines the steep-sided estuary of the River Gannel which flows past the popular sands of Crantock Beach.

Leave Crantock on an unclassified road SP 'Newquay'. In ¾ mile turn left on to another unclassified road and continue for 1 mile to the A3075. Turn left and return to Newquay.

CORNWALL'S STERNEST COAST

Great Atlantic rollers forever pound the towering cliffs of north Cornwall, spilling their energy in roaring white surf along the wide sandy beaches which have made Newquay and Padstow such popular resorts. The calm of antiquity is reflected inland, however, where a rolling landscape gently laps the rugged edge of stark Bodmin Moor.

NEWQUAY, Cornwall

Newquay's popularity as a holiday resort stems chiefly from its magnificent sandy beaches and the superb surfing which is probably the best in Cornwall. The most attractive area of the town itself is the 17th-century harbour. Here, some of the pilot gigs which used to guide in the cargo schooners during the 19th century have been preserved. On the headland west of the harbour is another relic from Newquay's past — the Huer's Hut. In the days when pilchards provided the town with a living, a man called a huer kept watch for shoals of pilchards entering the bay. When he saw the water reddening from the mass of fish, he alerted the town by shouting. To the west lies Trenance Park and Cornwall's only full-size zoo. Eight acres of landscaped grounds effectively display wild animals, tropical birds, wildfowl, reptiles, seals and penguins and there is a pets' corner to keep children happy.

Leave Newquay on the A392, SP 'Bodmin'. In ¾ mile, turn left on to the B3276, SP 'Padstow'. Continue to Mawgan Porth.

MAWGAN PORTH, Cornwall

The small safe bay at Mawgan Porth lies at the entrance to the lovely Lanherne Valley leading up to St Mawgan. There is a wooden monument shaped like a boat in this village which commemorates the lives of 10 seamen who were shipwrecked and swept ashore at Mawgan Porth. Remains of a settlement (AM) that supported a small community of fishermen and cattle breeders from the 9th to the 11th centuries are visible near the beach and the foundations of their courtyard houses and outline of the cemetery can be discerned.

From Mawgan Porth climb to Trenance. After another mile, on the left, is the track which leads to Bedruthan Steps.

BEDRUTHAN STEPS, Cornwall

Huge lumps of granite march along this beautiful, rugged beach. The rocks were, allegedly, named Bedruthan Steps because they were thought to be the stepping stones of the giant Bedruthan. This stretch of coast (NT) is one of the most spectacular in Cornwall and the great sands are usually deserted because a steep scramble down the cliff is the only access.

Continue on the B3276 and in 1¼ miles at the T-junction turn left, then ½ mile farther turn left again for the descent to Porthcothan.

The great crags of Bedruthan Steps rise up some 200ft from the deserted sands

PORTHCOTHAN, Cornwall

The sea reaches almost to the road at Porthcothan and the great cliffs on either side are more than a match for the angry attacks of the relentless Atlantic ocean. The shelter of the rocks obviously well suited smugglers because an underground passage emerges further up the valley, and it was along here that the daredevil smugglers hid their spoils and hauled up their luggers.

Turn inland from Porthcothan and after 1 mile turn left and continue to St Merryn.

ST MERRYN, Cornwall

A newer village has developed a little way from the old church and its protective cluster of cottages. The interior pillars of the church and font are made of locally cliff-quarried Catacleuse slate. This handsome dark blue-grey stone was the only slate that could be carved easily, which is why nearly all the carved work in Cornish churches is out of this slate. Old village stocks are kept in the church porch.

At the Farmers' Arms PH in St Merryn turn left SP 'Harlyn'. In 1 mile turn right for Harlyn Bay.

Most of Newquay, north Cornwall's largest resort, has been built along the cliffs above its large, sandy beaches

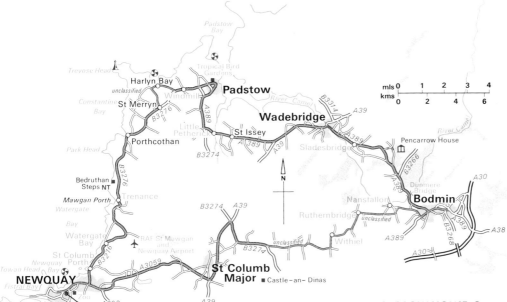

mls 0 1 2 3 4
kms 0 2 4 6

HARLYN BAY, Cornwall

For thousands of years an Iron-Age cemetery lay hidden beneath the sands near Harlyn Bay. In 1900 it was accidentally discovered and proved to have once been the site of over 100 graves. Five of the slate slabs have been preserved on the site and a small museum nearby contains the various other finds such as brooches, tools and combs which were buried with those far-off peoples.

Cross the river bridge and in 1 mile turn left to rejoin the B3276, SP 'Padstow'. Pass through Windmill and in ¾ mile keep left, then nearly ½ mile farther turn left again for Padstow.

PADSTOW, Cornwall

Padstow is one of north Cornwall's oldest and most charming fishing towns. However, its days as a fishing and export port ended in the mid-19th century when the Camel estuary silted up, and the picturesque harbour and crooked streets now throng with holiday-makers. An annual highlight in Padstow is May Day when the Hobby Horse Dance Festival takes place. The ritual of a masked man and a bizarre hobby horse dancing through the streets welcomes summer and is supposed to be the oldest dance festival in Europe. St Petroc's Church is a reminder of the early Christianity in Padstow, dating from the 6th century when St Petroc came here from Ireland to found a monastery. (Padstow is a derivation of Petrocstowe.) The original monastic site may have been the one now occupied by Prideaux Place (not open) just above the church. This is a handsome Elizabethan house — home of the Prideaux family for several hundred years — and a monument to the Prideaux lies in the church. Another interesting feature of Padstow is its tropical bird and butterfly gardens. A walk-in tropical house with free-flying birds and a butterfly exhibition where butterflies fly free in the summer, shows off these creatures in ideal conditions.

From the one-way system in Padstow follow SP 'Wadebridge' and ascend and at the top turn left on to the A398. In 2 miles turn left, continue through Little Petherick, and climb to St Issey.

ST ISSEY, Cornwall

About 20 figures placed in niches of Catacleuse stone stand inside St Issey's church. They were probably part of a tombchest at one time, but form part of the altar canopy now. The church tower collapsed in the last century but was rebuilt in 1873. A photograph from 1869 shows the tower falling and a policeman in a top hat looking helplessly on.

Remain on the A389 and in 2 miles turn left on to the A39 and continue to Wadebridge.

WADEBRIDGE, Cornwall

The centrepiece of this small market town is a fine medieval bridge crossing over the River Camel to Egloshayle. It was built by the vicar of Egloshayle, (the mother church of Wadebridge), because he deemed the ferry crossing to be too dangerous for his parishioners. The bridge, 320ft long, the longest in Cornwall, originally had 17 arches but 1 has since been blocked up. The foundations beneath the pillars are believed to have been based on packs of wool.

Cross the River Camel and on the far side turn right on to the A389, SP 'Bodmin'. A pleasant road then passes through Sladesbridge and after 2¼ miles a turning on the left leads to Pencarrow House.

PENCARROW HOUSE, Cornwall

Dense woods and rhododendrons cover an estate of 35 acres and in the middle hides modest, 18th-century Pencarrow House (OACT). The approach is mysterious; along a winding wooded drive and past an Iron-Age encampment ringed by dwarf oaks. Sir John Molesworth began the house in the 1700s and his descendants live there now. A great deal of the contents have been accumulated through prosperous marriages and the interior has been tastefully adapted to show the beautiful treasures off to maximum advantage.

Continue on the Bodmin road and recross the River Camel at Dunmere Bridge. A short climb then brings the tour into Bodmin.

BODMIN, Cornwall

Bodmin lies on the steep south-west edge of Bodmin Moor, equi-distant between Cornwall's north and south coasts, which makes it an ideal touring base. Approximately 12 miles square make up Bodmin Moor and very few roads cross its bleak face. The boulder-strewn slopes break out into steep granite tors, the highest being Rough Tor and Brown Willy, yet there is also a gentler aspect to the moor, of fields and wild flowers. St Petroc founded a monastery in Bodmin and his name lives on in the parish church, St Petroc's, which is the largest in Cornwall. At one time the town was renowned for its holy wells which cured eye complaints. One such well, St Guron's, stands near the church inscribed with the date 1700 and an advertisement extolling the well's powers.

Follow SP 'Redruth (A30)' and at the end of the town go forward. In ½ mile turn right, SP 'Wadebridge and Nanstallon'. In nearly another ½ mile keep left still SP 'Nanstallon'. In ¾ mile bear left, SP 'Ruthern', and go forward at the crossroads to Ruthernbridge. Here, turn left, SP 'Withiel', then in ¾ mile turn right and continue to Withiel. Here turn left, SP 'Roche', and at the church turn left again and in ½ mile turn right, SP 'St Wenn'. In 1¾ miles keep forward, SP 'St Columb', then in another mile join the B3274. In 2¼ miles turn left on to the A39 SP 'Truro', and continue along the St Columb Major bypass. From this road a detour may be made to St Columb Major.

ST COLUMB MAJOR, Cornwall

One of the chief churches in Cornwall belongs to St Columb Major. St Columba stands in a commanding position in a large churchyard and the tower has the unusual feature of 4 tiers. The good 16th-17th-century brasses inside are dedicated to the Arundell family who lived at Lanherne. Every Shrove Tuesday a local adaptation of the handball game of hurling takes place in the town's streets, using a traditional, applewood ball covered with silver. Two and a half miles south-east of St Columb Major is Castle an Dinas — an Iron-Age fort which still has 3 ramparts visible.

From the southern end of the St Columb Major Bypass the tour follows the A3059 Newquay road. In 5½ miles turn right on to the A392 for the return to Newquay.

The beach at Harlyn Bay, satellite of Newquay, is a popular bathing spot

PENZANCE, Cornwall

The most westerly town in England, Penzance enjoys a mild climate all year round. The town grew to prosperity through tin mining, and possibly smuggling, and was immortalized by Gilbert and Sullivan in *The Pirates of Penzance*. Evidence of its popularity in Regency times can be seen in the fine period buildings still standing in Chapel Street. Also here is a maritime museum with exhibits from 18th-century British warships wrecked off the Scilly Isles. There is a natural history museum in Penlee Park, and many exotic plants grow in Morab Gardens. About 2 miles inland are the Trengwainton Gardens (NT), with their exceptional collections of magnolias, rhododendrons and other shrubs. It was here that magnolias flowered for the first time in the British Isles.

MOUNT'S BAY, Cornwall

Mount's Bay curves in a series of wide coves and inlets between the Land's End peninsula in the west and The Lizard in the east. In spite of playing host to many visitors each year it is still a place of isolated bays and deserted, cliff-fringed beaches.

Leave Penzance on the A3077 'Newlyn', road skirting the harbour to Newlyn.

NEWLYN, Cornwall

This busy fishing port used to be famous for its artist colony. Many of the painters moved north to St Ives, but a few still live and work among the quaint old cottages and fish-cellars. The Passmore Edwards picture gallery shows some of the colony's work.

Cross a river bridge and immediately turn left on to an unclassified road which hugs the coast to Mousehole.

THE PENWITH PENINSULA

Storm-tumbled cliffs haunted by gulls and mermaid legends guard the wild Atlantic shoreline of Penwith. On the other side of Land's End is the great bight of Mount's Bay, where the 'nightmen' of folksong fame crept from secluded coves with 'baccy for the parson and brandy for the squire'.

The fairytale structure of St Michael's Mount dominates Mount's Bay.

MOUSEHOLE, Cornwall

Largely unchanged by time, Mousehole preserves the original character of old Cornwall in its granite houses and working harbour.

Turn left, drive to the harbour, and turn right then right again SP 'Paul', turn inland, and climb to Paul.

PAUL, Cornwall

Dorothy Pentreath, one of the last people to speak the ancient Cornish language is buried here. Inside the 15th-century church are several pieces of old armour.

Keep forward past Paul Church and after ½ mile meet a T-junction. Turn left on to the B3315 and continue for 2½ miles. A detour can be taken from the main route by turning left here on to an unclassifed road through the Lamorna Valley to Lamorna Cove.

LAMORNA COVE, Cornwall

Huge granite boulders and the rocky outcrops of this spectacular cove contrast with the gentler surrounding countryside. A granite quay and pier were built here in the last century to export granite from the quarries near by. Nowadays the cove is visited for its lovely scenery by tourists and artists.

Continue on the B3315 and in 3¼ miles, at a T-junction, turn left. Descend steeply, then climb to the edge of Treen.

TREEN, Cornwall

This tiny village lies near the fortified headland of Treryn Dinas on which stands Treen Castle (NT). Outside the local inn is a sign telling how in 1824 a nephew of Oliver Goldsmith overturned the 60 ton Logan Rock, a famous rocking stone on the headland, and how he was made to replace it at his own expense.

TREEN CASTLE (NT) Cornwall

It is believed that the defences of this excellent Iron-Age cliff castle were started between the 3rd and 2nd centuries BC. A huge bank and ditch cuts off the headland, and at the extreme tip of the rocks jutting out to sea is a bank faced with heavy masonry. Access is by footpath from Treen.

LOGAN ROCK, Cornwall

Pronounced 'loggan', the name of this curious rocking stone is derived from the Cornish verb *log*, meaning to move. It is reached by footpath from the village of Treen.

From the edge of Treen, remain on the B3315. In ¾ mile a detour from the main route can be taken by turning left on to an unclassified road for Porthcurno and the Minack Theatre.

PORTHCURNO AND THE MINACK THEATRE, Cornwall

The first transatlantic cable was brought ashore in this village. Porthcurno has an exceptionally good beach of almost white sand, and just to the south is the unique Minack Theatre — built out of living stone on the edge of the cliffs by Miss Rowena Cade in 1931. The auditorium is formed from ridges cut into the sloping rock, with the natural bedding adapted to make seats facing south and east over a stage right on the cliff edge.

Continue with the 'Land's End' road and after ½ mile turn right still with the B3315. After 2 miles turn left on to the A30 'Land's End' road, and drive to Land's End.

LAND'S END, Cornwall

Famous as England's most westerly point, Land's End is about 873 miles from the equally famous John O'Groats in Scotland. On a fine day the Isles of Scilly are visible 28 miles away to the west. A leisure and exhibition complex outlines the natural history of the area.

LONGSHIPS LIGHTHOUSE, Cornwall

Some 2 miles out to sea from Land's End the Longships Lighthouse rises 50ft high from a 60ft rock. Waves have been known to lash as high as the lantern during severe storms.

Wave torn rocks and the distant Longships Lighthouse starkly outlined against sunset at Land's End.

Ruined mine buildings, like the Carn Galver Mine at Morvah, add much to Cornwall's landscape

A short detour can be taken by turning left in St Just on to an unclassified road to Cape Cornwall.

CAPE CORNWALL, Cornwall
Features of this headland, the only 'cape' in England or Wales, include a mine chimney, prehistoric burial ground and a ruined chapel.

From St Just continue on the St Ives road B3306 to Pendeen.

On the headland at St Ives is a fishermen's chapel

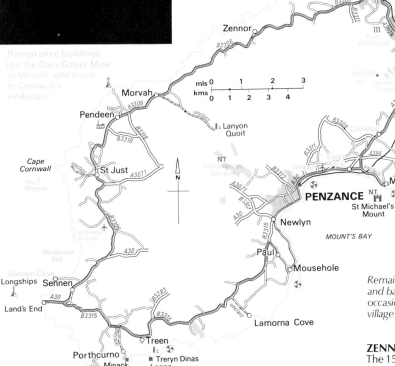

Lanyon Quoit is situated in an area rich in prehistoric remains.

Leave Land's End and return along the A30, past the 'Porthcurno' road, to Sennen.

SENNEN, Cornwall
According to legend Sennen, a small village with a past rich in local history, was the battleground for the last Cornish fight against invading Danes. The 15th-century church contains a medieval statue of the Virgin Mary and is the most westerly church in England. Sennen Cove offers good sand, excellent bathing, and superb scenery.

Continue on the A30. After 1¾ miles turn left on to the B3306, SP 'St Just' and pass Land's End Airport. After 3 miles turn left on to the A3071 and enter St. Just.

ST JUST, Cornwall
Also known as St Just-in-Penwith, this village is noted for the contents of its old church. Among these is a wall painting, an interesting inscribed stone of 5th-century date, and the shaft of a 9th-century Hiberno-Saxon cross. St Just itself is enchanting.

PENDEEN, Cornwall
Around the village are derelict remains of old mine workings; one that survived until 1986, the Geevor Mine, has an impressive tin-mining museum (may not re-open after 1986). The village church is a copy of Iona Cathedral in Scotland.

Leave Pendeen and continue along the B3306 to Morvah.

MORVAH, Cornwall
This little farming and former mining village is set on the edge of the Penwith moorland. About 1 mile south of the village are Chun Castle and Chun Quoit, respectively a circular Iron-Age fort built of stone and the remains of a large Neolithic dolmen, or tomb chamber.

Shortly beyond Morvah a detour can be taken right along an unclassified road for 2 miles to Lanyon Quoit.

LANYON QUOIT, Cornwall
Perhaps the best known and most visited of Cornwall's megaliths, this neolithic tomb (NT) resembles a huge three-legged stone table.

Remain on the B3306 through rocky and barren countryside, with occasional views of the coast; skirt the village of Zennor.

ZENNOR, Cornwall
The 15th-century church in this former tin-mining community is famous for the mermaid bench end. The writers Virginia Woolf and DH Lawrence both lived in the village in the 1920s. A folk museum here is well worth visiting.

Continue on B3306 to St Ives.

ST IVES, Cornwall
Until her recent death the sculptress Barbara Hepworth was the leading light in a famous artists' community that lived in this attractive fishing port and major holiday resort. Quaint old houses, narrow streets and alleys cluster beneath the 120ft granite tower of the 15th-century church. There are two fine sandy beaches (one for surfing), and a semi-circular harbour. Of interest are the St Ives Museum (civil and maritime history) the Barnes Museum of Cinematography, Barbara Hepworth Museum and Sculpture Garden, St Ives Society of Artists Gallery, Penwith Galleries and the Bernard Leach Pottery.

Leave St Ives on the A3074 and follow SP 'Hayle'. Pass through Carbis Bay and continue into Lelant.

LELANT, Cornwall
Lelant, on the Hayle estuary has a Norman and Perpendicular-style church with a 17th-century sundial and the Cornish Heritage Leisure Park.

At Lelant turn right and in 1 mile at a roundabout take 3rd exit A30 SP 'Penzance'. One mile beyond Crowlas take 2nd exit at roundabout onto the 'Marazion' road unclassified. Shortly turn left and cross a railway bridge to Marazion.

MARAZION, Cornwall
Good bathing and fishing can be enjoyed in this ancient port, and the marshland between Marazion and Ludgvan is the habitat for many species of bird. Marvellous views of famous St Michael's Mount can be enjoyed from here.

ST MICHAEL'S MOUNT Cornwall
This little granite island (NT) rises to a 250ft summit from the waters of Mount's Bay and is accessible by foot via a causeway at low tide, or by boat, from Marazion. Its splendid castle (NT) and priory (NT), both founded by Edward the Confessor in the 11th-century, stand high above a small harbour and hamlet. Inside the 14th-century chapel is an excellent collection of armour and furniture.

Return along the unclassifed road and turn left for Long Rock to rejoin the A30 for Penzance.

PLYMOUTH AND THE WESTERN MOOR

This is the country of Drake and Raleigh, of large adventures in small boats and salty tales that the historians have somehow missed. North are the water-sculpted tors and heathy slopes of western Dartmoor, a place of vast spaces patterned with the shadows of clouds.

PLYMOUTH, Devon

Sandwiched between the estuaries of the Plym and the Tamar, this popular yachting resort and important maritime city is the venue for national sailing championships and a stop-off point for round-the-world yachtsmen. It has been a naval base since the 16th century, and in the 17th the Pilgrim Fathers sailed from its Sutton Harbour to the New World of America in the *Mayflower*. Today Sutton Harbour is busy with large and small boats, and the craft and antique shops, pubs and restaurants of the Barbican make it an exciting district of modern Plymouth as well as a fascinating historic memorial. Most of the city centre was rebuilt after appalling war damage, and the area where Royal Parade is bisected by spacious Armada Way includes a fine shopping complex. The 200ft-high Civic Centre affords excellent cross-town views from its roof deck. A prominent statue of Sir Francis Drake shares the Hoe with Smeaton's Tower (open), which is the re-erected base of the old Eddystone Lighthouse and the impressive Naval War Memorial. Near by are the 17th-century Royal Citadel (AM) and the outstanding aquarium of the Marine Biological Association. Rising from the waters of the sound, almost in front of the Hoe, is the rocky, tree-scattered hump of Drake's Island (NT). The city's Church of St Andrew is the largest in Devon and dates from the 15th century. Close by are Prysten House, the city's oldest building (open), the Victorian Guildhall and the Elizabethan Merchant's House (open). Also of interest are the Elizabethan House and Wall Mural in the Barbican, Charles Church (city war memorial) and the Museum and Art Gallery containing works by Reynolds. Across the estuary is Mount Edgcumbe, which can be reached via the Cremyll Passenger Ferry from Plymouth.

MOUNT EDGCUMBE HOUSE & COUNTRY PARK, Cornwall

This beautiful Tudor mansion (open) was severely damaged during World War II but has since been completely restored. Its lovely gardens and parkland offer extensive views of Plymouth Sound.

DEVONPORT, Devon

Although Devonport started life with an identity of its own, the establishment of the important naval dockyard on the Hamoaze in 1691 resulted in its rapid development into the navy quarter of neighbouring Plymouth. Its fine 19th-century town hall was by the architect John Foulston, and older foundations include the Gun Wharf of 1718 and the Royal Naval Hospital, also of the 18th century.

THE TAMAR BRIDGES, Devon Devon

Spanning the Tamar river north-west of Plymouth city centre are two famous bridges that have opened up the West Country to tourism. The oldest is the Royal Albert, a railway bridge designed by the brilliant engineer Brunel and completed in 1859. Close by is a modern, single-span suspension road bridge opened in 1961 with a lightness and grace that contrast sharply with the heavy solidity of its elderly neighbour.

From Plymouth follow SP 'Exeter' to reach Marsh Mills roundabout. Take 3rd exit onto the Plympton road B3416 and cross the River Plym. Shortly on the left is a road to the Plym Valley Railway then in ½ mile pass a road on the right leading to Saltram House.

Monuments to their times — these two handsome bridges span the Tamar at Saltash.

Sir Francis Drake's statue stands on Plymouth Hoe.

SALTRAM HOUSE, Devon

This fine Tudor house (NT) has an 18th-century façade and contains a saloon and dining room by designer Robert Adam. Features of the lovely garden include an 18th-century summer house and a quaint orangery dating from 1773.

Continue on the B3416 for a further ¾ mile and meet a mini-roundabout. A short detour from the main route to the centre of Plympton can be made from here by keeping forward.

PLYMPTON, Devon

In medieval times Plymouth was an insignificant little hamlet called Sutton, and Plympton an important town with a wealthy priory. Since then the elder community has

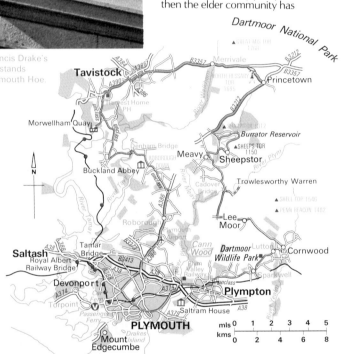

become a suburb of the successful younger. A Norman keep on a mound affords goods views. There are two medieval churches, a 16th-century guildhall, and an old grammar school where the painter Sir Joshua Reynolds, who was born in the town, was educated. At the Plym Valley Railway project (no trains running at present) a varied collection of locomotives can be seen.

From the mini-roundabout on the main route turn left SP 'Exeter', and in another ½ mile turn left again SP 'Sparkwell' and 'Cornwood'. In ¼ mile at a mini-roundabout turn right, and continue to Sparkwell. Beyond the village reach the Dartmoor Wildlife Park on the left.

DARTMOOR WILDLIFE PARK, Devon

A fine collection of British and European animals can be seen in this 25-acre zoo park. Excellent all-round views of the grounds are afforded by a tall observation tower.

Continue through Lutton to Cornwood.

CORNWOOD, Devon
The Hawns ravine on the River Yealm is a feature of this attractively situated village. Dendles Wood incorporates a national nature reserve, and there are numerous Bronze-Age enclosures and hut circles in the district. Fardell and Stert, family seats of the Raleighs and Drakes lie 1½ miles south.

At crossroads turn left SP 'Tavistock'. Begin a gradual ascent with Penn Beacon prominent on the right before skirting the industrial features of Lee Moor village.

Tunnel on the Tavistock Canal above Morwellham Quay

LEE MOOR, Devon
Colossal conical mountains of white waste dominate the landscape here, proclaiming Lee Moor as Devon's principal source of china clay.

Continue, with wide views, to a crossroads and turn right. In 1¾ miles reach Cadover Bridge on the River Plym and bear left. Trowlesworthy Warren nature trail is to the right here.

TROWLESWORTHY WARREN, Devon
This 1¾-mile nature trail flanks the south-west corner of Dartmoor alongside the River Plym. Prehistoric hut circles can be seen near the river's headwaters.

Ascend, and at the summit turn right SP 'Sheepstor, Meavy'. Descend into Meavy Valley, crossing the river to reach the edge of Meavy. A short detour can be made into the village by turning left here.

MEAVY, Devon
The stream from which this delightful village takes its name winds through woodlands over a rocky bed and pours over a small waterfall. Beside the Norman church on the village green is an ancient oak which is traditionally held to be the church's contemporary.

Continue forward on the main drive SP 'Princetown' and in ½ mile turn sharp right SP 'Burrator'. In ¾ mile turn right again SP 'Sheepstor' and cross the dam of Burrator Reservoir. In another ¾ mile turn left. A short detour to Sheepstor village can be made by bearing right here.

SHEEPSTOR & THE BURRATOR RESERVOIR, Devon
This enchanting hamlet is centred round an appealing little granite church. The picturesque Burrator Reservoir offers a dramatic backcloth, its sparkling waters reflecting the height of Sheeps Tor and the wooded slopes that rise from the opposite shore.

Skirt the reservoir on a narrow road and after 3 miles turn sharp right SP 'Princetown'. Ascend, and in ¾ mile meet crossroads and turn right again on to the B3212. Climb on to the wide, open moorland of Dartmoor National Park to reach Princetown. On the approach to Princetown are views left of 1,695ft North Hessary Tor and a BBC transmitter.

DARTMOOR NATIONAL PARK (WEST), Devon
Much of this tour is in the south-western part of this vast area, and near Princetown it climbs on to the rugged uplands of the moor itself. The landscape is dramatic and full of contrast, where jagged granite tors rise, from heather and bracken-clad slopes and peat bogs constantly replenished by the highest rainfall in Devon, though here and there great plantations of conifers are helping to dry the ground and bring back the forests that once stood here. Prehistoric crosses and hut circles are common in these parts.

PRINCETOWN, Devon
Sir Thomas Tyrwhitt founded the great convict prison here in 1806 and named the town in honour of his friend, the Prince Regent. Forced labour built many of the roads that allow modern motorists to tour comfortably through remote parts of the moor, and the town church was built by prisoners in 1883.

Turn left on to the B3357 'Tavistock' road, shortly passing the prison, then in 1 mile meet a T-junction and turn left again. Great Mis Tor rises to 1,768ft to the right, and views ahead encompass the Tamar valley and Bodmin Moor. Gradually descend from Dartmoor itself and pass Merrivale Quarry in the Walkham Valley to leave the Dartmoor National Park and enter Tavistock.

TAVISTOCK, Devon
There is an imposing town hall and remains of an abbey founded in the 10th-century. St Eustace's church, 15th-century, has interesting monuments and there is a statue of Sir Frances Drake born at Crowndale just south of the town. Light engineering and timber-working firms in this pleasant market town continue an industrial tradition that started at least as far back as the 14th century. Despite this activity the town remains unspoilt, an ideal touring base on the western fringe of the extensive Dartmoor National Park.;

Leave Tavistock on the A390 'Liskeard' road. In 2½ miles reach the Harvest Home PH and branch left on to an unclassified road SP 'Morwellham'. In 1 mile meet crossroads and go forward, SP 'Morwellham'. Follow a long descent to Morwellham Quay.

MORWELLHAM QUAY, Devon
This quay was once a busy copper-loading port on the River Tamar. Surviving installations now form part of a major industrial museum featuring the history of the port in particular and the development of the Devon copper mines in general.

Return to the crossroads and turn sharp right SP 'Bere Alston'. Continue along a high ridge between the Tamar and Tavy valleys, and after 2¾ miles turn sharp left SP 'Denham Bridge, Plymouth'. After a long descent cross the River Tavy at Denham Bridge and immediately turn right SP 'Plymouth'. Ascend to a T-junction and turn right SP 'Buckland Abbey'. In ½ mile meet crossroads and turn right, passing the entrance to Buckland Abbey on the right, then immediately left.

BUCKLAND ABBEY, Devon
Originally built by Cistercian monks in 1278, Buckland Abbey was considerably altered and adapted as a dwelling place by the Grenville family. The present house (NT) was sold to Sir Francis Drake in 1581, and nowadays contains a Drake Museum full of relics associated with the great sailor.

In 1¾ miles drive to crossroads at the edge of Roborough Down and turn left. Meet a T-junction and turn right on to the A386 (no SP) for Plymouth. Pass through Roborough, and Plymouth Airport on the return to the city centre.

SALISBURY, Wilts

The ancient city of Salisbury first came to importance following the abandonment of nearby Old Sarum in the 13th century. The bishop's see was transferred from the old to the new site, and in 1220 the cathedral was refounded in an early-English style that made it seem to soar from the ground rather than sit solidly on it. This illusion is accentuated by numerous slim columns of Purbeck stone and a magnificent 404ft spire that was added in the 14th century and is still the tallest in the country. The Cathedral Close preserves a beauty and atmosphere all of its own, and contains fine buildings dating from the 14th to the 18th centuries. Elsewhere in the town are 16th-century Joiner's Hall (NT), the 14th-century Poultry Cross (AM), and a great number of old inns. Interesting displays illustrating local history can be seen in the Salisbury and South Wiltshire Museum.

From Salisbury follow SP 'Yeovil A30' and drive to Wilton.

WILTON, Wilts

Wilton is an interesting town best known as an important carpet-making centre. Good Georgian houses can be seen in Kinsbury Square, and a curious country cross stands near the market house of 1738. Wilton House (open) was built on the site of Wilton Abbey in the 1540s, but was completely rebuilt by Inigo Jones after a serious fire. Subsequent work includes alterations by architect James Wyatt. Features of the lovely grounds (open) include fine cedars and a Palladian-style bridge over the Nadder.

At roundabout take the 1st exit, passing Wilton House on the left. In ½ mile reach the end of the village and turn right on to an unclassified road SP 'Great Wishford'. Go forward for 2¾ miles, with Grovely Woods to the left, then turn right into Great Wishford.

ON THE WILTSHIRE DOWNS

The grandeur of this tour is in the cathedral city of Salisbury and some of the county's finest stately homes. The beauty is in its fertile river valleys, and soft downland slopes that enfold timeless villages and open up panoramic views from their tree-crowned summits.

Salisbury's cathedral has been a source of inspiration for many artists, including John Constable.

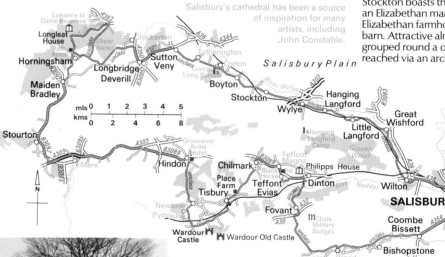

GREAT WISHFORD, Wilts

This delightful village is set in the Wylye Valley and has a church with a 15th-century crenellated tower. On Oak Apple Day (May 29) the villagers reaffirm their right to collect kindling from Grovely Woods.

Drive to the village church, turn left, and shortly afterwards turn right. Continue to Little Langford.

LITTLE LANGFORD, Wilts

Noted architect T H Wyatt rebuilt the local church in 1864, using material from the previous building. About ½ mile south west of the village is the notable iron-age hillfort of Grovely Castle.

Continue to Hanging Langford.

The bridge in the grounds of Wilton House was built in 1737 to a Palladian pattern.

HANGING LANGFORD, Wilts

Hanging Langford clings precariously to the lower flanks of hills at the edge of Grovely Wood. Some 2 miles south west of the hamlet is an earthwork that has yielded evidence of prolonged occupation.

Keep forward and drive to Wylye.

WYLYE, Wilts

Lovely flint-and-stone chequerwork cottages dating from the 17th century can be seen in this village, which stands on the Wylye River at the edge of Salisbury Plain.

SALISBURY PLAIN, Wilts

Most of the undulating 240 square miles of this windswept plateau is under cultivation, although some parts have been given over to military use. Many of its low chalk hills feature prehistoric burial mounds and other monuments. The borders of the plain are defined by the rivers Avon, Bourne, and Wylye.

From Wylye keep forward on the unclassified road SP 'Sutton Veny'. Drive along the Wylye Valley to Stockton.

STOCKTON, Wilts

Stockton boasts thatched cottages, an Elizabethan mansion, and an Elizabethan farmhouse with a great barn. Attractive almshouses are grouped round a common courtyard reached via an arched entry.

After 1 mile cross the railway line and turn right for Boyton.

BOYTON, Wilts

Flint and stone chequerwork common to this area can be seen in 13th-century and later Boyton Church, which was restored by the 19th-century architect T H Wyatt.

Drive through Corton and Tytherington, then keep left for Sutton Veny.

SUTTON VENY, Wilts

The ruined church of Sutton Veny dates from the 13th century and lies east of its 19th-century successor. Also here is a manor house dating from the 14th century.

At crossroads at the far end of the village turn left on to the B3095. Drive to Longbridge Deverill.

Overlooking the lake at Stourhead is the Pantheon, which contains casts of statues.

LONGBRIDGE DEVERILL, Wilts
John Thynne of Longleat House built the charming group of 17th-century almshouses here. His funeral helm hangs with two others in the tower of the local church.

At crossroads turn right on to the A350. In ½ mile turn left on unclassified road SP 'Crockerton' and then turn left SP 'Horningsham'. Continue through woodland passing Shear Water on the right. After 1¼ miles at T-junction turn right. Take the next turning right SP 'Longleat' to the outskirts of Horningsham. (To avoid Longleat Park toll forward through to Horningham/Bath Arms PH) turn right passing the Heavens Gate viewpoint and running alongside Longleat Estate. After 1¼ miles, before the A362 turn left to enter Longleat Park (toll).

LONGLEAT HOUSE, Wilts
This great Elizabethan mansion (open), the seat of the Marquess of Bath, stands on the site of a 13th-century priory and is a treasure house of old furniture, paintings, books, and interior decoration. It was one of England's first unified designs, and the grounds were landscaped by the brilliant 18th-century designer Capability Brown. The estate includes a large safari park (open), the first of its kind in Europe.

Leave the park with SP 'Way Out' and 'Warminster' via the Horningsham Gate.

HORNINGSHAM, Wilts
The thatched noncomformist Meeting House here, said to be one of the oldest of its kind in England, may date from the 16th century.

Drive to the Bath Arms (PH), meet crossroads, and go forward SP 'Shaftesbury' and 'Maiden Bradley'. In 1½ miles at a T-junction turn right for Maiden Bradley.

MAIDEN BRADLEY, Wilts
Wooded downland hills rise to 945ft Long Knoll above this pretty village, in which may be seen a number of attractive old houses.

At crossroads turn left on to the B3092 SP 'Mere', then pass the outskirts of Stourton.

STOURTON, Wilts
Good paintings and Chippendale furniture can be seen inside Stourhead House (NT), but this famous 18th-century mansion is best known for its superb grounds. These were laid out by Henry Hoare, who owned the estate, and show one of Europe's finest layouts of this period. In the park are classical garden temples and a delightful lake.

Continue for 1¼ miles, then turn right and then turn left SP 'Andover' to join the A303. Continue through open countryside for 3½ miles then turn right on to the B3089 SP 'Salisbury'. Continue to the A350 and turn left, then turn immediately right for Hindon.

HINDON, Wilts
Created by bishops of Winchester in the 13th century, this village was handsomely rebuilt by Wyatt after a fire and is an example of good 19th-century restoration.

Proceed from the Grosvenor Arms Hotel and turn right on to an unclassified road SP 'Tisbury'. Meet crossroads and turn right (no SP). Follow a narrow byroad to Newtown. Turn right SP 'Semley', then turn left SP 'Donhead' and 'Wardour'. Descend, and in ½ mile cross a railway. Shortly turn left SP 'Tisbury' and continue past the grounds of Wardour Castle.

WARDOUR CASTLE, Wilts
New Wardour Castle (open), the largest Georgian house in Wiltshire, was begun in 1769 for the 8th Lord Arundell. Its private chapel is larger than many a parish church, and very richly decorated.

WARDOUR OLD CASTLE, Wilts
Wardour Old Castle (AM) dates from the end of the 14th-century. It stands on a wooded bank overlooking an 18th-century artificial lake and is uniquely hexagonal in shape.

Keep forward for Tisbury.

TISBURY, Wilts
In the 7th century this village stood on an important Saxon track. Its cruciform church dates from the 12th century and shares the churchyard with a giant yew, 36ft in circumference, that is reputed to be more than 1,000 years old.

Turn right at the post office SP 'Salisbury'. Continue to the end of the village and turn right again. Proceed for ¾ mile and branch left SP 'Chilmark', passing Place Farm on the left.

PLACE FARM, Wilts
Formerly an abbey grange, this farm comprises a group of 14th to 15th-century domestic buildings. The 200ft-long tithe barn, is one of the largest in England.

Drive to Chilmark.

CHILMARK, Wilts
The creamy stone from Chilmark's quarries (closed) was used in Wilton House, Salisbury Cathedral, and the spire of Chichester Cathedral.

Turn left SP 'Salisbury', then right. Continue to the main road and turn right again, on to the B3089 for Teffont Magna. Keep right into the village, drive to the Black Horse (PH), and turn right on to an unclassified road. Continue with SP 'Tisbury' into Teffont Evias.

TEFFONT EVIAS, Wilts
Twin Teffont Magna and Teffont Evias stand close together in the beautiful Nadder Valley. The former boasts the delightful Fitz House of 1700, and the latter a Tudor mansion that was once the home of Sir James Ley, who became Lord Chief Justice of England and was immortalized by Milton in a sonnet.

In ¼ mile turn left with SP 'Salisbury' and cross a river bridge. Ascend to a main road and turn right to re-join the B3089. After ¾ mile at crossroads (the outskirts of Dinton) turn right on to an unclassified road for Fovant. A slight detour can be made to Philipps House by turning left at the crossroads.

PHILIPPS HOUSE, Wilts
Designed by Sir Jeffry Wyatville in 1816, this splendid neo-Grecian mansion (NT) stands in 200-acre Dinton Park and is let to the YWCA (open by appointment).

DINTON, Wilts
Three notable National Trust properties are to be found on the outskirts of this hillside village. Besides Philipps House there is the Tudor to 18th-century Hyde's House (not open) and ivy-covered Little Clarendon, which dates from the 15th-century (open on application).

On the main route, continue into Fovant.

FOVANT, Wilts
Huge regimental badges were cut in the chalk downs by soldiers stationed here during World War I. A memorial brass of 1492 can be seen in the local church.

Drive to the end of the village and turn right on to the A30. In ½ mile turn left on to an unclassified road SP 'Broad Chalke'. Ascend on to the downs, and after 1½ miles turn left. Drive to Broad Chalke, bear right then left through the village, and proceed to Bishopstone.

BISHOPSTONE, Wilts
Remarkable furnishings can be seen inside the local church, a beautiful cruciform building with superb stone vaulting and windows.

Continue to Coombe Bissett.

COOMBE BISSETT, Wilts
Just downstream from the fine 18th-century bridge that spans the river here is a picturesque packhorse bridge. Its wooden parapets are new, but the mounting stone is very old. Traces of every century from Norman times to the present day can be seen in the fabric of the attractive local church.

Turn left on to the A354 and return to Salisbury.

A picturesque old mill stands beside the River Ebble in Coombe Bissett.

SHAFTESBURY, Dorset
Situated on the edge of a 700ft plateau, Shaftesbury is an ancient town full of quaint corners and little eccentricities. Its most famous street, cobbled Gold Hill, plunges down the hillside with a graceful abandon. Thomas Hardy used the original town name Shaston when featuring it in his novels. Shaftesbury's history began with the abbey established here c880, a foundation that became the burial place of Edward the Martyr and grew to be one of the richest in the area until destroyed at the Dissolution in the 16th century. Only slight remains now exist (AM, open sometimes), but various relics are preserved in the Abbey Ruins Museum. In the Grosvenor Hotel is the famous Chevy Chase sideboard, which was carved from a single piece of oak in the 13th century.

Take the A30 'Sherborne, Yeovil' road and descend to the Blackmoor Vale. In 5 miles at East Stour, turn left on to the B3092 SP 'Sturminster Newton' and enter the Stour Valley. Continue to Marnhull.

MARNHULL, Dorset
Thomas Hardy called this village Marlott and made it the birthplace of his heroine in *Tess of the d'Urbervilles*. The 14th-century church has an attractive pinnacled tower overlooking Blackmoor Vale.

Continue to Sturminster Newton.

STURMINSTER NEWTON, Dorset
Important livestock markets are held in this southern Blackmoor Vale town. A fine six-arched medieval bridge spans the Stour, and both Sturminster Mill and the 14th-century Fiddleford Mill one mile to the east have been restored to working order.

Sherborne Abbey has beautiful 15th-century fan vaulting in the choir.

FARMLAND AND FOREST
Gentle hills and farmland watered by several rivers characterize the fertile Blackmoor Vale. In contrast are the rolling grass and woodlands of Cranborne Chase, a vast area that was once the private hunting preserve of kings.

Gold Hill, Shaftesbury's most picturesque street, overlooks the Blackmoor Vale.

Continue through Sturminster Newton on the 'Blandford' road. Cross a bridge and turn right on to the A357 SP 'Stalbridge' then pass through agricultural country to reach Lydlinch Common. Continue for ¾ mile and turn left on to an unclassified road SP 'Stourton Caundle'. Pass the edge of Stourton Caundle and proceed to Purse Caundle.

PURSE CAUNDLE, Dorset
Purse Caundle Manor is an excellent medieval house (open), notable for its great hall and chamber, and beautiful oriel window.

Proceed for ¼ mile and turn left on to the A30 SP 'Sherborne'. Continue to Milborne Port.

MILBORNE PORT, Dorset
Although stone is the predominant building material in this area, beautiful Venn House was brick built in Queen Anne style c1700. The local church preserves Saxon work, and a fine tympanum over the south door.

Proceed on the A30 to Sherborne. (For the town centre turn left)

SHERBORNE, Dorset
Winding streets of mellow stone-built houses dating from the 15th century onwards weave a fascinating web across this beautiful and historic town. From AD705 to 1075 Sherborne was a cathedral city, but the great church was adopted by a slightly later monastery that flourished until the Dissolution in the 16th century. Many of the foundation's buildings were adopted by other bodies and survive in a good state of preservation. Some were occupied by the famous Sherborne School, and the Abbey Gatehouse now accommodates the Sherborne Museum of local history. Over all stands the Norman to 15th-century Abbey Church, a magnificent building best known for its superb fan vaulting. The older of the town's two castles stands ½ mile east and dates from the 12th and 13th centuries. It was reduced to a picturesque heap of ruins (AM) in the Civil War. Sherborne's 16th-century castle was built for Sir Walter Raleigh, and contains fine furniture, paintings, and porcelain (open). It is set in 20-acre grounds designed by the 18th-century garden landscaper Capability Brown.

Follow SP 'Dorchester' to leave Sherborne on the A352. Pass through wooded country and continue through Middlemarsh. Make a winding ascent on the outer slopes to 860ft High Stoy to pass through a gap in the hills and reach Minterne Magna.

MINTERNE MAGNA, Dorset
Features of the attractive wild shrub garden that occupies 29 acres of ground round Minterne House (open) include bamboo-lined walks, great banks of Himalayan and Chinese rhododendrons, and a beautiful collection of azaleas.

Continue for 2 miles and branch left to enter Cerne Abbas. The turf-cut Giant can be seen to the left.

CERNE ABBAS GIANT, Dorset
This 180ft long figure (NT) is believed to be associated with fertility rites and may date from before the Roman occupation.

CERNE ABBAS, Dorset
The village of Cerne Abbas derives its name from a Benedictine abbey founded here in 987. Remains of this include a beautiful 15th-century guesthouse, and the contemporary tithe barn has been converted into a house. Early examples of heraldic stained glass can be seen in the windows of the local church.

In Cerne Abbas centre turn left on to an unclassified road, then in ¼ mile turn right on to the 'Piddletrenthide' road to reach that village.

PIDDLETRENTHIDE, Dorset
Attractive yellow-stone houses are scattered for nearly a mile along the banks of the River Piddle, or Trent. The 15th-century church has one of the finest towers in Dorset.

Turn right onto the B3143 and continue through Piddlehinton. Continue for 1¼ miles and turn left on to the Puddletown road B3142 to pass Waterston Manor and reach Puddletown.

PUDDLETOWN, Dorset
Thomas Hardy's Weatherbury in *Far from the Madding Crowd*, this village is one of the most attractive in Dorset and features a beautiful 15th-century church with an unusual panelled roof. Elizabethan and later Waterston Manor stands 2 miles northwest and was described by Hardy as Bathsheba's house in *Far from the Madding Crowd*. Between the village and Wareham are stretches of moorland that were part of the novel's Egdon Heath.

ATHELHAMPTON HOUSE, Dorset
Standing in 10 acres of formal landscape and water gardens about 1 mile east of Puddletown is the notable 15th- and 16th-century Athelhampton House, one of England's finest medieval houses (open).

Leave Puddletown by turning left on to the A354 SP 'Blandford'. Continue to Milborne St Andrew, then take an unclassified valley road to the left and drive to Milton Abbas.

Bulbarrow Hill is situated in a part of Dorset which is designated as an area of outstanding natural beauty

BULBARROW HILL, Dorset ST70

Excellent views over much of Dorset can be enjoyed from this 902ft hill, which is an official AA Viewpoint and one of the highest summits in this part of the country.

Follow SP 'Blandford', and in ½ mile bear left. In 3½ miles turn right and at the edge of Winterbourne Stickland turn left. In 4 miles cross the River Stour into Blandford Forum.

Milton Abbas was built by the owner of Milton Abbey to replace a village which he demolished because it spoilt his view

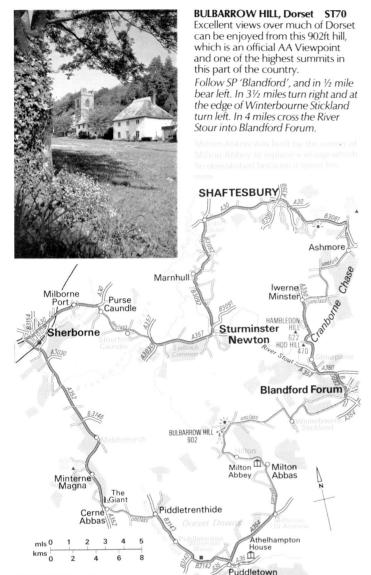

Leave Blandford Forum on the B3082 then A350 SP 'Warminster'. Continue along the Stour Valley and pass through Stourpaine. Just past the village on the left are the hills of Hambledon and Hod.

HAMBLEDON AND HOD HILLS, Dorset

Grass-covered Hambledon Hill rises to 622ft and is topped by earthworks raised at various times between the stone age and the Roman conquest. Its steep flanks, worth climbing for the tremendous views, were used by General Wolfe to train troops before embarking to take Quebec. To the south east is slightly lower Hod Hill, which features ancient earthworks and traces of a Roman camp that was built and manned cAD63.

Continue to Iwerne Minster.

IWERNE MINSTER, Dorset

The local Norman to 17th-century church has an attractive stone spire. Just outside the village is the site of a Roman villa.

From Iwerne Minster war memorial turn right on to the unclassified 'Tarrant Gunville' road. Climb on to the heights of Cranborne Chase and turn left on to the Shaftesbury road. Excellent views across Blackmoor Vale can be enjoyed from this section of route. Continue for 1¾ miles and at crossroads turn right for Ashmore.

ASHMORE, Dorset

Georgian houses mingle with flint, stone, and brick cottages round a duckpond and 19th-century church in this charming village. The village itself stands at 700ft in the chalk hills of Cranborne Chase and is the highest in Dorset. To the north is a summit, topped by a prehistoric earthwork, which commands views across the Chase to the Solent channel and the Isle of Wight.

Keep left of Ashmore village pond and in 1 mile join the B3081 to enter Wiltshire for a short distance. On the right is tree-capped Win Green, a 910ft hill which is accessible by track and is the highest point on Cranborne Chase. Re-enter Dorset and descend Zig-Zag Hill to enter Shaftesbury.

MILTON ABBAS, Dorset

Set in unspoilt rural surroundings, this peaceful village of thatched and whitewashed cottages was designed and built from scratch during the 18th century. It was probably the first integrally planned village in Britain. The Brewery Farm Museum is housed in the old brewery and contains antique agricultural implements, bygones, old photographs, and other relics.

From the foot of the village follow the 'Hilton' road past Milton Abbey.

MILTON ABBEY, Dorset

The beautiful abbey church dates from the 14th and 15th centuries and stands in front of a hill surmounted by a Norman chapel. Next to Milton Abbey is 15th-century Abbot's Hall, which was incorporated in a mansion by architects Sir William Chambers and James Wyatt. The huge 18th-century mansion here now is of exceptional interest and houses a school. It is open during the summer months.

Reach Hilton and in ¾ mile turn right and shortly right again for Bulbarrow Hill.

BLANDFORD FORUM, Dorset

All but 50 or so of the town's houses were destroyed by a terrible fire in 1731, which explains why handsome brick and stone architecture of the late 18th century is so much in evidence. Earlier survivals include the Ryves Almshouses of 1682, Dale House of 1689, and the early 17th-century Old House. Much of the countryside round Blandford is rich arable and dairy-farming land, watered by the beautiful River Stour to the south and fringed by the lovely countryside of Cranborne Chase to the north and west.

CRANBORNE CHASE, Dorset

Now an area of rolling grasslands scattered with fine beechwoods, the Chase covers over 100 square miles between Shaftesbury and Salisbury and was once a royal hunting forest. Subsequently the local hunting rights passed into the hands of the earls of Salisbury and Shaftesbury.

The atmosphere of rural tranquillity at Ashmore is enhanced by a duckpond

SHEPTON MALLET, Somerset

Shepton is short for the Saxon name Sheeptown, and Mallet was the Norman name of the lord of the manor. The wool trade brought wealth to the village in the 15th century and the magnificent church, with its high, fine tower, was built with the profits. Inside, the oak roof is lavishly decorated with 350 carved panels and about 300 carved bosses — all of different designs. In the market square stands the ornate market cross. Rebuilt in 1841, this has been the social and commercial centre of the village for 5 centuries; at one time even wives were put up for sale here, as well as more usual market goods. There is also a museum in the square where Roman relics and finds from the Mendip caves can be seen. Nearby are the medieval Shambles; these wooden market-benches were not slaughter houses (the usual meaning of Shambles) but market stalls.

Leave on the A371, SP 'Castle Cary'. After 1¾ miles turn right on to the A37, then ¼ mile farther take the A371.
Go through Prestleigh and opposite the Royal Bath and West showground, branch left on to the B3081 for Evercreech.

EVERCREECH, Somerset

Of all Somerset's beautiful Perpendicular church towers, this is perhaps the finest. An impression of great height is achieved by the tiers of tall pinnacles and bell-openings. The nave roof has 16 angels painted on its ceiling and gilded bosses. St Peter's overlooks a pleasant square with old cottages, almshouses and the village cross raised on well-worn steps.

At the crossroads turn left, SP 'Stoney Stratton', and 'Batcombe'. At the T-junction ½ mile later, turn right into Stoney Stratton, then in ¼ mile turn left, SP 'Batcombe'. After 1¾ miles bear left, then turn right, and at the next crossroads turn right again. In Batcombe, by the church, turn right on to the Bruton road and later join the B3081 for Bruton.

Superb landscaping at Stourhead

WEST SOMERSET AND THE WILTSHIRE BORDERS

The graceful spires of the great wool churches pierce the skies above the green, undulating landscape of West Somerset, and the glory of Stourhead's beautiful gardens and the excitements of Longleat's Safari Park draw visitors over the border into Wiltshire.

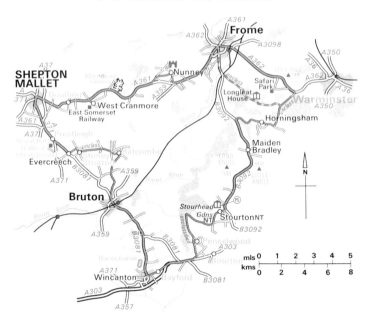

BRUTON, Somerset

Bruton was another of the chief textile towns in Somerset, and in 1290 one of the very first fulling mills in England was built on the banks of a nearby stream. The River Brue flows through the village and crossing it is the ancient packhorse bridge over which men and horses have trudged for centuries. A good view of the town is to be had from here, and several historic buildings hide among the narrow streets. There is, for instance, the 17th-century Hugh Sexey's Hospital, bequeathed to the town by a local stable boy who later found fame in London as auditor to Elizabeth I. Also of note is 16th-century King's Grammar

School which was founded by Edward VI. One of its most famous scholars was R. D. Blackmore, author of *Lorna Doone*. Bruton had a priory in the 12th century but all that remains of that now is a dovecot (NT) and part of the wall which both lie in a field behind the town.

From the one-way system in Bruton follow the B3081, SP 'Wincanton'. Continue through hilly countryside and after 4 miles pass Wincanton Racecourse before reaching Wincanton.

WINCANTON, Somerset

The town's medieval name, Wyndcaleton, came from the River Cale on which it stands on the edge of the Blackmoor Vale. Unfortunately a fire in the early 18th century destroyed most of Wincanton's buildings and left little of interest, apart from the church which has a 15th-century tower. Nevertheless it is a pleasant place with steep streets and makes an ideal base for touring the dairy hills of southern Somerset.

Turn left into Wincanton main street, SP 'Andover', and at the far end of the neighbouring village of Bayford turn left on to the A303. In 1½ miles turn left SP 'Penselwood', and in ½ mile turn left again. Later the tour bears left, SP 'Stourton', and the road gradually reaches 793ft. On the way down, after ¼ mile, turn sharp right (still SP 'Stourton'), and in 1½ miles by the ornamental lake, bear left and continue to Stourton.

Most famous of Frome's ancient lanes is Cheap Street, complete with water course

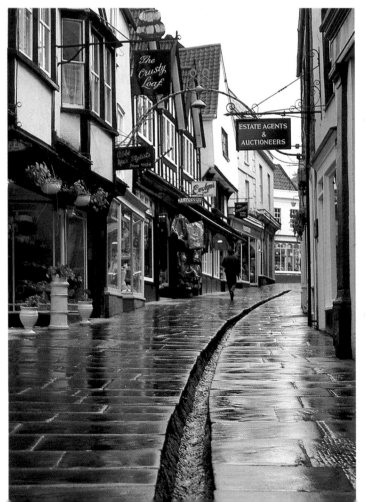

be explored; paved Cheap Street, with its central water conduit, leads picturesquely to the church, where Gentle Street winds up in steps towards the top of the town. The bridge over the Frome incorporates an 18th-century lock-up and nearby stand the Bluecoat School and Blue House, an attractive almshouse, built in 1726 and recently restored.

Leave on the A361 Glastonbury road. In 3¼ miles turn right onto an unclassified road, SP 'Nunney' and continue to Nunney.

NUNNEY, Somerset
Grey-stone, red-roofed cottages cluster round Nunney Castle (AM) — the tall, grey centrepiece of the village. Really a fortified manor house built in 1373, it is a fine sight with its 4 round towers and beautiful moat. Although the castle withstood Roundhead attacks well during the Civil War, it was eventually slighted by Cromwell. A footbridge over the moat and stream leads to the village church where there are a number of elaborate stone monuments to the de la Mares, owners of the castle.

In Nunney turn left, SP 'Shepton Mallet', cross the river bridge then turn left again. A mile later, at the T-junction, turn left, then at the main road turn right on to the A361. Continue for 4¼ miles and at the crossroads turn left for West Cranmore.

WEST CRANMORE, Somerset
Near the village the East Somerset Railway Centre can be found. A new engine house has been built here by artist and railway enthusiast David Shepherd, to house his 2 locomotives — *Black Prince* and *Green Knight*.

Return to the A361 and turn left, then continue through Doulting to complete the tour at Shepton Mallet.

STOURTON, Wilts
Lovely Stourton (NT) lies on the edge of the Stourhead estate overlooking the lake and gardens. The village consists of an extremely pleasing group of whitewashed 18th-century cottages facing St Peter's Church standing on its smooth open lawn, an inn and the graceful medieval Bristol High Cross — brought here in 1780. Inside the church are several monuments to the Hoare family, the famous bankers and creators of Stourhead.

Continue through the village, past the entrance to Stourhead Gardens.

STOURHEAD HOUSE AND GARDENS, Wilts
During the 18th-century the Hoares built the present Palladian mansion and dammed a nearby valley to form the beautiful lake in the gardens below. The original concept of the gardens was based on 4 ingredients — water, temples, trees and green grass. It was inspired by Henry Hoare's travels through Italy and the whole is a masterpiece of landscape gardening with the lake as a glittering centrepiece. Whatever the season there is always a heady profusion of colour at Stourhead, set against the timeless backdrop of ancient beech trees, rippling water and stone temples.

Leave the gardens and in ¼ mile turn left off on to the B3092, SP 'Frome', for Maiden Bradley.

MAIDEN BRADLEY, Wilts
Bradley House, home of the Dukes of Somerset, once stood on the edge of this neat and leafy village, but apart from 1 wing, this was demolished at the beginning of the last century. At Priory Farm lie the scant remains of a former leper hospital, founded in the 12th-century for the care of female patients, and later turned into an Augustinian Priory.

2 miles beyond Maiden Bradley turn right, SP 'Horningsham' and 'Longleat', and continue to Horningsham.

HORNINGSHAM, Wilts
At the heart of the village outside The Bath Arms, huddle a group of lime trees so intertwined that their branches form a close-weave canopy overhead. There are 12 of them and are thus locally known as the Apostles. Horningsham lies under the shadow of its famous neighbour, Longleat, and its valley borders the park. Possibly it is because of Longleat that Horningsham has what could be the oldest Non-conformist chapel in England. Many think that this small, thatched meeting house was built by Sir John Thynne, builder of Longleat, for his Scottish labour force.

Remain on the Longleat road and after ¾ mile pass Horningsham Church, then in ¼ mile turn left (still SP 'Longleat'). Follow this road through attractive woodland and after 1½ miles, pass the entrance to Longleat House on the left. (Access to the Longleat estate is via a toll road. If taken, leave the grounds by following SP 'Frome' and 'The West'. Later join the B3092 and enter Frome from the south to rejoin the main tour).

LONGLEAT, Wilts
Lions have made Longleat famous, but the hub of this huge estate belonging to the Marquess of Bath, the house, deserves its own notoriety. Builder Sir John Thynne originally transformed the Augustinian priory into a comfortable house, but sadly this suffered considerable fire damage in 1567 and the existing Elizabethan mansion is mostly Robert Smythson's work. The splendid exterior is more than matched by the inside: rich tapestries, Genoese velvet and ancient Spanish leather clothe the

walls, while Italianate painted ceilings and marble fireplaces ornament the state rooms. Much of the beautiful parkland, landscaped by Capability Brown and Humphry Repton, is occupied by the Safari Park. In the drive-through open reserves many wild animals, besides the lions, roam freely. The ornamental lake is the home of sealions and hippos and in the middle lies Ape Island. A narrow-gauge railway, an adventure playground and a pets' corner are just a few of the many other attractions at Longleat.

The main tour turns left on to the A362, SP 'Frome'. (After ½ mile note the turning on the left for Longleat Safari Park). Continue on the A362 to Frome.

FROME, Somerset
The old wool town of Frome, which takes its name from the river, is a busy, thriving place whose attractive character survives the summer traffic jams. Around its market place there is a network of old narrow streets to

COUNTIES OF GOLDEN HAM STONE

Dorset, a maze of country lanes; Somerset, the land of the 'summer-farm dwellers'. Both counties a blend of patchwork fields and timeless villages, each with a glorious church built of golden Ham stone once patronised by the lords of the magnificent manor houses.

SHERBORNE, Dorset

There is a great wealth of medieval buildings in Sherborne; a legacy of its ecclesiastical importance seeded in Anglo-Saxon times when St Aldhelm was first bishop of the cathedral. From 864 to 1539 this was a monastery, and during that time Sherborne became a great centre of learning. The monks rebuilt the abbey church in the 12th and 15th centuries, the latter project producing the Ham stone roofing for which it is famous. In the abbey lie 2 Anglo-Saxon kings, Ethelbad and Ethelbert, brothers of Alfred the Great. Sherborne School, founded in 1550, took over many of the abbey buildings after the Dissolution; its chapel is the Abbot's Hall, the Abbot's Lodging has been converted into studies, and also preserved as part of the school are the library and the Abbot's kitchen. One other part of the old monastery still surviving is the monks' washhouse, now the conduit in the main shopping centre, Cheap Street. Outside the town stand Sherborne's 2 castles. The first was built by Bishop Roger in the early 12th century, but was destroyed in the Civil War by Cromwell and remains a ruin in the parkland of the other (OACT). This was built by Sir Walter Raleigh in about 1594, who found the old castle unsuitable for conversion. It is set in gardens with lakeside lawns, a cascade and an orangery in grounds landscaped by Capability Brown. Also in the garden is the seat in which it is said the thoughtful Sir Walter was sitting, quietly smoking the newly discovered tobacco, when a servant doused him with a flagon of ale thinking he was on fire.

Leave Sherborne on the A30, SP 'Yeovil'. In 2½ miles pass, on the right, Worldwide Butterflies.

WORLDWIDE BUTTERFLIES, Somerset

Compton House (OACT), an Elizabethan mansion, is the rather unlikely home of a unique butterfly farm where species from around the world are bred. These entrancing insects can be studied in all stages of their development and there is a tropical jungle where particularly exotic butterflies live. The Palm House is another oasis of luxuriant vegetation and resembles an equatorial rain forest. The Lullingstone Silk Farm also occupies Compton House and the silk from here was used for Queen Elizabeth II's wedding dress.

Continue on the A30 to Yeovil.

YEOVIL, Somerset

This is a thriving town with a definite 20th-century flavour. It suffered disastrous fires in 1499, 1623 and 1640, and air raids in World War II which destroyed many old buildings. One long-standing spectator of the town's fortunes is the Ham stone church built at the end of the 14th century. Its simplicity and size make it impressive, and its greatest possession, a 15th-century brass lectern, is also refreshingly plain. The museum in Hendford Manor displays local archaeology and history, including Roman finds and a good collection of firearms.

Leave on the A37 SP 'Bristol'. In 1 mile branch left on to an unclassified road, SP 'Tintinhull'. Later pass the edge of Chilthorne Domer to reach Tintinhull.

TINTINHULL HOUSE, Somerset

Tintinhull House (NT) stands near the village green of Tintinhull. It dates from about 1600 when it was an unassuming farmhouse, but it was suddenly given architectural distinction by the addition of the west front in 1700. The interior remains plain, the carved staircase and some fine panelling being the only notable decorative features, both dating from the early 18th century. The garden, however, is for many the chief attraction. It consists of several hedged gardens and a sunken garden cunningly designed to give the impression of many varying levels. On the north side of the house there is a large lawn, shaded by a huge cedar tree, and on the west side a forecourt, another lawn and a memorial pavilion overlook a pond.

Leave Tintinhull on the Montacute road and follow this winding lane for 2 miles. At the T-junction turn left to enter Montacute for Montacute House.

MONTACUTE HOUSE, Somerset

Edward Phelips, who became Master of the Rolls, commenced the building of Montacute House (NT) in 1588, the year of the Armada. Built to impress — houses of that period reflected the power and position of the owner — Montacute is an almost magical building, liberally endowed with gables and turrets fashioned in a rich golden stone. The Phelips family faded from power in the mid-17th century, and the house became a quiet country house in a rural backwater for almost 300 years. The great hall has splendid 16th-century panelling, heraldic glass, plaster decoration and an elaborate stone screen and the 189ft gallery is the longest of the period. The house was empty when it came to the National Trust in 1931, but has since been filled with many valuable furnishings.

After passing the house and village square turn right into Townsend. Climb through pleasant woodland before turning right. Continue to Ham Hill Country Park and descend into Stoke-Sub-Hamdon.

STOKE-SUB-HAMDON, Somerset

Churches and houses all over Somerset and Devon are built from the golden stone quarried from Ham Hill up above Stoke village. Since Roman times stone has been hewn from this hill and its summit is much ridged and terraced by the earthworks of prehistoric peoples who built their forts here. Most of the houses of the village date back to the 17th century, and are built of Ham stone with mullioned windows and charming gables. The Priory (NT) was begun in the 14th century, but only the great hall (OACT) and the screens passage remain.

At the T-junction turn left, then turn right into North Street, SP 'Martock'. Later cross the A303 and in 1 mile turn right on to the B3165 and enter Martock.

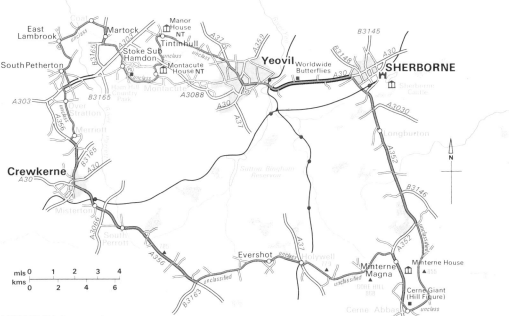

buttresses of the south transept; theories designate it either as a shrine or as a hermit's shelter. In September the town celebrates a 2-day fair, a custom centuries old and happily upheld.

Leave on the A356, SP 'Dorchester'. Pass through Misterton and South Perrott, then gradually ascend on to high ground. At the top follow an almost level road for 2 miles, then turn left on to an unclassified road for Evershot.

EVERSHOT, Dorset
This place among the hills is rather curious; it is a village yet its main street has raised pavements and old yellow and grey-stone houses, fitted with bow-fronted windows in the manner of a small town. George Crabbe, the poet, was rector of the little church here which has a rare silver Elizabethan chalice.

At the end of the village bear right. In 1¼ miles turn right then immediately left across the A37, SP 'Minterne Magna', and continue along the edge of Batcombe Hill. On reaching the A352, turn right for the hamlet of Minterne Magna.

MINTERNE MAGNA
Minterne House was built of Ham stone for Lord Digby between 1904 and 1906 by Leonard Stokes. Only the grounds are open, but, set in a lovely valley, they form a tapestry of rich colour made up of banks of rhododendrons, azaleas and magnolias.

Continue on the A352 towards Cerne Abbas. In 1¾ miles pass the Cerne Giant chalk figure (on the left), and turn left on to an unclassified road for the village centre. At the New Inn turn left, SP 'Buckland Newton'. Ascend on to high ground and at the top turn left, SP 'Sherborne'. In 3½ miles join the A352 for the return to Sherborne.

MARTOCK, Somerset
This is a charming little town enhanced by many old stone and thatched houses. The church, mainly 15th century, boasts the finest roof in the county. Virtually every inch of the tie-beam roof erected in 1513 is beautifully carved. Opposite the church is the old 14th-century manor house, one of 3 built here. The one from the 15th century lies ruined in a moated field nearby, while one from the 17th century stands close to the Georgian Market House at the end of the main street.

At the far end of the village (by the Bakers Arms PH) turn left on to an unclassified road, SP 'Coat'. At Coat turn left with the Kingsbury road, then in ¾ mile cross the river bridge and continue to East Lambrook.

EAST LAMBROOK, Somerset
In the village is East Lambrook Manor (OACT), a pretty little Tudor house with fine panelling, best known however for its gardens. These specialise in the growing of rare plants, and are laid out cottage-style as a memorial to the well-known gardener Margery Fish, as was the nursery for the propagation of rare species.

On entering the village turn left on to the South Petherton road. In 1 mile turn right for South Petherton.

SOUTH PETHERTON, Somerset
Tudor cottages, shops and villas, and a church with a roll call of vicars dating back to 1080 belong to South Petherton. Within the church walls lies the effigy of a curly-headed knight in chain mail, brought here after it was discovered by workmen digging a pit for a petrol storage tank. Also here is an extract from the diary of Richard Symonds, a Royalist soldier who stayed here in 1644, and whose writings provide a valuable insight of his contemporary world.

Branch left SP 'Illminster', and in just over ½ mile turn right on to the A303, then take the next turning left, SP 'Over Stratton'. At the far end of Over Stratton turn right then keep left and follow a pleasant byroad to Merriott. At the T-junction turn right (no sign), then at the A356 turn left and continue to Crewkerne.

CREWKERNE, Somerset
Crewkerne is a town of proud and ancient traditions, dating back to Anglo-Saxon times when it had the right of minting coins. In more recent times the town was famous for sail-making; it made sails for Nelson's *Victory*, and now does so for Americas Cup competitors. The Ham stone 15th-century church is the best building in Crewkerne, with a west front of cathedral-like proportions and glorious stained glass. An unsolved mystery are the 2 roofed-over

THE ISLE OF PURBECK

Superb views over this exceptionally beautiful peninsula can be enjoyed from high downs that drop sheer to the sea as massive limestone cliffs on the south side. East is the superb haven of Poole Harbour, which insinuates little creeks between heathery promontories and long, tree-covered spits.

THE ISLE OF PURBECK, Dorset

Most of this tour stays within the confines of the Isle of Purbeck, a wild and lovely peninsula that extends from Poole Harbour to Lulworth Cove and is crossed to the west by the Purbeck Hills. Like much of Dorset this is Thomas Hardy country, and reminders of the author and his many novels are everywhere. It is also a designated area of outstanding natural beauty.

SWANAGE, Dorset

This busy resort stands between towering downs that end as cliff-girded promontories on both sides of the sandy bay. Winding, switchback streets weave down to a shopping and amusement area concentrated on the only level piece of ground in the town – the sea front. Farther round the bay is the small pier and quay, where the Bournemouth ferry docks and anglers fish. An attractive group of old buildings clusters round the Mill Pond, off the Main Street and near the parish church is the town museum.

DURLSTON COUNTRY PARK, Dorset

Accessible from Swanage by road or a 1-mile footpath, this fascinating area of wild clifftop has many unusual features. Imposing Durlston Castle is built of Purbeck stone and occupies a lovely site near the headland. On Durlston Head itself is a 40-ton globe map of the world, fashioned from Portland stone quarried in the district, and $\frac{1}{4}$ mile away near the Anvil Lighthouse are the Tilly Whim caves – old quarries once used by smugglers.

Leave Swanage on the A351 SP 'Wareham'. In 1½ miles turn left on to the B3069 SP 'Kingston' to pass through Langton Matravers, a picturesque hillside village of local stone. At the end of the village turn left on to an unclassified road for Worth Matravers.

WORTH MATRAVERS, Dorset

This village is an enchanting combination of steep streets and stone cottages. A rough road south leads to the tiny Norman chapel and fine views on lonely St Alban's (or Aldhelm's) Head, while a toll road to the west leads to the cliff-encircled Chapman's Pool.

From Worth Matravers take the Corfe Castle road and in 1¼ miles at a T-junction turn left to rejoin the B3069. Continue to Kingston, with good views to Corfe Castle.

KINGSTON, Dorset

Features of 19th-century Kingston Church, considered one of the finest in the area, include black Purbeck marble pillars and a beautiful stone-vaulted chancel.

From Kingston a pleasant detour from the main route can be taken via a toll road to 600ft Swyre Head. In clear weather both the Isle of Portland and Isle of Wight can be seen from here. On the main route, bear right with the B3069 and make a sharp, winding descent to meet the A351. Turn left to enter Corfe Castle.

CORFE CASTLE, Dorset

Dominated by the picturesquely ruined stronghold from which it takes its name, this Purbeck-stone village owes its existence to the curiously symmetrical hill on which the castle stands. The mound rises exactly in the centre of a gap in the Purbeck Hills and was probably first fortified by King Alfred against the Danes. When the Normans came they occupied the site and began the magnificent 12th- to 15th-century castle (open) whose remains can be seen today. After the Civil War Cromwell made sure that it could never again be used against him by blowing it up with gunpowder. A river curls round the

Ammonites are the most easily identified of many fossil types found in Dorset

Corfe Castle dominates its surroundings. The River Frome flows to the south of Wareham

base of the steep hill. On the village side is a deep moat spanned by a bridge, and in a garden off the main street is a perfect replica of the village and castle in miniature. Various old relics from the village can be seen in the local museum, and an interesting (though very informal) fossil museum occupies a shed near the castle gates.

Continue along the 'Wareham' road and just past the castle turn left on to an unclassified road and skirt the castle hill to reach Church Knowle. Drive through Church Knowle and meet crossroads. A detour can be taken from the main route by turning left and following toll roads through the estate of Smedmore House to Kimmeridge and Kimmeridge Bay.

KIMMERIDGE, Dorset

Thatched and slate-roofed cottages make up this tiny village, which is situated near the shallow bay from which it takes its name. A toll road leads to the coast.

KIMMERIDGE BAY, Dorset
Very low cliffs of black shale ring this wide, sandless bay, and the beach is littered with great chunks of rock literally packed with fossil ammonites. A condition of entry to the beach nowadays is that hammers and chisels should be left behind. A well sunk here in 1959 produces some 10,000 tons of crude oil each year.

SMEDMORE HOUSE, Dorset
Nearly all the land round Kimmeridge village and bay forms part of the Smedmore estate, and it is by permission of the big house that visitors are allowed on to the toll roads that lead to the attractive coast. The house itself (open) shows a combination of Jacobean, Queen Anne, and Georgian styles. Inside is a good collection of antique dolls.

To continue on the main route, turn right at the crossroads outside Church Knowle and cross the Purbeck Hills. Left are views of Creech Barrow and to the right is the attractive Blue Pool.

BLUE POOL, Dorset
Once an ugly scar left by the extraction of clay, this flooded pit (open) has been transformed into one of the county's most famous beauty spots by the re-establishment of coniferous woodland on its banks. Particles of clay suspended in the water make it brilliant blue when conditions are right. A short distance to the north is Furzebrook where a rail-connected terminal exports oil from the Wych Farm oil-field beside Poole Harbour.

Continue to Stoborough Green and turn left on to the A351 to reach Wareham.

WAREHAM, Dorset
Situated between the tidal River Frome and the River Trent (or Piddle), this quiet port has an ancient quay which now serves anglers and pleasure craft. In Saxon times the settlement was defended by earthworks, and their grass-covered remains still almost encircle the town. Much of Wareham was rebuilt after a great fire in 1762, which explains why so many attractive Georgian houses can be seen here. The parish church preserves original Saxon work and contains an effigy of Lawrence of Arabia. To the north of the town are the sandy heathlands and coniferous plantations of 3,500-acre Wareham Forest.

From Wareham go forward SP 'Poole' and at all roundabouts follow signs 'Poole'. After 4½ miles at the A35 roundabout take the 2nd exit SP 'Lytchett Minster B3067' and pass through Lytchett Minster to reach Upton. Here turn right on to the A350 SP 'Hamworthy'. The road ahead at this point leads to the Upton Country Park.

Continue on the A350 and pass through residential Hamworthy before crossing a bridge to reach Poole Old Town.

POOLE, Dorset
Elizabeth I granted Poole county status which it kept until the late 19th century, and today it is a busy mixture of industrial centre and tourist resort. Its good beach and sheltered harbour have made it popular with holidaymakers, and its position close to a lovely and historic area of heaths and pinewoods makes it ideal as a touring base. Many fine old buildings stand in Poole's historic precinct, including the 18th-century Guildhall and a medieval merchant's house called Scaplen's. Both buildings contain local interest

Kimmeridge Bay, which is famous for its fossils, is overlooked by a ruined tower that was built in the early 19th century.

museums. Poole has a well-known pottery and also the RNLI Headquarters which has a small museum. There are also a maritime museum, aquarium, zoo and the rock and gem centre.

POOLE HARBOUR & BROWNSEA ISLAND, Dorset
Archaeological evidence suggests that Phoenician sailors were using this vast harbour as early as 800BC. It is the second largest natural harbour in the world, and has a coastline that measures over 100 miles if all its indentations are considered. Its largest island is Brownsea, which is accessible by boat from Poole Quay

and is famous as the site of Lord Baden-Powell's first scout camp. Part of its wild heath, wood, and reed-fringed marshland is protected as a nature reserve (NT) and is a haven for many forms of wildlife, including the rare red squirrel.

Follow signs 'Bournemouth' at all roundabouts and continue to follow 'Bournemouth' signs to reach the Poole Civic Centre gyratory system. From here follow signs 'Sandbanks' B3369 to skirt Poole Harbour. In 2½ miles a short detour to Compton Acres Gardens at Canford Cliffs can be made by turning left on to the B3065 and following the signs.

COMPTON ACRES GARDENS, Dorset
These famous private gardens (open) are amongst the finest in Europe and cover some 15 acres overlooking Poole Harbour, Brownsea Island and the Purbeck Hills beyond. There are seven separate and secluded gardens; English, Heather, Japanese, Italian, Roman, Rock and Water, each with its own individual beauty. Most of them contain a priceless collection of bronze and marble statues from all over the world. The careful lay-out of the gardens also include paths, bridges and stepping stones over streams and ponds.

On the main route continue with the B3369 to Sandbanks.

SANDBANKS, Dorset
The sandy beaches of this mile-long peninsula are backed by large houses and a car ferry operates from Haven Point for Studland and Swanage.

At the one-way system join the ferry lane and cross the entrance of Poole Harbour by ferry, then follow an unclassified road to Studland.

STUDLAND, Dorset
Built mainly of red brick, this village contains a fine Norman church and offers 2 miles of sandy beach sheltered by dunes. Moorland extends west from here to Wareham, and on the heathland 1 mile north west is a 500-ton ironstone rock known as the Agglestone.

BALLARD DOWNS AND OLD HARRY ROCKS, Dorset
Views from Studland Bay extend to the headland of Handfast Point and the isolated chalk stacks of the Old Harry Rocks. A little farther south the great bulk of Ballard Down dominates Swanage and offers good coastal views.

From Studland turn inland on the B3351. In 1 mile turn left on to an unclassified road SP 'Swanage' and climb round Ballard Down to return to Swanage.

The less sightly aspects of 20th-century life are softened by sunset at Poole Harbour.

IN SEARCH OF ANCIENT MAN

Near Uffington the great turf-cut figure of a horse leaps across a downland slope beneath the ramparts of a prehistoric hillfort. Elsewhere in the Vale of the White Horse are the massive stones of Wayland's Smithy, the enigmatic mound of Silbury Hill, and dozens of hilltop tumuli.

Tithe barns like the one at Great Coxwell were specially built to store the tithe, or one tenth of all produce, which was once levied from all land holders.

SWINDON, Wilts
In 1900 Old and New Swindon were combined to form Wiltshire's largest town. The small old town is still recognisable in fragments such as the remains of Holy Rood Church in the grounds of a 17th-century house, The Lawn, the old Town Hall and the Market Square. New Swindon grew out of the Great Western Railway's decision to site its repair and locomotive works here, and much of its history is detailed in the fascinating Great Western Railway Museum, the Railway Village House has been refurbished to show life at the turn of the century.

Leave the County Roundabout with SP 'Oxford A420'. In 1¼ miles after two roundabouts turn left on to the B4006 SP 'Stratton'. At traffic signals in Stratton St Margaret turn left, then turn right, and continue to Highworth.

HIGHWORTH, Wilts
Several 17th-century houses and an impressive church with a good west tower are features of this old hilltop village.

Continue on the A361. Later pass the village of Inglesham and a riverside park on the left.

INGLESHAM, Wilts
The tiny church in Inglesham stands where the River Thames meets the derelict Severn Canal and the River Coln. Inside are attractive box pews, a 15th-century screen, and a beautiful late Saxon carving of the Madonna and Child.

Wayland's Smithy is one of many outstanding prehistoric monuments which stand near the Ridgeway.

Continue on the A361. Cross the Thames via the old Halfpenny Bridge and drive into Lechlade.

LECHLADE, Glos
Lechlade marks the upper limit for large craft using the River Thames. The old Halfpenny Bridge spans the river here, and St John's Bridge stands ½ mile to the east. The local church is noted for the curious figures on its tower buttresses.

Turn right, then right again, on to the A417 Faringdon road. In ¾ mile by the nearside of the Trout Inn, turn left on to the B4449 SP 'Bampton'. A detour from the main route can be made here to Buscot village and Buscot Park by keeping forward on the A417.

BUSCOT, Oxon
Almost 4,000 acres of Buscot village and Park, including lovely woods and farmlands that run down to the Thames, are owned or protected by the National Trust. The late 18th-century house contains a noted collection of paintings, and the attractive grounds feature a water garden by landscaper Harold Peto. The Old Parsonage is an early 18th-century house in 10-acre grounds.

Continue along the unclassified road crossing the River Leach. After 1¼ miles turn right leading to Kelmscott village.

KELMSCOTT, Oxon
Poet and painter William Morris lived in Kelmscott's Elizabethan manor house and is buried in the local churchyard. The village itself is a charming collection of greystone buildings standing on the banks of the upper Thames.

Continue for a further 2¾ miles and meet a T-junction. Turn right on to the A4095 SP 'Faringdon' and shortly cross the historic Radcot Bridge.

RADCOT, Oxon
Many centuries ago the forces of Richard II and Henry IV met in battle at the 14th-century bridge here, and 300 years later Prince Rupert's cavalry defeated Cromwell's parliamentarian horsemen in nearby Garrison Field.

Continue to Faringdon.

FARINGDON, Oxon
Poet Laureate Henry Pye built Faringdon House in 1870, and Lord Berners added a folly to its park in 1935 to help relieve local unemployment. Faringdon Church lost its spire in the Civil War. The town itself is a market centre known for its dairy produce.

Follow SP 'Swindon A420', and after ½ mile turn right into Highworth Road (B4019). After another 1¼ miles turn left on to an unclassified road for Great Coxwell.

GREAT COXWELL, Oxon
William Morris thought the great 13th-century tithe barn (NT) at Coxwell's Court Farm 'as noble as a cathedral'. Measuring 152ft long by 51ft high and 44ft wide, this huge stone building is certainly one of the finest of its kind in England today.

Turn left (no SP), then in ½ mile at a T-junction turn right, then turn left on to the A420. Take the 1st turning right on to an unclassified road for Little Coxwell, and continue to Fernham. Turn left on to the B4508, then in ¼ mile branch right on to an unclassified road for Uffington, in the Vale of the White Horse.

UFFINGTON, Oxon
Good views can be enjoyed from here of the famous 374ft-long prehistoric white horse cut into the chalk slopes of 856ft White Horse Hill.

Drive to the nearside of the village and turn right, then take the 2nd turning right SP 'White Horse Hill'. In 1 mile cross the main road and ascend White Horse Hill to reach Uffington Castle and associated monuments.

UFFINGTON CASTLE, THE RIDGEWAY, & WAYLAND'S SMITHY, Oxon
The iron-age hillfort (AM) of Uffington stands on the ancient Ridgeway above the famous White Horse in the Berkshire Downs. The Ridgeway is a pre-Roman track that follows the crest of the downs and is now the route of a long-distance footpath. Just off it in a grove of trees is the megalithic long barrow of Wayland's Smithy (AM). This excellent example has lost part of its earth mound, so its chambers are open to view. Wayland is a smith in Norse mythology, and tradition was that anyone who left a horse and coin here overnight would find his mount shod in the morning.

Follow exit signs from Uffington Castle, descend to a main road, and turn right on to the B4507 with further views of the White Horse to the right. After another 2 miles meet crossroads and turn right on to an unclassified road SP 'Lambourn'. Ascend on to the Berkshire Downs and in 4¼ miles turn right on to the B4001 for Lambourn. Continue across the Lambourn Downs to Lambourn.

LAMBOURN, Berks

Racehorses are trained on downland gallops near this lovely village, and the crystal Lambourn River is everything a chalk trout stream should be. The local cruciform church, which dates from Norman times, houses several old brasses and the village stocks.

Meet crossroads and turn right on to the B4000, then drive to the next turning left SP 'Baydon'. A short detour can be made from the main route to Ashdown House by keeping straight ahead on the B4000 for 3½ miles.

ASHDOWN HOUSE, Oxon

Ashdown House (NT) was built from chalk-rock blocks in the latter half of the 17th century. More than a quarter of its interior is taken up by a magnificent staircase.

On the main route, turn left from the B4000 on to the 'Baydon' road and in 2¼ miles meet a T-junction. Turn right and continue to Baydon.

BAYDON, Wilts

A 13th-century font can be seen in Baydon Church, which has Norman origins but acquired its west tower later. Baydon House farmhouse is of mid 18th-century date.

Turn left and continue to the downland village of Aldbourne.

ALDBOURNE, Wilts

Aldbourne, one of Wiltshire's most attractive villages, lies south east of a one-time hunting area known as Aldbourne Chase.

Turn left on to the B4192 SP 'Hungerford', then in 1¾ miles turn right on to an unclassified road and continue to Ramsbury.

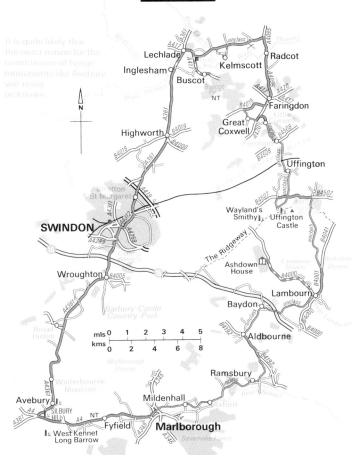

RAMSBURY, Wilts

Excellent Jacobean and Georgian buildings can be seen in this charming River Kennet village, and the church contains ancient sculptured stones.

Turn right and keep forward through the village to Axford and Mildenhall.

MILDENHALL, Wilts

Mildenhall, pronounced 'Minall', lies on the River Kennet to the north of Savernake Forest. A late Celtic vessel known as the Marlborough Bucket was unearthed at Folly Farm, which stands near by on the site of the Roman town *Cunetio*.

Continue to Marlborough.

MARLBOROUGH, Wilts

High downs rise to the north and south of this historic River Kennet town. Legend has it that Merlin, the magician of King Arthur's court, was buried under the town's castle mound. The town may well be old enough for this claim, but many of its more ancient foundations were damaged or destroyed by a series of bad fires and by the Civil War. Its High Street, one of the widest in England, is a reminder of the way things used to be. William Morris was a pupil at the famous 19th-century Marlborough College.

Leave Marlborough on the A4 SP 'Chippenham' and drive to Fyfield.

FYFIELD, Wilts

To the north of this attractive village is the high Fyfield Down nature reserve, which is as much protected for its prehistoric monuments as for its abundant wildlife. South of Fyfield are the sarsen stones of the Grey Wethers (NT), and about 1 mile north east of the village at Lockeridge Dene is a dolmen known as the Devil's Den.

Continue on the A4 to Silbury Hill.

SILBURY HILL & THE WEST KENNET LONG BARROW, Wilts

Situated close to the A4 road near Avebury, these superb prehistoric monuments are among the best known in Europe. Silbury Hill (AM), an enormous artificial mound that covers almost 6 acres, is still as enigmatic as when 18th-century Cornish miners employed to explore it by the Duke of Northumberland emerged baffled and empty-handed. A footpath from the A4 leads ¾ mile to the West Kennet Long Barrow (AM), the finest monument of its kind in England. Excavations during the 19th century uncovered skeletons and pottery in the tomb's passage and end chamber, but the side chambers remained undiscovered until 1955.

Drive to the Beckhampton roundabout and take the 3rd exit to leave by the A4361 SP 'Swindon'. In 1 mile keep left for Avebury.

AVEBURY, Wilts

Many experts consider Avebury the most significant prehistoric monument (AM) in Europe. It is certainly one of the largest stone circles in the world, comprising 100 standing-stone positions enclosing some 28 acres of land. Inside the large outer circle, which has quite a few gaps due to superstitious destruction in the past, are two smaller rings about 300ft in diameter. At one time a 50ft-wide avenue of stones ran 1 mile to connect with a pair of concentric circles on Overton Hill. The village itself is a collection of handsome old buildings between the stones and the banks of the monument, featuring a small museum of archaeology, the Great Barn and Museum of Wiltshire Folk and a multi-period church. Avebury Manor is a 16th-century house (open) (NT).

Continue on the 'Swindon' road to Winterbourne Monkton, with views of the Marlborough Downs to the right. Later descend to Wroughton.

WROUGHTON, Wilts

South of the village stands Barbury Castle an ancient hill fort dating from AD 566. The 130 acres of surrounding countryside is a country park.

Drive to the end of the village and turn left for the return to Swindon.

TRURO, Cornwall

Although it lies on the River Truro — a finger of the Fal estuary — and its history belongs to the sea, Truro serves its county now as administrative capital and cathedral city. During the Middle Ages it was important in the export of mineral ore and from the 13th to 18th centuries was one of the 4 Cornish stannary towns that controlled the quality of tin. The city's 18th-century popularity with wealthy sea merchants left a legacy of fine Georgian architecture to rival that of Bath. Truro became a fashionable focal point of society and the old theatre and assembly rooms next to the cathedral were particularly popular meeting places. However, it is in Lemon Street and Walsingham Place that the finest buildings can be seen from this elegant era. The cathedral is a relatively recent feature of Truro. For 800 years the See of Cornwall was shared with Devon, but when it was reconstituted in 1897 a new cathedral was begun. Built in early English style, it incorporated the old Church of St Mary and was completed in 1910. Inside, the main features are the baptistry, a massive Jacobean monument and the wall of the north choir. For a comprehensive picture of Cornwall's history visit the County Museum in River Street. Here too is an excellent array of Cornish minerals, together with unusual collections of porcelain and pottery. There is a small art gallery as well, containing paintings, engravings and drawings.

Leave Truro on the A39, SP 'Bodmin'. Continue through wooded country to Tresillian, situated on the creek of the Tresillian River. Cross the bridge and in 1 mile keep forward on the A390, SP 'St Austell', to Probus.

PROBUS, Cornwall

This tiny village boasts the tallest church tower in Cornwall, rising in 3 tiers to 126ft. Built during the 16th century of granite, it is richly decorated with figures, heads, animals and tracery, and lichen has given it all a pleasant greenish hue. It is strange to find this lofty tower here because the style resembles that of Somerset's churches and this ranks among the best examples.

Beyond the village pass on the right the County Demonstration Garden.

COUNTY DEMONSTRATION GARDEN AND ARBORETUM, Cornwall

Keen gardeners will find this place fascinating. Detailed displays show all aspects of gardening, including layout, the selection of plants and flowers to suit particular requirements and the effect of different weather conditions on gardens. Attractive exhibitions of fruit, herbs, flowers and vegetables

CATHEDRAL CITY BY THE SEA

In all her Georgian elegance, Truro lies demurely between shady creeks of woodland and water and the strange white moonscape of St Austell's hills of china clay. Away from these the tour runs through hidden fishing villages by way of twisting lanes, high-banked and narrow.

Truro Cathedral, although built in the 20th century, harmonises well with the town's Georgian architecture

illustrate a wealth of information and interest for those either with or without a garden.

Continue on the St Austell road and in ½ mile pass the entrance to Trewithen House and Gardens.

TREWITHEN HOUSE AND GARDENS, Cornwall

This simple, elegant manor house (OACT) of Pentewan stone was built for the Hawkins family in 1723. The interior is mainly Palladian yet each room has its own individuality: the oak room is panelled with oak, the dining room is decorated in grey-green and white and the drawing room is embellished with Chinese fretwork. The surrounding gardens are typical of Cornwall — huge banks of rhododendrons and magnolias ornament landscaped woodland affording frequent glimpses of sweeping parkland.

Remain on the A390 and continue through Grampound and Sticker to St Austell.

ST AUSTELL, Cornwall

White, unnatural peaks rise up to the north of St Austell, giving the moors an almost lunar appearance. They are the great spoil-heaps of white china clay which forms the basis of the

town's main industry. Before the discovery of this valuable natural resource in 1775 by William Cookworthy, St Austell was just another small tin-mining town. Clay pits were opened soon after this date and today the clay is one of Britain's major export materials. The town itself has more the appearance of a market town than an industrial one, and numbering among its pleasant buildings are the town hall, the Quaker Meeting House, the White Hart Hotel and Holy Trinity Church.

Leave St Austell on the B3273 and continue to Mevagissey.

MEVAGISSEY, Cornwall

Narrow streets wind up from the harbour of Mevagissey and colour-washed cottages cover the cliffsides haphazardly. Like many Cornish coastal villages, fishing has always provided Mevagissey with a livelihood and pilchard fishing in particular brought wealth to the village in the 18th and 19th centuries, although smuggling contributed substantially to the riches too. Besides frequent shark and mackerel fishing trips, other attractions in the village include a folk museum and a model railway. The former occupies an 18th-century boatbuilder's workshop and concentrates on local crafts, mining and agricultural equipment and seafaring relics. The latter runs through varied model terrain which includes an Alpine ski resort and a china clay pit.

Return along the B3273 and in 1 mile turn left on to an unclassified road, SP 'Gorran'. After another 1¼ miles turn left again and continue to Gorran. Beyond the village keep left, SP 'Gorran Haven', then take the next turning right and bear right again to reach Gorran Haven.

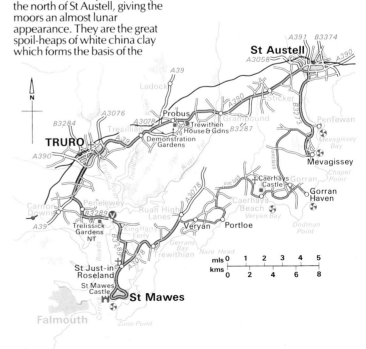

GORRAN HAVEN, Cornwall

This tiny, remote village rivalled Mevagissey in the heyday of pilchard fishing. It is a charmingly unspoilt resort now, with one village street and a pebbly beach.

Return for 1 mile to the T-junction and turn left, then in 250 yards turn left again, SP 'Caerhays'. Touch the coast again at the attractive Caerhays Beach where to the right stands Caerhays Castle.

CAERHAYS CASTLE, Cornwall

Perched above a bay, this castellated mansion (not open) looks like a fairy castle when seen from the cliff road. It was built by John Nash in 1808 for J.B. Trevannion — whose family had owned the estate since the 14th century.

A steep climb leads to St Michael's Caerhays Church. In ¾ mile take the 2nd turning left, SP 'St Mawes and Veryan', then keep left. After 1¼ miles keep left again then turn left, SP 'Veryan' and 'Portholland'. In ¾ mile turn left and nearly ½ mile farther left again, SP 'Portloe'. In just over ¼ mile bear right then descend to Portloe.

PORTLOE, Cornwall

A stream flows through this minute fishing village down to the sea. Between the steep cliffs there is a small rocky beach which is good for swimming. Traditional south Cornish beach boats work here full time, each handling about 100 crab pots.

Beyond the village ascend, then in 1 mile go over the crossroads and continue to Veryan.

VERYAN, Cornwall

Hidden in a wooded valley is the delightful inland village of Veryan. Its most distinguishing feature is its 5 Round Houses. These, placed 2 at each end of the village and 1 in the middle, are round, white-washed cottages with conical thatched roofs. A local story has it that a parson built them for his 5 daughters and he made them round so that the devil would have no corners to hide in.

Turn left, then right on to the St Mawes road. In ½ mile turn left on to the A3078. Pass through Trewithian to reach St Just in Roseland.

ST JUST IN ROSELAND, Cornwall

Tucked away up a creek of the Carrick Roads lies a tiny hamlet that more than lives up to its picturesque name; St Just was believed to be a 6th-century Celtic saint. There is little more to this place than the church, the rectory and a cottage or two, but it has one of the most beautiful churchyards in the country and it is this which has made St Just in Roseland so famous. The church lies at the bottom of a steeply wooded combe descending from the road. Enter it through a lychgate and at this point you can look down on the church tower. The way down passes through luxuriant trees and shrubs — many familiar such as rhododendrons, hydrangeas and camelias; many not so well known — such as the Chilean myrtle, bamboos and the African strawberry tree. On either side of the path stand granite blocks inscribed with biblical verses and quotations. Another lychgate at the bottom (with an unusual granite cattle grid) leads out of the churchyard. This glorious garden is largely due to One Revd C.W. Carlyon (church rector) who began planting the shrubs in the mid-19th century.

Continue on the A3078 and in 1 mile turn right into Upper Castle Road, SP 'St Mawes via Castle'. Pass St Mawes Castle to enter the resort of St Mawes.

ST MAWES, Cornwall

St Mawes commands a fine view over the Carrick Roads and it was this strategic position which provided such an ideal site for Henry VIII's defensive castle (AM) built in the early 1540s at the southernmost tip of the town. In fact the castle saw very little action and its great tower and battlements still stand today in excellent repair. The resort itself is smart and relatively unspoilt by tourism, backing up steeply behind the quay which was busy with sea trade in the Middle Ages.

Follow the road around the harbour and return to St Just in Roseland. Here, branch left on to the B3289 and later descend to the King Harry Ferry. On the far side climb steeply and pass Trelissick Gardens on the left.

TRELISSICK GARDENS, Cornwall

Although a house (not open) has stood here since the mid-18th century, it was not until the late 19th century that the grounds (NT) were landscaped. The Copelands, who inherited the house in 1937, continued to improve them and gave the gardens their present shape. Smooth expanses of lawn enclosed by dense shrubs and woods pierced by winding walks characterise Trelissick. Two specialities here are a collection of over 130 species of hydrangea and a dell full of giant cedar and cypress trees.

The tour continues on the B3289 and after ½ mile, at the crossroads, turn right, SP 'Truro'. Beyond Penelewey turn right again on to the A39 for the return to Truro.

Both fishing boats and pleasure craft share Mevagissey's lively harbour

BETWEEN BODMIN AND THE SEA

Majestic cliffs indented by tiny harbours are typical of north Cornwall. So also are the long sands of Bude Bay, the eerie enchantment of Arthur's Castle at Tintagel, and the dark counterpoint of Bodmin Moor rising inland.

WADEBRIDGE, Cornwall
One of the finest medieval bridges in England can be seen here. Built c 1485 and widened in 1849, it spans the River Camel with 17 arches and measures 320ft long. It is thought that packs of wool may have been sunk into the river bed to make firm bases for the piers.

Leave Wadebridge on the A39 'Bude' road. Cross the bridge and turn left, then in ½ mile turn left on to the B3314 SP 'Port Isaac'. After 3 miles turn left again on to an unclassified road SP 'Rock'. In a further 1½ miles turn left into Pityme then take the next turning right SP 'Polzeath'. A detour from the main route can be made by continuing ahead for 1 mile to Rock.

ROCK, Cornwall
Rock lies opposite Padstow on the lovely Camel Estuary. The small Church of St Michael, at nearby Porthilly, was dug from drifting sand and houses a simple Norman font.

Continue along the main tour route and pass through Trebetherick to reach Polzeath.

POLZEATH, Cornwall
Safe bathing and excellent sands that offer some of the best surfing in Cornwall are the main attractions of Polzeath. The village stands on Padstow Bay and the wide Camel estuary, within easy reach of beautiful walking country (NT) round Portquin. Fine views over Portquin Bay can be enjoyed from Pentire Head, to the north.

Tintagel Castle is divided in two by a breathtaking chasm

Leave Polzeath and ascend sharply. After 2 miles branch left SP 'Port Isaac'. In ½ mile turn left on to the B3314 for St Endellion.

ST ENDELLION, Cornwall
Although inland from sheltered Portquin Bay, St Endellion occupies an exposed site and often feels the full force of the gales for which this part of the country is known. Its beautiful compact church was built from Lundy Island granite. Inside, under the 18th-century tower arch, are several quaint bell-ringer's rhymes. A number of amusing and somewhat irreverent Georgian epitaphs can be seen on old gravestones in the churchyard.

Continue along the B3314 for 1 mile, then turn left on to the B3267 for Port Isaac.

PORT ISAAC, Cornwall
In the old part of this outstandingly picturesque fishing village the houses huddle together along a steep coombe and down to the harbour.

Turn right onto an unclassified road and descend to Port Gaverne. Pass through the village and climb inland. After 2½ miles rejoin the B3314 and continue to Delabole.

DELABOLE, Cornwall
At one time most of the roofs in Cornwall came from the ancient slate quarry in this village, which is estimated to have been worked continuously for at least 350 years. Britain's deepest man-made hole, it has a depth of 500ft and a circumference of 1½ miles.

Since the 19th century Boscastle has declined as a port but developed as a resort.

Continue on the B3314 for 1¾ miles, then turn left on to an unclassified road SP 'Tintagel'. After ½ mile keep forward to join the B3263 then keep left. Just before the village of Trewarmet a road to the left offers a pleasant detour to Trebarwith Strand.

TREBARWITH STRAND, Cornwall
The good beach in this cove is crossed by a natural slate causeway, which leads down to the water's edge from the high-water line.

Continue through Trewarmett on the main tour route and drive to Tintagel.

TINTAGEL, Cornwall
The name Tintagel is highly evocative of the Arthurian legends, but the only King Arthur's Hall here nowadays is the modern home of the Fellowship of the Round Table. The local post office (NT) is a superb slate-built structure that dates from the 14th century and was originally a small manor house. Norman workmanship is very evident in the local church, but its origins are probably farther back in Saxon times. A Norman font and Roman milestone can be seen inside.

TINTAGEL CASTLE, Cornwall
Near Tintagel is the romantic ruined castle (AM) that, according to legend, was the birthplace of King Arthur. Its remains post-date that giant of Western folklore by some 7 centuries, but traces of a Celtic monastery (AM) founded early enough to have accommodated him can be seen close by. The castle itself was built on its wave-lashed promontory, now almost cut in half by the sea, by Reginald, Earl of Cornwall and illegitimate son of Henry I, in the 12th century. Views from here take in the entire North Cornish coast from Pentire Point to Hartland Point.

From the Wharncliffe Arms Hotel in Tintagel follow the B3263 'Boscastle' road, and shortly pass through Bossiney. Continue for another ½ mile to reach Rocky Valley.

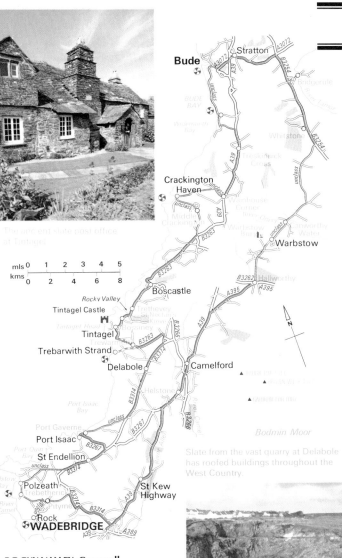

Rockpools are a feature of Widemouth Bay, which is situated to the south of Bude.

ROCKY VALLEY, Cornwall
Trees, stone, and water all contribute their own particular magic to the wonderful scenery of Rocky Valley, a deep cut sloping down to the sea. About 1 mile along the valley is its most magnificent feature, the 40ft waterfall of St Nectan's Kieve. Nectan (or Knighton) was a Celtic hermit saint said to have had an oratory beside the kieve (basin).

Continue on the B3263, pass through Trethevey and after 1¾ miles turn left with the B3263 SP 'Bude'. Descend steeply through a hairpen bend to Boscastle.

BOSCASTLE, Cornwall
The tiny harbour here is at the head of a deep S-shaped inlet between high cliffs, and the combined Valency and Jordan rivers meet incoming tides with dramatic effect when the moon is full and the rivers are running at full spate. Even on a calm day the sea can be impressive. A local blowhole amply demonstrates the force of the water. Boscastle itself is an attractive village arranged round a long, broad street that climbs steeply through woodland. Close to the harbour is a witches' museum of interesting (and often gruesome) relics associated with magic and witchcraft. At one time the local seal population was severely reduced by hunters, but this industry is now controlled.

Leave Boscastle, cross a river bridge, and ascend (1 in 6). After 2¾ miles turn left and immediately turn left on to an unclassified road SP 'Crackington Haven'. Later descend steeply into the village of Crackington Haven.

CRACKINGTON HAVEN, Cornwall
This tiny seaside village stands on a rugged stretch of coast and has a good surfing beach. High Cliff, to the south, drops 700ft in a series of weathered faces and terraces.

Leave Crackington Haven and ascend. After 3 miles reach the village of Wainhouse Corner and turn left on to the A39 SP 'Bude'. Continue past Treskinnick Cross, then 1¼ miles farther turn left on to an unclassified road SP 'Widemouth'. After ¾ mile follow the wide sweep of Widemouth Bay to Bude.

BUDE, Cornwall
This small resort near the mouth of the River Neet was once the port for the Bude Canal which ran inland to Launceston. The town's history is displayed in the Historical and Folk Museum on the canal wharf. Also in the town is the World of Nature Exhibition covering local natural history and geology and including an aquarium.

Leave Bude on the A3072 'Bideford' road. After 1¼ miles turn left on to the A39, and in ¼ mile, turn right rejoining the A3072, SP 'Holsworthy'. Drive into Stratton.

STRATTON, Cornwall
This picturesque grouping of attractive houses and thatched cottages has a peaceful atmosphere that belies its turbulent history. In 1643 a Civil War battle was fought here and is re-enacted every May by the Sealed Knot Society. The Tree Inn was the headquarters of Sir Bevil Grenville before he led his Cavaliers to victory at Stamford Hill, just north of the village. Local legend recalls Anthony Payne, a 7ft giant who was born in the Tree Inn and was a retainer in Sir Bevil's household. The village church dates from the 15th century and houses good 16th-century brasses.

Continue on the A3072 'Holsworthy' road. After 2¾ miles at the Red Post Cross turn right on to the B3254 SP 'Launceston'.

Drive along the B3254 to Whitstone and ¾ mile beyond the village turn right on to an unclassified road SP 'Week St Mary'. Continue for 1¼ miles, meet crossroads, and drive straight on towards Canworthy Water. After 2 miles on this narrow road turn right for Canworthy Water. Here keep straight on and after 1 mile ascend to Warbstow.

WARBSTOW, Cornwall
Warbstow Bury is one of the finest Iron-Age hillforts in Cornwall. Situated at 750ft it provides extensive views in all directions except the south-west.

Continue to Hallworthy, turn right on to the A395, and in another 2¾ miles turn left on to the A39 SP 'Wadebridge'. Continue to Camelford.

CAMELFORD, Cornwall
One of the more obscure Arthurian legends places Camelford as having been the site of Camelot, the fabulous city of King Arthur and his Knights of the Round Table. Slaughter Bridge, which crosses the Camel River 1 mile north of the town, is one of several contenders for the title 'Arthur's last battleground'.

The North Cornwall Museum and Gallery contains many items on Cornish rural life.

Leave Camelford on the A39 and keep straight on. Pass through Helstone, crossing the River Allen at Knightsmill, and continue to St Kew Highway.

ST KEW HIGHWAY, Cornwall
Old stocks are preserved in the porch of the village church, and inside is a very fine Elizabethan pulpit decorated with ornamental panels. Also here is a stone inscribed with characters of the Celtic Ogham script, an ancient form of writing.

Remain on the A39 and return to Wadebridge.

WELLS, Somerset

Wells is a delightful cathedral city situated at the foot of the Mendip Hills. The west front of its fine 13th-to 15th-century cathedral is adorned with statues, and inside are a graceful branching staircase and a 14th-century clock. With its associated buildings the cathedral forms part of England's largest medieval ecclesiastical precinct. The Vicar's Close preserves picturesque 14th-century houses, and across the cathedral green is the moated Bishop's Palace (open), where Wells' famous swans ring a bell near the drawbridge for food. Other interesting old buildings include a medieval tithe barn (AM) and the 15th-century parish church. Wells Museum includes a display on the Mendip Caves.

An interesting detour from the main route to the caves of Wookey Hole can be made at Wells: leave the city on the A371 'Cheddar' road and in ¼ mile turn right on to the unclassified 'Wookey Hole' road. Continue for 1¾ miles to Wookey Hole. Please note that route directions for the main tour start after the following entry.

WOOKEY HOLE, Somerset

Inhabited for some 650 years from 250BC this gigantic system was hollowed out of the Mendip limestone by the River Axe. Finds relating to the period of habitation can be seen in the associated museum. The old mill at the cave entrance demonstrates the art of paper making, and is a store for Madame Tussaud's waxwork museum and Lady Bangor's fairground collection.

Leave Wells by the A39 'Glastonbury' road and proceed to Glastonbury.

GLASTONBURY, Somerset

High above the skyline of this ancient town is the 520ft pinnacle of Glastonbury Tor, a place associated in myth with fabulous Avalon and the Celtic Otherworld. Glastonbury was probably founded in Celtic times, but according to legend it was created by Joseph of Arimathea. Other traditions connect St Patrick and King Arthur with the abbey, and it is said that Arthur is actually buried here. The well preserved remains that exist today date from the 12th and 13th centuries, and include St Mary's Church, the abbey church, and a number of monastic buildings (open). By far the best preserved is the superb Abbot's Kitchen. Features of the town itself include 2 medieval churches, the George and Pilgrim Inn, a 15th-century abbey courthouse known as the Tribunal (open) containing late prehistoric finds from lake dwellings at Meare and Godney and the Abbey Barn which houses the Somerset Rural Life Museum.

Leave Glastonbury on the B3151 'Meare' road and proceed through low-lying country to Meare.

THE POLDEN AND MENDIP RANGES

Low-lying areas of unpopulated countryside are dominated by the bare Mendip summits and lower Polden Hills. Here are the cradle of early English Christianity, the supposed site of King Arthur's fabulous Camelot, and old battlefields that have seen decisive turning points in the country's history.

MEARE, Somerset

From c300BC to cAD100 a lake settlement of houses on stilts and brushwood existed here. Few traces of this survive, but excavations have yielded many interesting finds that are displayed in Taunton and Glastonbury Museums. A 14th-century building known as the Fish House (AM) was used by the monks of Glastonbury to house their fishermen, and the contemporary manor house was a summer residence for the abbots.

Over 400 statues survive on the west front of Wells Cathedral. They were made during the 13th century and were inspired by sculpture in Continental cathedrals.

Continue on the B3151 for 1¼ miles and turn left on to an unclassified road SP 'Shapwick'. Meet a T-junction and turn left again. Continue across level wooded countryside to Shapwick. By Shapwick Church turn right on to the 'Bridgwater' road and ascend the gradual slope of the Polden Hills.

THE POLDEN HILLS, Somerset

These low hills (part NT), rising to less than 300ft at their highest point, extend from Glastonbury to a point near Bridgwater and dominate the surrounding marshy levels.

About ¾ mile from Shapwick cross a main road, then continue for ¼ mile and turn right on to the A39. Proceed along a low ridge for 5 miles, then descend and bear sharp left over the King's Sedgemoor Drain. Cross the M5 and enter Bridgwater.

BRIDGWATER, Somerset

It was here that the Duke of Monmouth proclaimed himself King in 1685, prior to suffering a crushing defeat at nearby Sedgemoor. Of interest are the town's wide main street, the tall spire of St. Mary's church and the Admiral Blake Museum.

From Bridgwater follow SP 'Langport' on the A372 and recross the M5. Drive across Sedgemoor.

SEDGEMOOR, Somerset

In 1685 the last battle on English soil took place here when James II defeated James Duke of Monmouth. The King won a decisive victory at the expense of the lives of some 1,400 of Monmouth's followers. The rebels who survived were subsequently dealt with by the travelling 'Bloody Assize' of the notorious Judge Jeffries.

Continue through Weston Zoyland, then after another 2¼ miles skirt Middlezoy. In 1 mile turn right on to the A361 and follow SP 'Taunton to enter Othery. Continue on to Burrow Bridge.

BURROW BRIDGE & BURROW MUMP, Somerset

Wide views are afforded by the hill, or mump (NT), here; an extensive collection of Victorian engines is housed in an old pumping station (open) opposite the Mump.

Cross the River Parrett and immediately turn left (no SP) on to an unclassified road. Follow SP 'Stathe, Langport', reach Stathe, and follow SP 'Curry Rivel'. After ¾ mile branch right, and in 1 mile ascend Red Hill (NT) for excellent views over Sedgemoor. At the road summit bear right and in ¾ mile turn left on to the A378 to enter Curry Rivel. In ¼ mile turn right on to an unclassified road SP 'Drayton, Muchelney'. Proceed through Drayton to reach Muchelney.

MUCHELNEY, Somerset

The Benedictine abbey whose extensive remains (AM) survive here was not the first foundation on the site. Excavations have revealed a rare Saxon chapel, dating from around the 7th century, beneath ruined Norman monastic buildings. Priest's House is a good 14th-century thatched building (NT).

Leave Muchelney by bearing left with SP 'Langport'. Continue for 1 mile, meet a T-junction, and turn right to enter Huish Episcopi.

Turn right by Somerton Church into unclassified New Street SP 'Ilchester, Yeovil'. Continue for $\frac{1}{2}$ mile and turn right on to the B3151. After 2¾ miles turn right then left across the A372. In 1½ miles at the edge of Ilminster reach a mini-roundabout and take the 1st exit SP 'Yeovilton'.

ILCHESTER, Somerset
In Roman times this quiet River Yeo town was an important military station. Its superb Town Hall houses a 13th-century mace - the oldest staff of office in England.

Wookey Hole was formed by the River Axe.

Wells Cathedral's 14th-century astronomical clock.

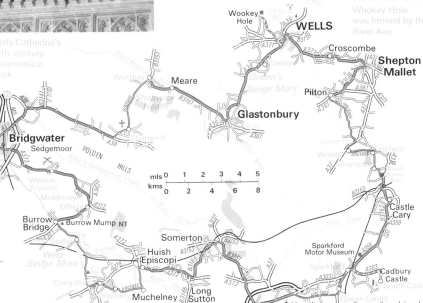

The Market Cross in Somerton was rebuilt in 1673.

HUISH EPISCOPI, Somerset
Glass by Burne-Jones and a fine Norman doorway are features of the local church, but its crowning glory is a 15th-century tower considered to be the finest in the county.

Turn right on to the A372 'Wincanton, Yeovil' road, and later pass the edge of Long Sutton.

LONG SUTTON, Somerset
This attractive village is grouped round a notable 15th-century church and boasts a 17th-century manor house.

In ½ mile turn left on to the B3165 SP 'Somerton', and in 2¼ miles turn right SP 'Ilchester' to enter Somerton.

SOMERTON, Somerset
Somerton was the capital of Somerset under the West Saxons and is particularly known for its attractive market place. All around the square and along the back streets are handsome old buildings, including the Town Hall of c1700 and the 17th-century Hext Almshouses. Somerton Church carries a magnificent tie-beam roof dating from the 15th century.

On the main route, continue for 1½ miles and pass the entrance to the Royal Naval Air Station for the Fleet Air Arm Museum, Yeovilton.

YEOVILTON, Somerset
Yeovilton's Fleet Air Arm Museum portrays the development of naval aviation since 1903 and displays over 40 historic aircraft.
Proceed for ¼ mile and turn right on to an unclassified road SP 'Queen Camel'. In 2½ miles go forward on to the A359 SP 'Sparkford, Frome' to enter Queen Carmel. Proceed for ¾ mile and turn right on to the A303 to enter Sparkford. Here a detour to Cadbury Castle can be taken. Proceed along the A303 for 1½ miles and turn right on to an unclassified road for South Cadbury.

CADBURY CASTLE, Somerset
Once it was thought that the myths linking this hilltop fort with King Arthur's Camelot had been disproved by excavations revealing evidence of Stone- and Bronze-Age occupation. However, digging in 1966 suggested that the site had been re-defended during Arthur's period. The Saxon King Ethelred (the Unready) established a mint here.

From Sparkford bear right to cross a railway bridge, then turn immediately left on to the A359 'Frome' road passing the Sparkford Motor Museum. Continue for 3 miles and branch left on to the B3152 SP 'Castle Cary'. Continue 1½ miles to enter Castle Cary.

CASTLE CARY, Somerset
Several fine old houses and a pretty duckpond are grouped together at the heart of this pleasant small town. The local lock-up, an unusual circular structure once used for the restriction of petty mischief makers, dates from the 18th century.
Leave Castle Cary with SP 'Bath, Bristol (A371)'. After 1 mile turn left on to the A371 SP 'Shepton Mallet'. Shortly bear right across a railway bridge, then proceed for $\frac{1}{2}$ mile to the Brook House Inn and turn left on to an unclassified road SP 'Alhampton'. In 1 mile enter Alhampton and turn right SP 'Ditcheat'. Proceed to Ditcheat and at a T-junction turn left (no SP). Continue to the Manor House Inn and turn right, then shortly bear left SP 'East Pennard'. Proceed to Wraxall, and at crossroads turn right on to the A37 'Shepton Mallet' road. Ascend Wraxall Hill and after 1 mile at crossroads turn left on to an unclassified road SP 'East Pennard'. In ½ mile turn right SP 'Pilton' to reach Pilton.

PILTON, Somerset
One of the most picturesque villages in the area, lovely Pilton has an ancient cruciform tithe barn (AM) and a church with a magnificent 15th-century roof.

Meet crossroads and turn left, then descend to the church and turn left SP 'Shepton Mallet'. Meet a T-junction and turn right on to the A361. Proceed for 1 mile, then turn left on to the B3136 for Shepton Mallet.

SHEPTON MALLET, Somerset
Wool from flocks grazing the windswept Mendip Hills made the fortune of this pleasant market town. Several good 17th- and 18th-century buildings survive from this period, plus a fine church with an intricately carved nave roof.

Leave the town with SP 'Wells A371' to enter Croscombe.

CROSCOMBE, Somerset
Steep wooded hills surround this stone-built village, which has an old church containing amazing 17th-century pastoral and heraldic carvings in rich black oak.

Continue along the A371 to re-enter Wells.

WESTON-SUPER-MARE, Avon

Good beaches and lavish entertainment facilities are features of this large Bristol Channel resort. Among many places of interest are a marine lake with boating, an aquarium, and a model village. The resort's wide seafront road is lined by several public gardens and overlooks the low Flat Holme and Steep Holme offshore islands. Both these are particularly rich in birdlife. An Iron-Age earthwork (AM) can be seen 1 mile north on Worlebury Hill.

Leave Weston-super-Mare on the A370 'Bristol' road. Pass through suburbs and cross the M5 then flat countryside to reach Congresbury. Turn left, cross the River Yeo, then turn left again on to the B3133 SP 'Yatton, Clevedon'. Proceed through Yatton then cross and pass through Kenn. Cross the M5 and in ½ mile reach the Clevedon Distributor Road. For a detour to visit Clevedon Court and Clevedon Craft Centre turn right and follow signs. For a detour to Clevedon town centre keep forward.

CLEVEDON COURT, Avon

This superb 14th-century house (NT) is one of the oldest of its type to have survived anywhere in Britain. It carries an even older 13th-century tower and is considered typical of its period, with a screen passage dividing the buttery and kitchen from the great hall and the lord of the manor's living quarters. During the 18th and 19th centuries it became a popular meeting place for the avant-garde of the day. Clevedon Craft Centre lies ½ mile to the south and visitors can watch displays of wood carving and turning here at the weekends.

CLEVEDON, Avon

Situated at a junction of hill ranges, Clevedon is a quiet Severn estuary residential town and resort. The pier, designed to cope with the 40ft tidal range in this area is being restored

The main route turns left SP 'Sea Front' on to an unclassified road and in 1¼ miles turn left on to the B3130 for the front. In a further ½ mile bear left, pass the pier, and keep forward for 1½ miles to meet a T-junction, then turn left on to B3124, SP 'Portishead'. In ½ mile at the Walton-in-Gordano crossroads turn left on to an unclassified road (no SP). Continue high above the shores of the Bristol Channel, then enter a built-up area and turn left into Nore Road (no SP). Continue above the coast and in 1¼ miles pass the AA Portishead viewpoint. Pass Battery Point and descend into Portishead.

PORTISHEAD, Avon

Portishead is a residential town, small resort and former port situated on the lower slopes of a wooded hillside overlooking the Bristol Channel.

BEACHES AND GORGES

In many ways tiny Avon is the envy of much larger counties. Its port city of Bristol is one of the most historic in England, its resort offers miles of sandy beaches, and its interior is riddled by limestone cave systems that extend deep into Somerset.

Birnbeck Pier at Weston-super-Mare.

Leave Portishead on the A369 'Bristol' road. After 2¾ miles reach the M5 junction roundabout and take 4th exit SP 'Clifton' (toll) to enter hill country. Continue through Abbot's Leigh. Proceed for 1¼ miles and turn left on to the B3129 SP 'Clifton'. In ½ mile reach the Clifton Suspension Bridge.

CLIFTON SUSPENSION BRIDGE AND AVON GORGE, Avon

Here, where the sheer limestone cliffs of the Avon Gorge constrict that river to a silver ribbon some 245ft below, is the spectacular suspension bridge by the brilliant engineer Isambard Kingdom Brunel. Started in 1836, it was not completed until 1864, 5 years after his death.

Cross the bridge and in 200yds turn left SP 'Motorway M5'. After a short distance turn left again into Clifton Down Road. After ¼ mile meet crossroads and turn left on to the B4468 SP 'Weston'. The right turn here leads to Bristol Zoo. Descend Bridge Valley Road into the Avon Gorge. At the bottom turn left on to

Clevedon Court, though much altered, preserves many 14th-century features, including the south entrance.

the A4, pass underneath the suspension bridge, and after ¼ mile keep left SP 'City Centre' to remain in Hotwell Road. Enter Bristol city centre.

BRISTOL, Avon

During the 16th century ships out of Bristol sailed to every part of the known world opening up international trading routes in a way never before imagined. In 1843 Brunel launched his SS *Great Britain*, the largest iron ship of the time, and in 1970 its rusting hulk was rescued from the Falkland Islands and returned to the Bristol dry dock in which it was originally built. Extensive renovation has restored it as a proud memorial (open) to its great designer and the city of its birth. Nowadays the city's dock areas are at Avonmouth and Portbury which are more fitted to coping with the vast ships of 20th-century world traffic. Bristol's many lovely old buildings include a cathedral that contains examples of Norman, Early-English, Gothic and Victorian architecture. St Mary Redcliffe, one of the city's finest churches, was built and extended between the 13th and 15th centuries and carries a massive tower with a 285ft spire. The 16th-century Red Lodge (open) houses interesting work carvings and furnishings of contemporary and later date, and the Georgian House (open) features furniture from the 18th-century. Outside the Corn Exchange are the original metal 'nails' upon which merchantmen once put their payments, hence the expression 'to pay cash on the nail'. Various displays and exhibitions can be seen in St Nicholas' Church Museum and the City Museum and Art Gallery.

Other features of the Floating Harbour area are the Bristol Exhibition and Watershed Arts Complexes, the Arnolfini Gallery, National Lifeboat Museum and Bristol Industrial Museum, and the Maritime Heritage Centre.

Follow SP 'Weston (A370)' and in 1½ miles cross the impressive Cumberland Basin and Avon bridges, then keep forward to join the A370 'Long Ashton' bypass. Proceed through pleasant countryside and pass the villages of Flax Bourton and Backwell (Farleigh), then 1½ miles beyond Backwell (West Town), meet crossroads, and turn left on to an unclassified road SP 'Bristol Airport'. Ascend deep and thickly-wooded Brockley Combe, then emerge and in 1½ miles meet a T-junction. Turn right on to the A38 'Taunton' road and pass Bristol Airport on the right. Descend Red Hill, cross the River Yeo, then in ½ mile branch left on to an unclassified road SP 'Burrington, Blagdon'. Ahead are views of Beacon Batch Hill. After 1 mile turn right on to the A368 SP 'Burrington Combe' then take the 2nd turning left on to the B3134. Ascend Burrington Combe.

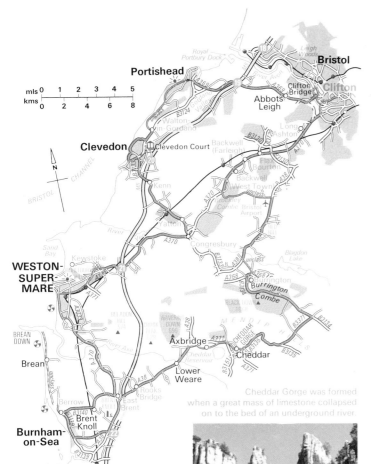

The SS *Great Britain* at Bristol.

BURRINGTON COMBE, Somerset
High above Burrington village is 1,065ft Beacon Batch, the summit of Black Down and the highest point of the bleak Mendip range. The dramatic gorge of Burrington Combe inspired the Rev. Toplady to write the hymn *Rock of Ages*.

Climb to over 900ft, with glimpses to the left of Blagdon Lake, then cross high farmland for several miles. Meet crossroads and turn right on to the B3371 SP 'Cheddar'. Proceed through open scenery, then descend into a shallow valley and turn right on to the B3135. Make the long winding descent of Cheddar Gorge.

CHEDDAR GORGE & VILLAGE, Somerset
Every year many thousands of people come here to drive through the spectacular rock scenery of Cheddar Gorge. Curiously weathered limestone outcrops, softened in many places by the foliage of precariously rooted shrubs, hang over the road from 450ft cliffs. Underground the region is honeycombed by caves and potholes, many of which feature weird crystalline formations created by water action. Particularly good examples can be seen in Cox's and Gough's caverns (open). Various archaeological finds are displayed in the Cheddar Caves Museum.

Leave Cheddar with SP 'Bristol' and 'Weston-super-Mare' and in 1 mile turn left and immediately right on to the A371, SP 'Axbridge, Weston'. On the left is the popular yachting centre of Cheddar Reservoir. Branch left and drive into Axbridge.

Cheddar Gorge was formed when a great mass of limestone collapsed on to the bed of an underground river.

AXBRIDGE, Somerset
Among many interesting and attractive old buildings in this Mendip town is King John's Hunting Lodge (NT), which dates from early Tudor times. The local manor house (not open) is also of note.

Drive to the end of Axbridge and follow SP 'Taunton, (A38)'. In ½ mile turn left on to the A38 and proceed across the flat ground of the Axe Valley. Views of 690ft Wavering Down and 628ft Crook Peak can be enjoyed to the right. Continue to Lower Weare.

LOWER WEARE, Somerset
Collections of waterfowl and a variety of small pets can be seen here at the Ambleside Water Gardens and Aviaries. Particular features of the gardens are their attractive ponds and varied shrubs.

Continue and pass through Rooks Bridge with the isolated 457ft mound of Brent Knoll increasingly prominent ahead. Cross the M5, then in ¼ mile meet a roundabout and keep left. In 1½ miles at the next roundabout take the 3rd exit on to the B3140 SP 'Burnham-on-Sea'. Proceed for 1½ miles, then meet another roundabout and keep forward to enter Burnham-on-Sea.

BURNHAM-ON-SEA, Somerset
This red-brick town is expanding to cope with holidaymakers who come to enjoy its miles of sandy beaches in larger numbers every year. Bridgwater Bay Nature Reserve lies a little to the south west.

Turn right SP 'Berrow, Brean'. After 1¼ miles reach Berrow and turn right SP 'Weston-super-Mare'. A detour from the main route to Brean can be made here by keeping forward on to an unclassified road and in ½ mile turning left.

Evening light on the vast sands at Burnham-on-Sea.

BREAN & BREAN DOWN, Somerset
At the base of 320ft Brean Down (NT), adjacent to 7 miles of sandy beaches, is the Brean Down Bird Sanctuary (open). Many species from all over the world can be seen here.

On the main route, proceed to Brent Knoll.

BRENT KNOLL, Somerset
This village takes its name from a nearby 457ft hill surmounted by an ancient camp. Inside the 15th-century church are bench ends bearing animal carvings that depict the tale of a greedy abbot who once tried to seize revenue from an unfortunate parish priest.

Meet a T-junction in the village and turn left. Skirt the base of Brent Knoll to reach East Brent, then at crossroads turn left on to the A370. Continue for 3 miles to re-enter Avon and pass the edge of Bleadon. After 2 miles meet a T-junction, turn right and return to Weston-super-Mare along the sea-front.

THOMAS HARDY'S WESSEX

Hardy's novels featured many places, thinly disguised, from his beloved Dorset. Here the visitor can find his barren island and wind-blasted heaths, earthworks overlooking thatch and stone villages from the tops of green downs, and salt lagoons held behind by giant shingle banks.

Chesil Bank stretches for 12 miles from Fortuneswell on the Isle of Portland to Abbotsbury.

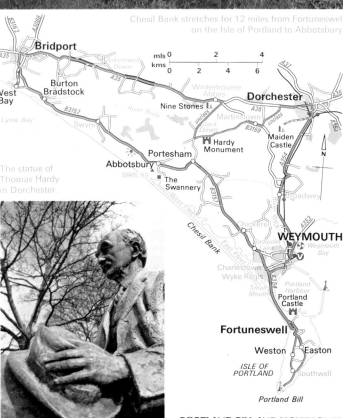

WEYMOUTH, Dorset

Weymouth's early claim to fame was as the only safe port for miles around, but the town became fashionable for seaside holidays after King George III began coming here in 1789. Georgian terraces still line the wide Esplanade, and quaint little back streets wind round the old harbour. Known for years for the comings and goings of cross-Channel ferries, cargo boats, and pleasure craft, the resort offers sun and sea bathing. Among Weymouth's places of interest are the Museum of Local History and No. 3 Trinity Street. The latter is actually two 17th-century cottages with contemporary furnishings (open).

Leave Weymouth by the A354 SP 'Portland'. Cross Small Mouth, the only outlet for the waters of the Fleet, with Chesil Bank (or Beach) to the right.

CHESIL BANK, Dorset

This 20- to 30ft-high pebble ridge is 200yds wide and extends approximately 12 miles from Portland to Abbotsbury. It is separated from the mainland by a channel and tidal lagoon called the East and West Fleet, and joins the mainland at Abbotsbury. Severe storms are commonplace along the coast here, and bathing from the bank is dangerous.

Weymouth Harbour was used extensively by cargo and passenger vessels for many years.

ISLE OF PORTLAND, Dorset

Dorsetman Thomas Hardy referred to this small, almost treeless limestone peninsula as 'The Rock of Gibraltar' and used it in his novels as the 'Isle of Slingers'. Up until the 19th century it was of small importance, but then convict labour from the local prison was used to build the important naval harbour and breakwater that stand here today. The prison is now a Borstal institution. An old lighthouse on Portland Bill now serves as a bird-watching station. The interior of the island is pitted with excavations left by the extraction of the prized Portland Stone, which was used by Wren for St Paul's Cathedral. All round the coast are the deserted quays where it was loaded before road transport became a practicable possibility.

Continue on the A354 to Fortuneswell and Portland Castle.

FORTUNESWELL, Dorset

East of the village high cliffs drop to the waters of Portland Harbour. Close by is the highest spot in the peninsula, a 490ft eminence bristling with the 19th-century forts and batteries of the vast Verne Citadel.

PORTLAND CASTLE, Dorset

Built by Henry VIII in 1520, this fortress (AM) was part of a defensive chain that stretched from Kent in the east to Cornwall in the west. Its 14ft thick walls were built to absorb cannon fire.

The statue of Thomas Hardy in Dorchester.

At roundabout take 2nd exit then climb steeply through Fortuneswell with SP 'Portland Bill'. Fine views can be enjoyed from the car park at the top of the ascent. Reach Easton.

EASTON, Dorset

Thatched Avice's Cottage, a 17th-century Portland Island dwelling now containing a museum, was featured as the heroine's home in Thomas Hardy's novel *The Well Beloved*. Near by is the single pentagonal tower of Bow and Arrow Castle, said to have been built by William Rufus in the 11th-century. It derives its name from the many small loopholes which pierce the walls. Pennsylvania Castle was built during the 19th century for the Governor of Portland.

Bear left unclassified and proceed to Southwell. At the Eight Kings (PH) turn left for Portland Bill.

PORTLAND BILL AND LIGHTHOUSE, Dorset

This barren mass of limestone drops to only 20ft above the sea at the southern tip of the Isle. Nearby Pulpit Rock is a pinnacle rising from the sea in a series of crags and caves. For years its labyrinthine tunnels were used by smugglers.

Return to the Eight Kings (PH) and turn left to reach Weston, passing one of the Portland stone quarries on the way.

WESTON, Dorset

Portland stone, a superb material made famous by architect Sir Christopher Wren while he was rebuilding London after the Great Fire, is quarried near this village.

Drive through Weston, climb to the top of Portland Hill, and turn left. Descend into Fortuneswell and cross to the mainland. After 1 mile turn left on to the B3157 SP 'Bridport' and proceed through Charlestown and Chickerell to reach Portesham.

PORTESHAM, Dorset

This village has an attractive green and stands at the foot of hills dotted with ancient monuments. Those nearest include burial mounds and standing stones.

Proceed on the B3157 to reach Abbotsbury.

ABBOTSBURY, Dorset

This very attractive stone-built village has a notable 15th-century tithe barn and gateway from an ancient Benedictine monastery and a 15th- to 16th-century church with a pulpit bearing the marks of Civil War bullets. Abbotsbury Gardens, 20 beautiful acres of rare sub-tropical plants are 1½ miles west of the village. Excellent views are afforded by Chapel Hill, named after the 15th-century chapel standing on its exposed summit.

ABBOTSBURY SWANNERY, Dorset

Swans, once considered a table delicacy, were bred here as long ago as 1393 to provide food for the monastery at Abbotsbury village. The swannery (open) lies ½ mile south of the village in the lagoon formed by Chesil Bank. Some 560 swans and various species of geese, ducks, and other water birds live here.

Continue on the 'Bridport' road and ascend steep Abbotsbury Hill for excellent views over low-hedged fields to the sea. Pass through Swyre to reach Burton Bradstock.

BURTON BRADSTOCK, Dorset

The restored 15th-century church in this picturesque thatched village has an embattled central tower. Unusually stratified cliffs of geological interest can be seen to the east.

Leave Burton Bradstock and proceed for 2 miles; a short detour can be made to West Bay.

WEST BAY, Dorset

A port since the 13th century, West Bay is still used for fishing but additionally caters for small cargo boats and pleasure craft. At one time it served as a harbour for Bridport, which lies 1½ miles north, but nowadays it supplements its port business with resort facilities.

Continue on B3157 to reach Bridport.

BRIDPORT, Dorset

For over 750 years Bridport has been associated with rope and net making, and it is still Europe's principal centre for the production of fishing nets, lines, and cordage. These fascinating local trades are featured in a permanent exhibition at Bridport Museum and Art Gallery. Also here are exhibits showing the archaeology, geology, and natural history of the area. After the battle of Worcester in 1651 Charles II came here to hide, rather incautiously, at the best inn in town; this is now a chemist's shop.

Excavations at Maiden Castle in 1937 revealed the bones of men killed whilst defending the fort against the Romans.

Leave Bridport on the A35 'Dorchester' road and enjoy fine views from Askerswell Down. Proceed to the Nine Stones.

NINE STONES, Dorset

This ancient stone circle (AM) beside the A35 ½ mile west of Winterbourne Abbas is the most notable of many tumuli and configurations of stones in the Dorchester area.

Continue through Winterbourne Abbas. At the end of the village bear right on to the B3159 SP 'Weymouth', then right again on to an unclassified road SP 'Hardy Monument'. Climb on to heathland and turn left to reach the monument.

Dorchester Museum displays many exhibits in elegant Victorian surroundings.

HARDY MONUMENT, Dorset

Admiral Hardy, who was beside Lord Nelson at his death during the battle of Trafalgar, is commemorated here by an obelisk on top of Black Down. Tremendous views can be enjoyed from the hill top (NT).

Continue for 2 miles to a T-junction, and turn right on to the B3159 to enter Martinstown. Drive to the end of the village and branch left on to an unclassified road. In 1¼ miles at a T-junction turn right on to A35. Continue to Dorchester.

DORCHESTER, Dorset

Thomas Hardy was born 2 miles north-east of Dorchester in a cottage (NT, open by appointment), at Higher Bockhampton. The town itself is featured in several of his novels as 'Casterbridge', and the original manuscript of *The Mayor of*

Casterbridge can be seen among other relics in the County Museum. Excellent finds from periods before and after the Romans founded their major walled town of *Durnovaria* here cAD43 are also displayed, and foundations of a Roman villa complete with tessellated pavement can be seen at Colliton Park. After the Monmouth rebellion Judge Jeffries held his notorious 'Bloody Assize' at the Antelope Hotel in 1685, sentencing 292 local men to various degrees of punishment for their treachery. Up to 74 of them were hanged in the town, and their heads were impaled on the railings of St Peter's Church as a grim warning against treason. The rest were deported. Much later in 1834 the infant trades union movement was dealt a public blow at the trial of 6 agricultural workers later to become known as the Tolpuddle Martyrs. They were tried in the courtroom of the old Shire Hall, now a Tolpuddle memorial (open), and were sentenced to transportation for joining forces to request a wage increase for local farmworkers. Also of interest in the town are the Dorset Military Museum, the Dinosaur Museum, and the 17th-century Napper's Mite almshouses.

Leave Dorchester on the A354 'Weymouth' road. An unclassified road on the right leads to Maiden Castle.

MAIDEN CASTLE, Dorset

Situated 2 miles south west of Dorchester, this vast prehistoric hillfort (AM) occupies 120 acres of land and is the finest of its kind in Britain. It was large enough to have accommodated 5,000 people, and probably developed from a simple bank and ditch defence against neighbouring tribes. After successfully storming it the Romans used the castle as a base and built a temple cAD367 within its ramparts.

Continue along the A354 and drive over downland. Pass through Broadwey and return to Weymouth.

The magnificent abbey at Bath provides a majestic backdrop to the famous Roman baths.

Key to Town Plans

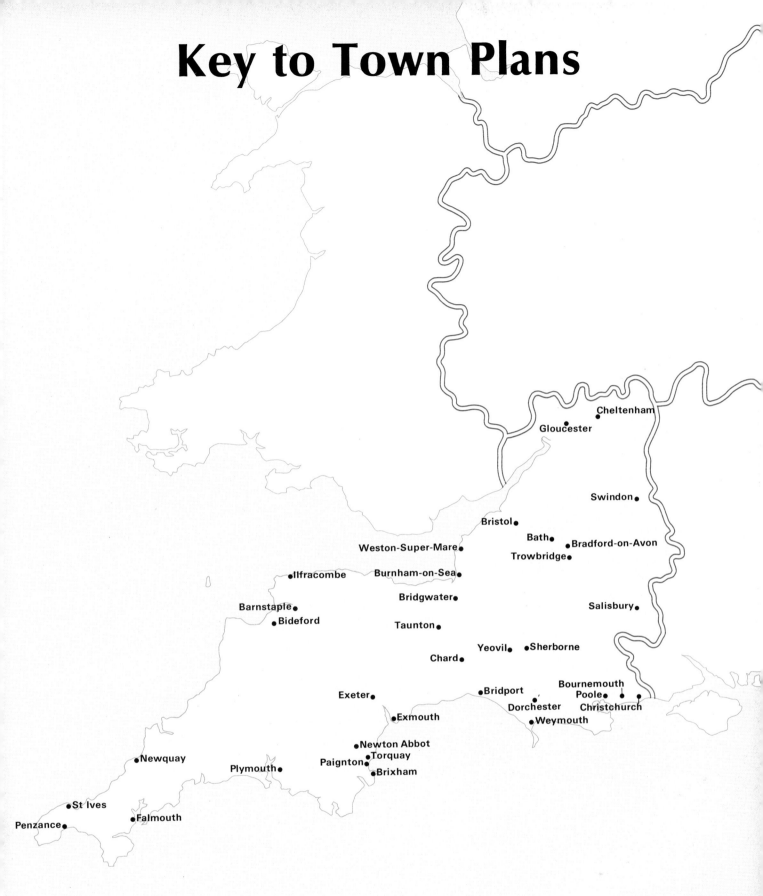

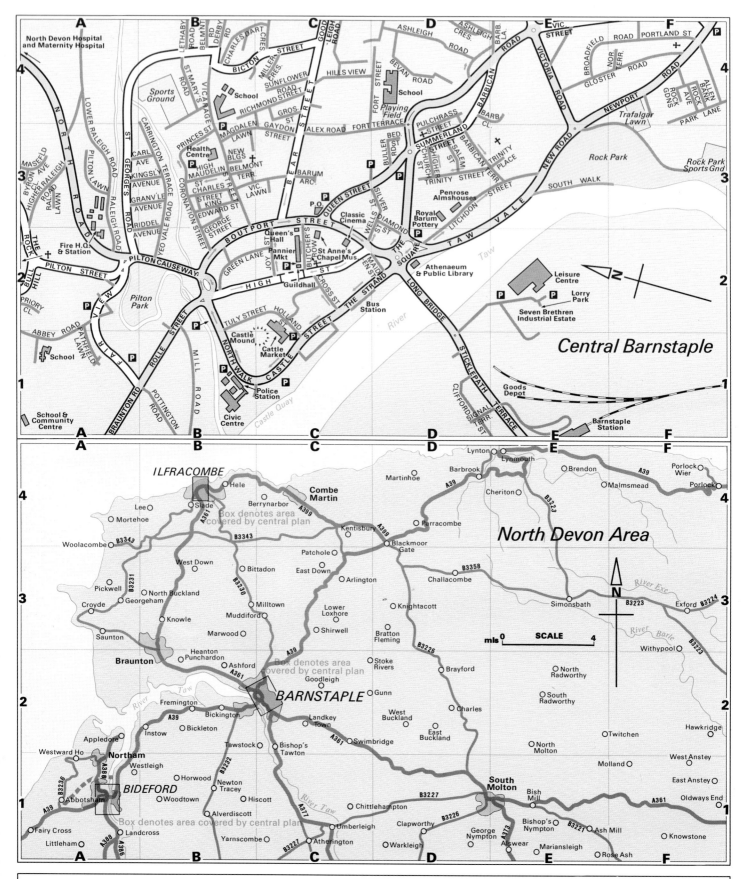

Barnstaple

During the 18th century the wool trade created a prosperity in Barnstaple to which the town's elegant Georgian buildings testify. Queen Anne's Walk, a colonnade where merchants conducted business, is both a fine example of this period and a reminder that Barnstaple has always been a trading centre. This tradition continues as today it is one of the area's busiest market towns. Of the many picturesque shopping streets Butchers Row is particularly attractive.

Ilfracombe This is North Devon's well-established "Queen of the Coast". Originally a fishing harbour, Ilfracombe evolved in the 19th century – when enterprise was all – into one of the typical seaside resorts that mushroomed all over England. Here, terraces of large Victorian hotels and houses follow the contours of the hills down to the harbour and a welter of little coves. The town is also the main departure point for Lundy Island.

Bideford South-west of Barnstaple and Ilfracombe, Bideford too has always made its living by trading and the sea. Sir Richard Grenville, a Bideford man famous for his fight against the Spaniards in the Azores, gained a charter for the town from Elizabeth I and it prospered as a port and shipbuilding centre until the 18th century. A nautical air still pervades Bideford and the long, tree-lined quay is popular.

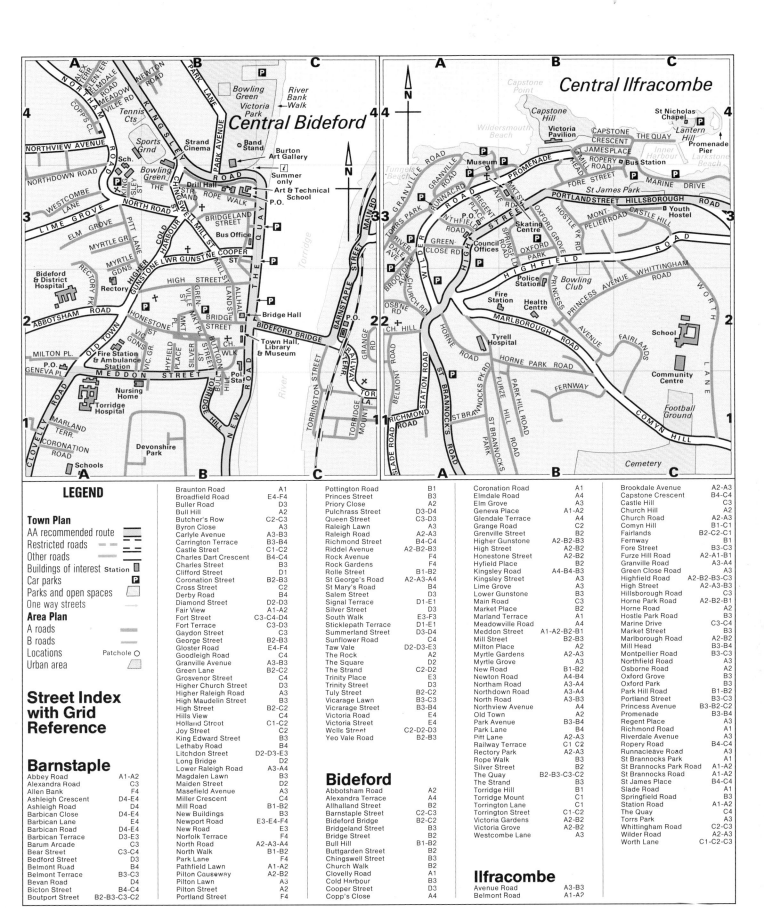

Central Bideford

Central Ilfracombe

LEGEND

Town Plan
AA recommended route
Restricted roads
Other roads
Buildings of interest   Station
Car parks
Parks and open spaces
One way streets

Area Plan
A roads
B roads
Locations   Patchole
Urban area

Street Index with Grid Reference

Barnstaple

Abbey Road	A1-A2
Alexandra Road	C3
Allen Bank	F4
Ashleigh Crescent	D4-E4
Ashleigh Road	D4
Barbican Close	D4-E4
Barbican Lane	E4
Barbican Road	D4-E4
Barbican Terrace	D3-E3
Barum Arcade	C3
Bear Street	C3-C4
Bedford Street	D3
Belmont Road	B4
Belmont Terrace	B3-C4
Bevan Road	D4
Bicton Street	B4-C4
Boutport Street	B2-B3-C3-C2
Braunton Road	A1
Broadfield Road	E4-F4
Buller Road	D3
Bull Hill	A2
Butcher's Row	C2-C3
Byron Close	A3
Carlyle Avenue	A3-B3
Carrington Terrace	B3-B4
Castle Street	C1-C2
Charles Dart Crescent	B4-C4
Charles Street	B3
Clifford Street	D1
Coronation Street	B2-B3
Cross Street	C2
Derby Road	D3
Diamond Street	D2-D3
Fair View	A1-A2
Fort Street	C3-C4-D4
Fort Terrace	C3-D3
Gaydon Street	C3
George Street	B2-B3
Gloster Road	E4-F4
Goodleigh Road	C4
Granville Avenue	A3-B3
Green Lane	B2-C2
Grosvenor Street	C4
Higher Church Street	D3
Higher Raleigh Road	A3
High Maudelin Street	B3
High Street	B2-C2
Hills View	C4
Holland Street	C1-C2
Joy Street	C2
King Edward Street	B3
Lethaby Road	B4
Litchdon Street	D2-D3-E3
Long Bridge	D2
Lower Raleigh Road	A3-A4
Magdalen Lawn	B3
Maiden Street	D2
Masefield Avenue	A3
Miller Crescent	C4
Mill Road	B1-B2
New Buildings	B3
Newport Road	E3-E4-F4
New Road	E3
Norfolk Terrace	F4
North Road	A2-A3-A4
North Walk	B1-B2
Park Lane	F4
Pathfield Lawn	A1-A2
Pilton Causeway	A2-B2
Pilton Lawn	A3
Pilton Street	A2
Portland Street	F4
Pottington Road	B1
Princes Street	B3
Priory Close	A2
Pulchrass Street	D3-D4
Queen Street	C3-D3
Raleigh Lawn	A3
Raleigh Road	A2-A3
Richmond Street	B4-C4
Riddel Avenue	A2-B2-B3
Rock Avenue	F4
Rock Gardens	F4
Rolle Street	B1-B2
St George's Road	A2-A3-A4
St Mary's Road	B4
Salem Street	D3
Signal Terrace	D1-E1
Silver Street	D3
South Walk	E3-F3
Sticklepath Terrace	D1-E1
Summerland Street	D3-D4
Sunflower Road	C4
Taw Vale	D2-D3-E3
The Rock	A2
The Square	D2
The Strand	C2-D2
Trinity Place	E3
Trinity Street	D3
Tuly Street	B2-C2
Vicarage Lawn	B3-C3
Vicarage Street	B3-B4
Victoria Road	E4
Victoria Street	E4
Well Street	C2-D2-D3
Yeo Vale Road	B2-B3

Bideford

Abbotsham Road	A2
Alexandra Terrace	A4
Allhalland Street	B2
Barnstaple Street	C2-C3
Bideford Bridge	B2-C2
Bridgeland Street	B3
Bridge Street	B2
Bull Hill	B1-B2
Buttgarden Street	B2
Chingswell Street	B3
Church Walk	B2
Clovelly Road	A1
Cold Harbour	B3
Cooper Street	D3
Copp's Close	A4
Coronation Road	A1
Elmdale Road	A4
Geneva Place	A1-A2
Glendale Terrace	A4
Grange Road	C2
Grenville Street	B2
Higher Gunstone	A2-B2-B3
High Street	A2-B2
Honestone Street	A2-B2
Hyfield Place	B2
Kingsley Road	A4-B4-B3
Kingsley Street	A3
Lime Grove	A3
Lower Gunstone	B3
Main Road	C3
Market Place	B2
Marland Terrace	A1
Meadowville Road	A4
Meddon Street	A1-A2-B2-B1
Mill Street	B2-B3
Milton Place	A2
Myrtle Gardens	A2-A3
Myrtle Grove	A3
New Road	B1-B2
Newton Road	A4-B4
Northam Road	A3-A4
Northdown Road	A3-A4
North Road	A3-B3
Northview Avenue	A4
Old Town	A2
Park Avenue	B3-B4
Park Lane	B4
Pitt Lane	A2-A3
Railway Terrace	C1 C2
Rectory Park	A2-A3
Rope Walk	B3
Silver Street	B2
The Quay	B2-B3-C3-C2
The Strand	B3
Torridge Hill	B1
Torridge Mount	C1
Torrington Lane	C1
Torrington Street	C1-C2
Victoria Gardens	A2-B2
Victoria Grove	A2-B2
Westcombe Lane	A3

Ilfracombe

Avenue Road	A3-B3
Belmont Road	A1-A2
Brookdale Avenue	A2-A3
Capstone Crescent	B4-C4
Castle Hill	C3
Church Hill	A2
Church Road	A2-A3
Comyn Hill	B1-C1
Fairlands	B2-C2-C1
Fernway	B1
Fore Street	B3-C3
Furze Hill Road	A2-A1-B1
Granville Road	A3-A4
Green Close Road	A3
Highfield Road	A2-B2-B3-C3
High Street	A2-A3-B3
Hillsborough Road	C3
Horne Park Road	A2-B2-B1
Horne Road	B2
Hostle Park Road	B3
Marine Drive	C3-C4
Market Street	B3
Marlborough Road	A2-B2
Mill Head	B3-B4
Montpellier Road	B3-C3
Northfield Road	A3
Osborne Road	B3
Oxford Grove	B3
Oxford Park	B3
Park Hill Road	B1-B2
Portland Street	B3-C3
Princess Avenue	B3-B2-C2
Promenade	B3-B4
Regent Place	A3
Richmond Road	A1
Riverdale Avenue	A3
Ropery Road	B4-C4
Runnacleave Road	A1
St Brannocks Park	A1
St Brannocks Park Road	A1-A2
St Brannocks Road	A1-A2
St James Place	B4-C4
Slade Road	A1
Springfield Road	B3
Station Road	A1-A2
The Quay	C4
Torrs Park	A3
Whittingham Road	C2-C3
Wilder Road	A2-A3
Worth Lane	C1-C2-C3

BARNSTAPLE
This ancient town stands on the Taw estuary and until the 19th century was an important port. The bridge across the river was originally built in the 1400s but has since been widened and extensively altered.

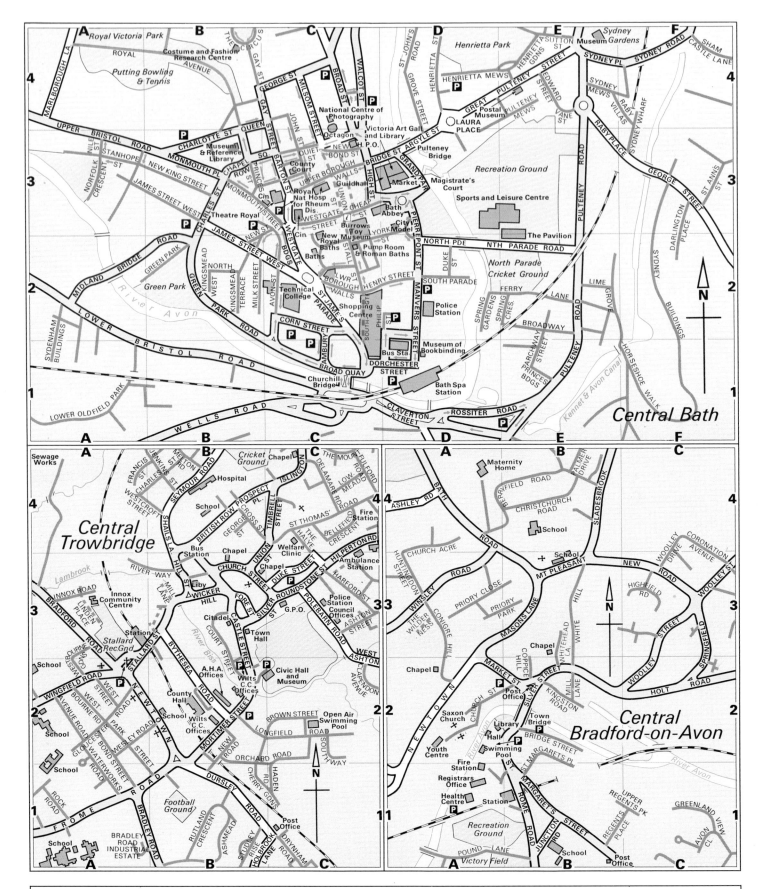

Bath

This unique city combines Britain's most impressive collection of Roman relics with the country's finest Georgian townscape. Its attraction to Romans and fashionable 18th-century society alike was its mineral springs, which are still seen by thousands of tourists who visit the Roman Baths every year. They are now the centre-piece of a Roman museum, where exhibits give a vivid impression of life 2000 years ago. The adjacent Pump Room to which the waters were piped for drinking was a focal point of social life in 18th- and 19th-century Bath.

The Georgian age of elegence also saw the building of Bath's perfectly proportioned streets, terraces and crescents. The finest examples are Queen Square, the Circus, and Royal Crescent, all built of golden local stone. Overlooking the Avon from the west is the great tower of Bath Abbey – sometimes called the "Lantern of the West" because of its large and numerous windows.

Bath has much to delight the museum-lover. Near the abbey, in York Street, is the Burrows Toy Museum – a treasure-trove of playthings spanning two centuries. The Assembly Rooms in Bennett Street, very much a part of the social scene in Georgian Bath, are now the home of the Museum of Costume, and nearby, in Circus Mews, is the Carriage Museum, which vividly recalls coaching days.

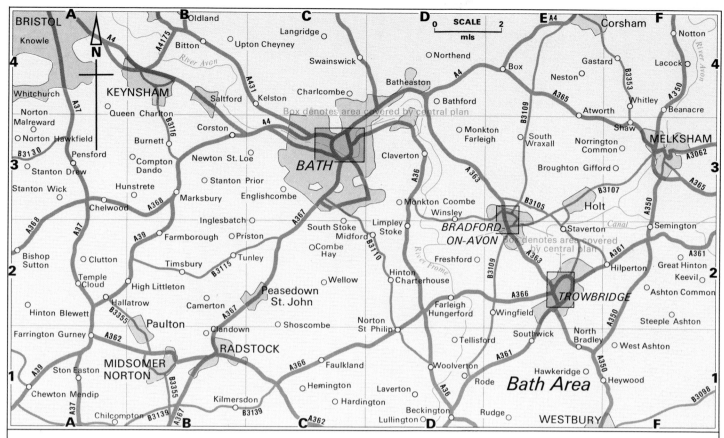

Key to Town Plan and Area Plan

Town Plan

A A Recommended roads
Other roads
Restricted roads
Buildings of interest   Library
Car Parks   P
Parks and open spaces
Churches   †
One Way Streets

Area Plan

A roads
B roads
Locations   Box O
Urban Area

Street Index with Grid Reference

Central Bath

Ambury	C1-C2
Archway Street	E1-E2
Argyle Street	D3-D4
Avon Street	C2
Barton Street	C3
Bridge Street	C3-D3
Broadway	E2
Broad Street	C3-C4
Broad Quay	C1
Chapel Row	B3
Charles Street	B2-B3
Charlotte Street	B3-B4
Cheap Street	C3
Claverton Street	C1-D1
Corn Street	C2
Darlington Place	F2-F3
Dorchester Street	C1-D1
Duke Street	D2
Edward Street	E4
Ferry Lane	D2-E2
Gay Street	B4-C4-C3
George Street	B4-C4
George Street	F2-F3
Grand Parade	D3
Great Pulteney Street	D4-E4

Green Park	A2-B2
Green Park Road	B1-B2-C2-C1
Grove Street	D3-D4
Henrietta Gardens	E4
Henrietta Mews	D4-E4
Henrietta Street	D4
Henry Street	C2-D2
High Street	C3
Horseshoe Walk	F1
James Street West	A3-B3-B2-C2
John Street	C3-C4
Kingsmead North	B2
Kingsmead Terrace	B2
Kingsmead West	B2
Laura Place	D3-D4
Lime Grove	E2-F2-F1
Lower Bristol Road	A2-A1-B1-C1
Lower Borough Walls	C2
Lower Oldfield Park	A1
Manvers Street	D1-D2
Marlborough Lane	A4
Midland Bridge Road	A2-B2-B3
Milk Street	B2
Milsom Street	C3-C4
Monmouth Place	B3
Monmouth Street	B3-C3
New Street	B2-B3-C3
New Bond Street	C3
New King Street	A3-B3
Nile Street	A3
Norfolk Crescent	A3
North Parade	D2
North Parade Road	D2-E2
Philip Street	C1-C2
Pierrepont Street	D2-D3
Princes Buildings	E1
Princes Street	B3
Pulteney Mews	E4
Pulteney Road	E1-E2-E3-E4
Queen Square	B3-B4-C4-C3
Quiet Street	C3
Raby Place	E4-E3-F3
Raby Villas	E4-F4
Rossiter Road	D1-E1
Royal Avenue	A4-B4
St Ann's Street	F3
St Jame's Parade	C2
St John's Road	D4
Sham Castle Lane	F4
Southgate	C1-C2
South Parade	D2
Spring Crescent	E2
Spring Gardens	D2
Stall Street	C2-C3
Stanhope Street	A3
Sutton Street	E4
Sydenham Buildings	A1-A2
Sydney Buildings	F1-F2-F3
Sydney Mews	E4-F4
Sydney Place	E4-F4
Sydney Road	F4
Sydney Wharf	F3-F4
The Circus	B4
Union Street	C3
Upper Borough Walls	C3
Upper Bristol Road	A4-A3-B3
Vane Street	E4
Walcot Street	C3-C4
Wells Road	A1-B1-C1

Westgate Buildings	C2-C3
Westgate Street	C3
York Street	C2-D2-D3

Trowbridge

Ashmead	B1
Ashton Street	C3
Avenue Road	A2
Bellefield Crescent	C4
Bond Street	A1-A2
Bradford Road	A2-A3
Bradley Road	A1-B1
British Row	B4
Brown Street	B2-C2
Bythesea Road	B2-B3
Castle Street	B2-B3
Charles Street	A4-B4
Cherry Gardens	B1-C1
Church Street	B3-C3
Clapendon Avenue	C2
Court Street	B2-B3
Cross Street	B4-C4
Delamare Road	C4
Drynham Road	C1
Duke Street	C3-C4
Dursley Road	B1-C1
Fore Street	B3
Francis Street	A4-B4
Frome Road	A1-B1
Fulford Road	C4
George Street	B4
Gloucester Road	A2
Haden Road	C1
Harford Street	C3
Hill Street	B3
Hilperton Road	C3-C4
Holbrook Lane	B1-C1
Innox Road	A3
Islington	C4
Jenkins Street	A4-B4
Linden Place	A3
Longfield Road	B2-C2
Lowmead	C4
Melton Road	B4
Mill Lane	B3
Mortimer Street	B2
New Road	B1-B2
Newtown	A2-B2
Orchard Road	B1-B2-C2-C1
Park Street	A2-A1-B1
Polebarn Road	C3
Prospect Place	B4-C4
River Way	A3-B3
Rock Road	A1
Roundstone Street	C3
Rutland Crescent	B1
St Thomas' Road	C4
Seymour Road	C4
Shails Lane	B3-B4
Silver Street	B3-C3
Southway	C2
Stallard Street	A2-A3-B3
Studley Rise	B1
The Hayle	C4
The Mount	C4
Timbrell Street	C4

Union Street	B3-B4-C4-C3
Waterworks Road	A1-A2
Wesley Road	A2-B2
West Street	A2
West Ashton	C2-C3
Westbourne Gardens	A2-A3
Westbourne Road	A2
Westcroft Street	A4-B4
Wicker Hill	B3
Wingfield Road	A2

Bradford-on-Avon

Ashley Road	A4
Avon Close	C1
Bath Road	A3-A4-B4-B3
Berryfield Road	A4-B4
Bridge Street	B2
Christchurch Road	B4
Church Acre	A4
Church Street	A2-B2
Conigre Hill	A2-A3
Coppice Hill	B2-B3
Coronation Avenue	C3-C4
Greenland View	C1
Highfield Road	C3
Holt Road	B2-C2
Huntingdon Street	A3
Kingston Road	B2
Junction Road	B1
Market Street	A2-B2
Masons Lane	A3-B3
Mill Lane	B2
Mount Pleasant	B3
Newtown	A1-A2-A3
New Road	B3-C3
Palmer Drive	B4
Pound Lane	A1-B1
Priory Close	A3-B3
Priory Park	A3-B3
Regents Place	B1-C1
Rome Road	B1
St Margaret's Place	B1-B2
St Margaret's Street	B2-B1-C1
Silver Street	B2
Sladesbrook	B3-B4
Springfield	C2-C3
The Wilderness	A3
Upper Regents Park	B1-C1
White Hill	B2-B3
Whitehead Lane	B2-B3
Winsley Road	A3-A4
Woolley Drive	C3-C4
Woolley Street	C2-C3

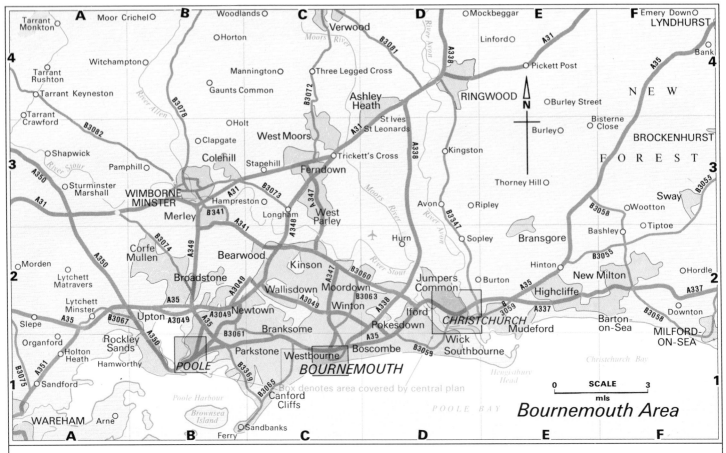

Bournemouth Area

Box denotes area covered by central plan

SCALE 0 — 3 mls

Street Index with Grid Reference

Bournemouth

Albert Road	C3-D3
Avenue Road	B3-C3
Bath Road	D2-E2-E3-E4-F4
Beacon Road	C1
Bodorgan Road	C4
Bourne Avenue	B3-C3
Braidley Road	B3-B4
Branksome Wood Road	A4
Cambridge Road	A2-A3
Central Drive	B4
Chine Crescent	A1-A2
Chine Crescent Road	A1-A2
Christchurch Road	F4
Cotlands Road	F4
Cranbourne Road	B2-C2
Crescent Road	A3-B3
Dean Park Crescent	C4-D4
Dean Park Road	C4
Durley Chine Road	A1-A2
Durley Gardens	A1-A2
Durley Road	A1-A2-B1
East Overcliff Drive	E2-F2-F3
Exeter Crescent	C2
Exeter Lane	C2-D2
Exeter Park Road	C2-D2
Exeter Road	C2-D2
Fir Vale Road	D3-D4
Gervis Place	C3-D3
Gervis Road	E3-F3
Glenfern Road	D3-E3-E4
Grove Road	E3-F3
Hahnemann Road	A1-B1-B2
Hinton Road	D2-D3-E2
Holdenhurst Road	F4
Lansdowne Road	E4-F4
Lorne Park Road	E4
Madeira Road	D4-E4
Marlborough Road	A2
Meyrick Road	F3
Norwich Avenue	A2-A3-B3
Norwich Avenue West	A3
Old Christchurch Road	D3-D4-E4-F4
Parsonage Road	D3-E3
Poole Hill	A2-B2
Poole Road	A2
Priory Road	C1-C2

Richmond Hill	C3-C4
Russell Cotes Road	E2
St Michael's Road	B2-B1-C1
St Peter's Road	D3-E3
St Stephen's Road	B3-B4-C4-C3
Stafford Road	E4
Suffolk Road	A3-B3
Surrey Road	A3
Terrace Road	B2-C2
The Triangle	B2-B3
Tregonwell Road	B2-C2-C1
Undercliffe Drive	D1-D2-E1-E2-F2
Upper Hinton Road	D2-D3-E2
Upper Norwich Road	A2-B2
Upper Terrace Road	B2-C2
Wessex Way	A3-A4-B4-C4-D4-E4
West Cliff Gardens	B1
West Cliff Promenade	B1-C1-D1-C1
West Cliff Road	A1-B1
Westhill Road	A2-B2-B1-C1
Westover Road	D2-D3
West Promenade	C1-D1
Wimborne Road	C4
Wootton Gardens	E3-E4
Yelverton Road	C3-D3

Christchurch

Albion Road	A4
Arcadia Road	A4
Arthur Road	B3
Avenue Road	A3-B3-B4
Avon Road West	A3-A4-B4
Bargates	B2-B3
Barrack Road	A4-A3-B2-B3
Beaconsfield Road	B2-C3
Bridge Street	C2
Bronte Avenue	B4
Canberra Road	A4
Castle Street	B2-C2
Christchurch By-Pass	B2-C2-C3
Clarendon Road	A3-B3
Douglas Avenue	A2-B2
Endfield Road	A4
Fairfield	B3
Fairmile Road	A4-B4-B3
Flambard Avenue	B4
Gardner Road	A3-A4
Gleadowe Avenue	A2-B2
Grove Road East	A3-B3

Grove Road West	A3
High Street	B2
Iford Lane	A1
Jumpers Avenue	A4
Jumpers Road	A3-A4-B4
Kings Avenue	A2-B2
Manor Road	B2
Millhams Street	B2-C2
Mill Road	B3-B4
Portfield Road	A3-B3
Queens Avenue	B1
Quay Road	B1
St John's Road	A2
St Margarets Avenue	B1
Sopers Lane	B1-B2
South View Road	A1-B1
Stony Lane	C4-C3-C2
Stour Road	B3-B2-A1-A2
The Grove	A4
Tuckton Road	A1
Twynham Avenue	B2-B3
Walcott Avenue	A4-B4
Waterloo Place	C2
Wickfield Avenue	B1-B2
Wick Lane	A1-B1-B2
Willow Drive	A1-B1
Willow Way	A1-B1
Windsor Road	A3

Poole

Ballard Road	B1-C1
Church Street	A1
Dear Hay Lane	A2-B2
Denmark Road	C3
East Quay Road	B1
East Street	B1
Elizabeth Road	C3
Emerson Road	B1-B2
Esplanade	B3
Garland Road	C4
Green Road	B2-B1-C1
Heckford Road	C3-C4
High Street	A1-B1-B2
Hill Street	B2
Johns Road	C3-C4
Jolliffe Road	C4
Kingland Road	B2-C2
Kingston Road	C3-C4
Lagland Street	B1-B2

Longfleet Road	C3
Maple Road	C3-C4
Mount Pleasant Road	C2-C3
Newfoundland Drive	C1
New Orchard	A1-A2
North Street	B2
Old Orchard	B1
Parkstone Road	C3-C2
Perry Gardens	B1
Poole Bridge	A1
St Mary's Road	C3
Seldown Lane	C2-C3
Shaftesbury Road	C3
Skinner Street	B1
South Road	B2
Stanley Road	B1
Sterte Avenue	A4-B4
Sterte Road	B2-B3-B4
Stokes Avenue	B4-C4
Strand Street	A1-B1
Tatnam Road	B4-C4
The Quay	A1-B1
Towngate Bridge	B2-B3
West Quay Road	A1-A2-B2
West Street	A1-A2-B2
Wimborne Road	B3-C3-C4

LEGEND

Town Plan

AA Recommended route	
Other roads	
Restricted roads	
Buildings of interest	Town Hall
AA Centre	AA
Car Parks	P
Parks and open spaces	
One way streets	

Area Plan

A roads	
B roads	
Locations	Mudeford O
Urban area	

Bournemouth

Until the beginning of the 19th century the landscape on which Bournemouth stands was open heath. Its rise began when a scattering of holiday villas were built by innovative trend-setters at a time when the idea of seaside holidays was very new. Soon a complete village had taken shape. In the next 50 years Bournemouth had become a major resort and its population catapulted to nearly 59,000.

Today's holidaymakers can enjoy Bournemouth's natural advantages – miles of sandy beaches, a mild climate and beautiful setting, along with a tremendous variety of amenities. These include some of the best shopping in the south – with shops ranging from huge departmental stores to tiny specialist places. Entertainments range from variety shows and feature films to opera, and the music of the world-famous Bournemouth Symphony Orchestra.

Poole has virtually been engulfed by the suburbs of Bournemouth, but its enormous natural harbour is still an attraction in its own right. At Poole Quay, some 15th-century cellars have been converted into a Maritime Museum, where the town's association with the sea from prehistoric times until the early 20th century is illustrated, and the famous Poole Pottery nearby offers guided tours of its workshops.

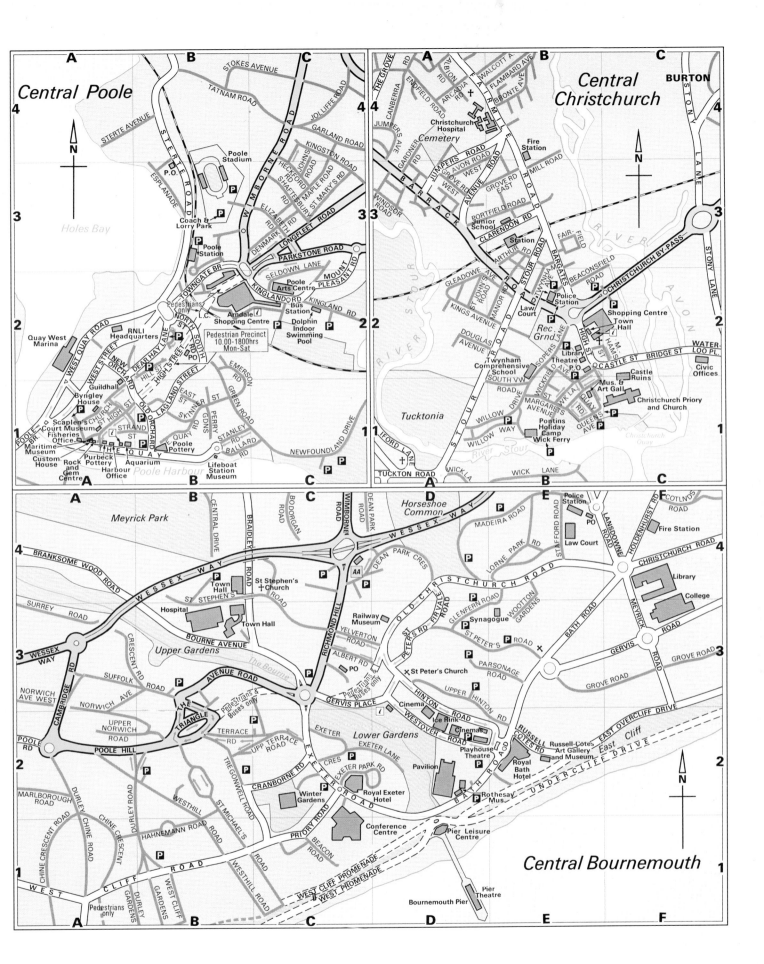

Central Poole

STOKES AVENUE
TATNAM ROAD
STERTE AVENUE
ESPLANADE
P.O.
Poole Stadium
Holes Bay
Coach & Lorry Park
Poole Station
JOLIFFE ROAD
GARLAND ROAD
KINGSTON ROAD
HECKFORD ROAD
MAPLE ROAD
SHAFTESBURY RD
ST MARY'S RD
ELIZABETH RD
DENMARK RD
LONGFLEET ROAD
PARKSTONE ROAD
SELDOWN LANE
MOUNT PLEASANT RD
KINGLAND RD
KINGLANDORD
Poole Arts Centre
Bus Station
Dolphin Indoor Swimming Pool
Arndale Shopping Centre
Pedestrians only
TOWNGATE BR
KINGLAND RD
RNLI Headquarters
Quay West Marina
Pedestrian Precinct 10.00-1800hrs Mon-Sat
NORTH ST
SOUTH RD
High St
PO
WEST QUAY ROAD
WEST STREET
NEW ORCHARD
DEAR HAY LANE
HILL ST
LAGLAND STREET
EMERSON RD
GREEN ROAD
Guildhall
Byngley House
Scaplen's Court Museum
Fisheries Office
Maritime Museum
Custom House
Rock and Gem Centre
Purbeck Pottery
Harbour Office
POOLE BR
OLD ORCHARD
HIGH ST
EAST ST
SKINNER ST
GONS
PERRY
STANLEY RD
BALLARD RD
NEWFOUNDLAND DRIVE
STRAND ST
THE QUAY
Poole Pottery
Aquarium
Lifeboat Station Museum
Poole Harbour

Central Christchurch

BURTON
THE GROVE
FAIRMILE
CANBERRA
ENDFIELD ROAD
ARCADIA RD
ALBION RD
WALCOTT A.
FLAMBARD AVE
BRONTE AVE
STONY LANE
Christchurch Hospital
Cemetery
Fire Station
MILL ROAD
JUMPERS AVE
GARDNER ROAD
GROVE AVENUE
JUMPERS ROAD
AVON ROAD WEST
GROVE RD EAST
WINDSOR ROAD
PORTFIELD ROAD
BARRACK ROAD
Junior School
CLARENDON RD
Station
ARTHUR RD
GLEADOWE AVE
ST JOHNS ROAD
MANOR ROAD
STOUR ROAD
TWYNHAM AVE
BARGATES
FAIR-FIELD
BEACONSFIELD ROAD
CHRISTCHURCH BY PASS
RIVER
Police Station
Law Court
KINGS AVENUE
DOUGLAS AVENUE
WICKFIELD AVE
Twynham Comprehensive School
SOUTH VW
Shopping Centre
Town Hall
HIGH ST
Library
Theatre
PO
Castle Ruins
Civic Offices
WATER-LOO PL.
CASTLE ST
BRIDGE ST
Mus. & Art Gall
Christchurch Priory and Church
RIVER STOUR
Tucktonia
SOPERS LANE
MARGARETS AVENUE
WILLOW DRIVE
WILLOW WAY
Pontins Holiday Camp
Wick Ferry
QUEENS AVE
Christchurch Quay
IFORD LANE
TUCKTON ROAD
WICKLA
WICK LANE
River Stour

Central Bournemouth

Meyrick Park
BRANKSOME WOOD ROAD
WESSEX WAY
CENTRAL DRIVE
BRADLEY RD
BODORGAN ROAD
WIMBORNE ROAD
DEAN PARK ROAD
Horseshoe Common
WESSEX WAY
Police Station
PO
Fire Station
SCOTLNDS ROAD
St Stephen's Church
Town Hall
ST STEPHEN'S RD
MADEIRA ROAD
LORNE PARK RD
STAFFORD ROAD
LANSDOWNE ROAD
HOLDENHURST RD
CHRISTCHURCH ROAD
Library
College
Hospital
Town Hall
BOURNE AVENUE
Upper Gardens
SURREY ROAD
RICHMOND HILL
Railway Museum
YELVERTON ROAD
ALBERT RD
OLD CHRISTCHURCH ROAD
ST PETER'S RD
FIRVALE ROAD
GLENFERN ROAD
Synagogue
WOOTTON GARDENS
ST PETER'S ROAD
BATH ROAD
METRICK ROAD
GERVIS ROAD
GROVE ROAD
WESSEX WAY
NORWICH AVE WEST
CAMBRIDGE RD
CRESCENT ROAD
SUFFOLK RD
NORWICH AVE
UPPER NORWICH ROAD
POOLE RD
THE TRIANGLE
AVENUE ROAD
POOLE HILL
Pedestrians & buses only
TERRACE RD
PO
St Peter's Church
PARSONAGE ROAD
UPPER HINTON RD
HINTON ROAD
GERVIS PLACE
Cinema
Ice Rink
Cinemas
GROVE ROAD
MARLBOROUGH ROAD
DURLEY ROAD
CHINE CRESCENT ROAD
WESTHILL
ST MICHAEL'S ROAD
HAHNEMANN ROAD
UPP TERRACE ROAD
EXETER RD
EXETER LANE
Lower Gardens
Westover Road
WESTOVER ROAD
Playhouse Theatre
RUSSELL COTES RD
Russell-Cotes Art Gallery and Museum
East Cliff
EAST OVERCLIFF DRIVE
Royal Bath Hotel
CRANBORNE RD
EXETER PARK RD
Winter Gardens
Royal Exeter Hotel
PRIORY ROAD
BEACON ROAD
Conference Centre
Pavilion
BATH ROAD
Rothesay Mus
UNDERCLIFF DRIVE
WESTHILL ROAD
WEST CLIFF ROAD
WEST CLIFF GARDENS
DURLEY GARDENS
Pedestrians only
WEST CLIFF PROMENADE
WEST PROMENADE
Pier Leisure Centre
Pier Theatre
Bournemouth Pier

BOURNEMOUTH
The pier, safe sea-bathing, golden sands facing south and sheltered by steep cliffs, and plenty of amenities for the holiday maker make Bournemouth one of the most popular resorts on the south coast of England.

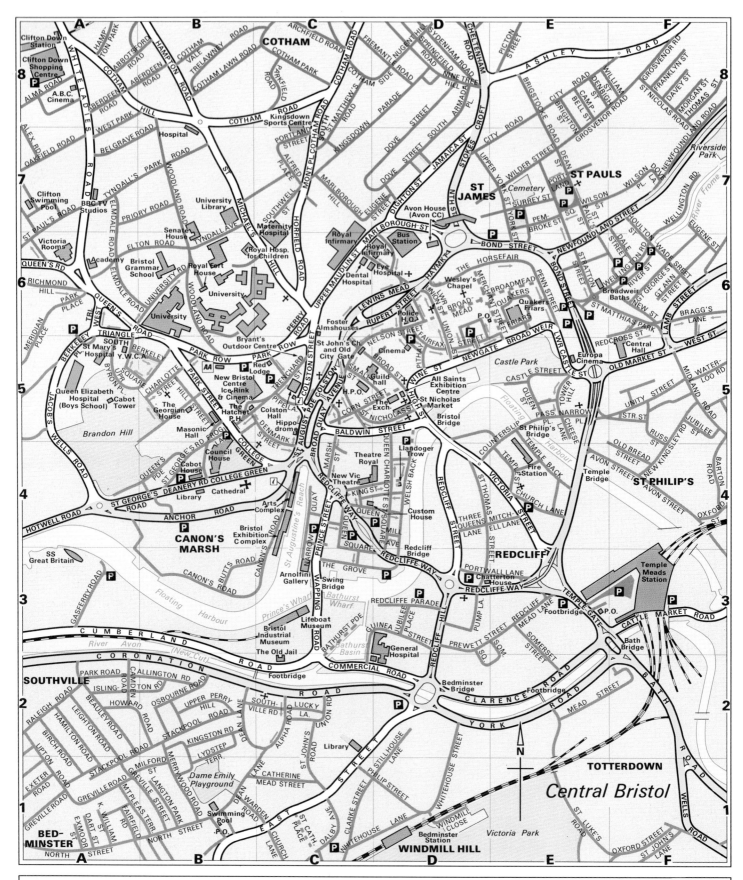

Bristol

One of Britain's most historic seaports, Bristol retains many of its visible links with the past, despite terrible damage inflicted during bombing raids in World War II. Most imposing is the cathedral, founded as an abbey church in 1140. Perhaps even more famous than the cathedral is the Church of St Mary Redcliffe. Ranking among the finest churches in the country, it owes much of its splendour to 14th- and 15th-century merchants who bestowed huge sums of money on it.

The merchant families brought wealth to the whole of Bristol, and their trading links with the world are continued in today's modern aerospace and technological industries. Much of the best of Bristol can be seen in the area of the Floating Harbour – an arm of the Avon. Several of the old warehouses have been converted into museums, galleries and exhibition centres. Among them are genuinely picturesque old pubs, the best-known of which is the Llandoger Trow. It is a timbered 17th-century house, the finest of its kind in Bristol. Further up the same street – King Street – is the Theatre Royal, built in 1766 and the oldest theatre in the country. In Corn Street, the heart of the business area, is a magnificent 18th-century corn exchange. In front of it are the four pillars known as the 'nails', on which merchants used to make cash transactions, hence 'to pay on the nail'.

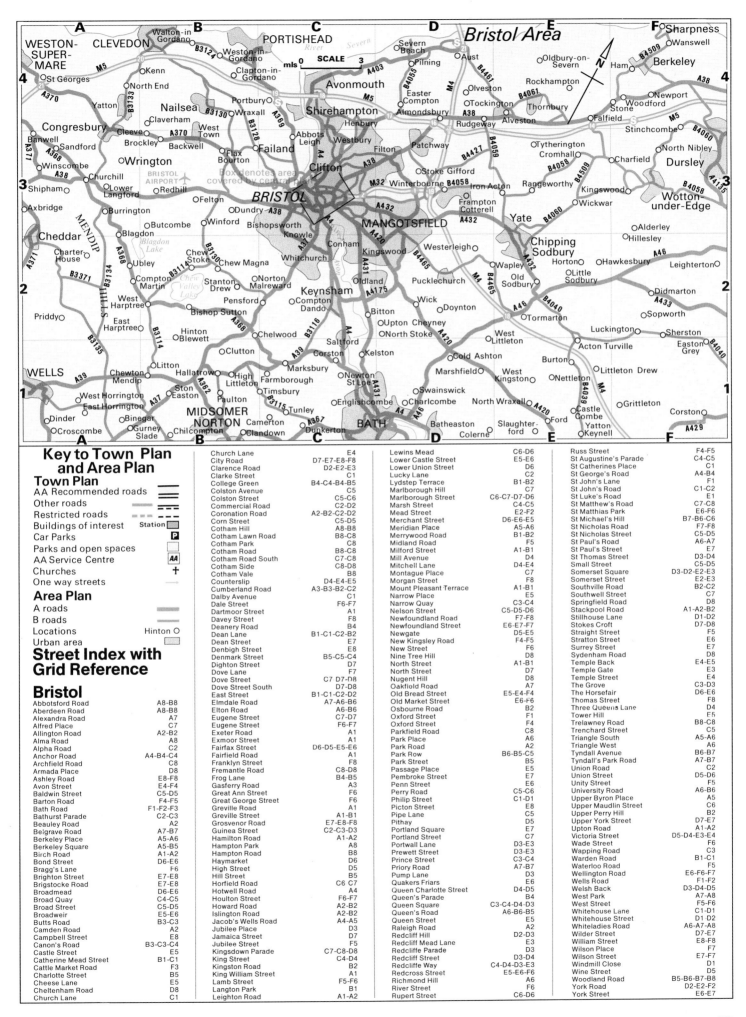

Key to Town Plan and Area Plan

Town Plan

AA Recommended roads
Other roads
Restricted roads
Buildings of interest   Station
Car Parks
Parks and open spaces
AA Service Centre
Churches
One way streets

Area Plan

A roads
B roads
Locations   Hinton O
Urban area

Street Index with Grid Reference

Bristol

Abbotsford Road	A8-B8
Aberdeen Road	A8-B8
Alexandra Road	A7
Alfred Place	C7
Allington Road	A2-B2
Alma Road	A8
Alpha Road	C2
Anchor Road	A4-B4-C4
Archfield Road	C8
Armada Place	D8
Ashley Road	E8-F8
Avon Street	E4-F4
Baldwin Street	C5-D5
Barton Road	F4-F5
Bath Road	F1-F2-F3
Bathurst Parade	C2-C3
Beauley Road	A2
Belgrave Road	A7-B7
Berkeley Place	A5-A6
Berkeley Square	A5-B5
Birch Road	A1-A2
Bond Street	D6-E6
Bragg's Lane	F6
Brighton Street	E7-E8
Brigstocke Road	E7-E8
Broadmead	D6-E6
Broad Quay	C4-C5
Broad Street	C5-D5
Broadweir	E5-E6
Butts Road	B3-C3
Camden Road	A2
Campbell Street	E8
Canon's Road	B3-C3-C4
Castle Street	E5
Catherine Mead Street	B1-C1
Cattle Market Road	F3
Charlotte Street	B5
Cheese Lane	E5
Cheltenham Road	D8
Church Lane	C1

Church Lane	E4
City Road	D7-E7-E8-F8
Clarence Road	D2-E2-E3
Clarke Street	C1
College Green	B4-C4-B4-B5
Colston Avenue	C5
Colston Street	C5-C6
Commercial Road	C2-D2
Coronation Road	A2-B2-C2-D2
Corn Street	C5-D5
Cotham Hill	A8-B8
Cotham Lawn Road	B8-C8
Cotham Park	C8
Cotham Road	B8-C8
Cotham Road South	C7-C8
Cotham Side	C8-D8
Cotham Vale	B8
Countership	D4-E4-E5
Cumberland Road	A3-B3-B2-C2
Dalby Avenue	C1
Dale Street	F6-F7
Dartmoor Street	A1
Davey Street	F8
Deanery Road	B4
Dean Lane	B1-C1-C2-B2
Dean Street	E7
Denbigh Street	E8
Denmark Street	B5-C5-C4
Dighton Street	D7
Dove Lane	F7
Dove Street	C7-D7-D8
Dove Street South	D7-D8
East Street	B1-C1-C2-D2
Elmdale Road	A7-A6-B6
Elton Road	A6-B6
Eugene Street	C7-D7
Eugene Street	F6-F7
Exeter Road	A1
Exmoor Street	A1
Fairfax Street	D6-D5-E5-E6
Fairfield Road	A1
Franklyn Street	F8
Fremantle Road	C8-D8
Frog Lane	B4-B5
Gasferry Road	A3
Great Ann Street	F6
Great George Street	F6
Greville Road	A1
Greville Street	A1-B1
Grosvenor Road	E7-E8-F8
Guinea Street	C2-C3-D3
Hamilton Road	A1-A2
Hampton Park	A8
Hampton Road	B8
Haymarket	D6
High Street	D5
Hill Street	B5
Horfield Road	C6 C7
Hotwell Road	A4
Houlton Street	F6-F7
Howard Road	A2-B2
Islington Road	A2-B2
Jacob's Wells Road	A4-A5
Jubilee Place	D3
Jamaica Street	D7
Jubilee Street	F5
Kingsdown Parade	C7-C8-D8
King Street	C4-D4
Kingston Road	B2
King William Street	A1
Lamb Street	F5-F6
Langton Park	B1
Leighton Road	A1-A2

Lewins Mead	C6-D6
Lower Castle Street	E5-E6
Lower Union Street	D6
Lucky Lane	C2
Lydstep Terrace	B1-B2
Marlborough Hill	C7
Marlborough Street	C6-C7-D7-D6
Marsh Street	C4-C5
Mead Street	E2-F2
Merchant Street	D6-E6-E5
Meridian Place	A5-A6
Merrywood Road	B1-B2
Midland Road	F5
Milford Street	A1-B1
Mill Avenue	D4
Mitchell Lane	D4-E4
Montague Place	C7
Morgan Street	F8
Mount Pleasant Terrace	A1-B1
Narrow Place	E5
Narrow Quay	C3-C4
Nelson Street	C5-D5-D6
Newfoundland Road	F7-F8
Newfoundland Street	E6-E7-F7
Newgate	D5-E5
New Kingsley Road	F4-F5
New Street	F6
Nine Tree Hill	D8
North Street	A1-B1
North Street	D7
Nugent Hill	D8
Oakfield Road	A7
Old Bread Street	E5-E4-F4
Old Market Street	E6-F6
Osbourne Road	B2
Oxford Street	F1
Oxford Street	F4
Parkfield Road	C8
Park Place	A6
Park Road	A2
Park Row	B6-B5-C5
Park Street	B5
Passage Place	E5
Pembroke Street	E7
Penn Street	E6
Perry Road	C5-C6
Philip Street	C1-D1
Picton Street	E8
Pipe Lane	C5
Pithay	D5
Portland Square	E7
Portland Street	C7
Portwall Lane	D3-E3
Prewett Street	D3-E3
Prince Street	C3-C4
Priory Road	A7-B7
Pump Lane	D3
Quakers Friars	E6
Queen Charlotte Street	D4-D5
Queen's Parade	B4
Queen Square	C3-C4-D4-D3
Queen's Road	A6-B6-B5
Queen Street	E5
Raleigh Road	A2
Redcliff Hill	D2-D3
Redcliff Mead Lane	E3
Redcliffe Parade	D3
Redcliff Street	D3-D4
Redcliff Way	C4-D4-D3-E3
Redcross Street	E5-E6-F6
Richmond Hill	A6
River Street	F6
Rupert Street	C6-D6

Russ Street	F4-F5
St Augustine's Parade	C4-C5
St Catherines Place	C1
St George's Road	A4-B4
St John's Lane	F1
St John's Road	C1-C2
St Luke's Road	E1
St Matthew's Road	C7-C8
St Matthias Park	E6-F6
St Michael's Hill	B7-B6-C6
St Nicholas Road	F7-F8
St Nicholas Street	C5-D5
St Paul's Road	A6-A7
St Paul's Street	E7
St Thomas Street	D3-D4
Small Street	C5-D5
Somerset Square	D3-D2-E2-E3
Somerset Street	E2-E3
Southville Road	B2-C2
Southwell Street	C7
Springfield Road	D8
Stackpool Road	A1-A2-B2
Stillhouse Lane	D1-D2
Stokes Croft	D7-D8
Straight Street	F5
Stratton Street	E6
Surrey Street	E7
Sydenham Road	D8
Temple Back	E4-E5
Temple Gate	E3
Temple Street	E4
The Grove	C3-D3
The Horsefair	D6-E6
Thomas Street	F8
Three Queens Lane	D4
Tower Hill	E5
Trelawney Road	B8-C8
Trenchard Street	C5
Triangle South	A5-A6
Triangle West	A6
Tyndall Avenue	B6-B7
Tyndall's Park Road	A7-B7
Union Road	C2
Union Street	D5-D6
Unity Street	F5
University Road	A6-B6
Upper Byron Place	A5
Upper Maudlin Street	C6
Upper Perry Hill	B2
Upper York Street	D7-E7
Upton Road	A1-A2
Victoria Street	D5-D4-E3-E4
Wade Street	F6
Wapping Road	C3
Warden Road	B1-C1
Waterloo Road	F5
Wellington Road	E6-F6-F7
Wells Road	F1-F2
Welsh Back	D3-D4-D5
West Park	A7-A8
West Street	F5-F6
Whitehouse Lane	C1-D1
Whitehouse Street	D1-D2
Whiteladies Road	A6-A7-A8
Wilder Street	D7-E7
William Street	E8-F8
Wilson Place	F7
Wilson Street	E7-F7
Windmill Close	D1
Wine Street	D5
Woodland Road	B5-B6-B7-B8
York Road	D2-E2-F2
York Street	E6-E7

89

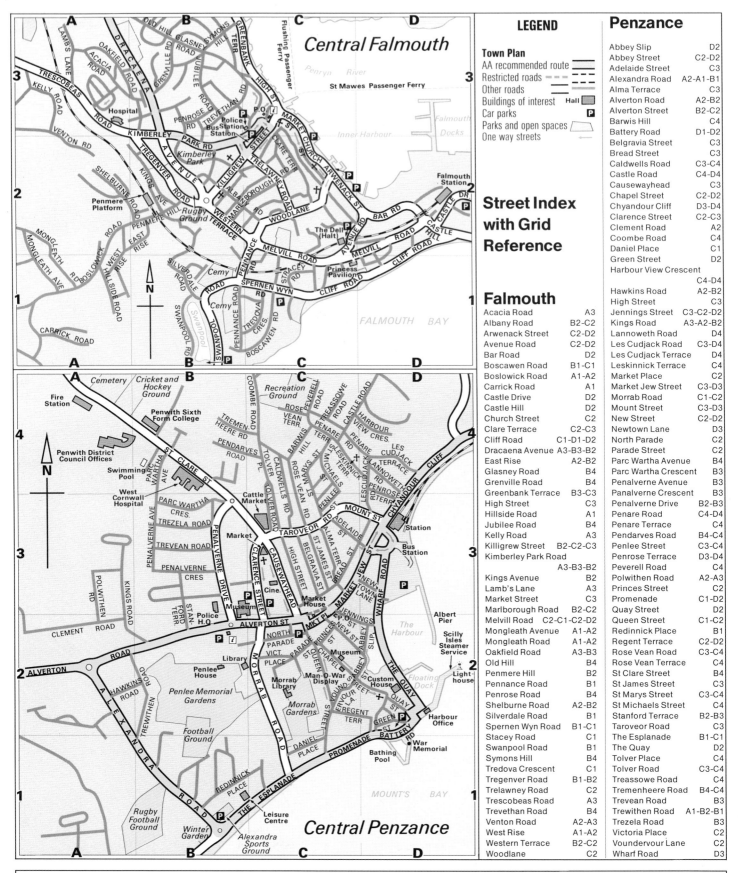

LEGEND

Town Plan
AA recommended route
Restricted roads
Other roads
Buildings of interest — Hall
Car parks — P
Parks and open spaces
One way streets

Street Index with Grid Reference

Falmouth

Acacia Road	A3
Albany Road	B2-C2
Arwenack Street	C2-D2
Avenue Road	C2-D2
Bar Road	D2
Boscawen Road	B1-C1
Boslowick Road	A1-A2
Carrick Road	A1
Castle Drive	D2
Castle Hill	D2
Church Street	C2
Clare Terrace	C2-C3
Cliff Road	C1-D1-D2
Dracaena Avenue	A3-B3-B2
East Rise	A2-B2
Glasney Road	B4
Grenville Road	B4
Greenbank Terrace	B3-C3
High Street	C3
Hillside Road	A1
Jubilee Road	B4
Kelly Road	A3
Killigrew Street	B2-C2-C3
Kimberley Park Road	A3-B3-B2
Kings Avenue	B2
Lamb's Lane	A3
Market Street	C3
Marlborough Road	B2-C2
Melvill Road	C2-C1-C2-D2
Mongleath Avenue	A1-A2
Mongleath Road	A1-A2
Oakfield Road	A3-B3
Old Hill	B4
Penmere Hill	B2
Pennance Road	B1
Penrose Road	B4
Shelburne Road	A2-B2
Silverdale Road	B1
Spernen Wyn Road	B1-C1
Stacey Road	C1
Swanpool Road	B1
Symons Hill	B4
Tredova Crescent	C1
Tregenver Road	B1-B2
Trelawney Road	C2
Trescobeas Road	A3
Trevethan Road	B4
Venton Road	A2-A3
West Rise	A1-A2
Western Terrace	B2-C2
Woodlane	C2

Penzance

Abbey Slip	D2
Abbey Street	C2-D2
Adelaide Street	C3
Alexandra Road	A2-A1-B1
Alma Terrace	C3
Alverton Road	A2-B2
Alverton Street	B2-C2
Barwis Hill	C4
Battery Road	D1-D2
Belgravia Street	C3
Bread Street	C3
Caldwells Road	C3-C4
Castle Road	C4-D4
Causewayhead	C3
Chapel Street	C2-D2
Chyandour Cliff	D3-D4
Clarence Street	C2-C3
Clement Road	A2
Coombe Road	C4
Daniel Place	C1
Green Street	D2
Harbour View Crescent	C4-D4
Hawkins Road	A2-B2
High Street	C3
Jennings Street	C3-C2-D2
Kings Road	A3-A2-B2
Lannoweth Road	D4
Les Cudjack Road	C3-D4
Les Cudjack Terrace	D4
Leskinnick Terrace	C4
Market Place	C2
Market Jew Street	C3-D3
Morrab Road	C1-C2
Mount Street	C3-D3
New Street	C2-D2
Newtown Lane	D3
North Parade	C2
Parade Street	C2
Parc Wartha Avenue	B4
Parc Wartha Crescent	B3
Penalverne Avenue	B3
Panalverne Crescent	B3
Penalverne Drive	B2-B3
Penare Road	C4-D4
Penare Terrace	C4
Pendarves Road	B4-C4
Penlee Street	C3-C4
Penrose Terrace	D3-D4
Peverell Road	C4
Polwithen Road	A2-A3
Princes Street	C2
Promenade	C1-D2
Quay Street	D2
Queen Street	C1-C2
Redinnick Place	B1
Regent Terrace	C2-D2
Rose Vean Road	C3-C4
Rose Vean Terrace	C4
St Clare Street	B4
St James Street	C3
St Marys Street	C3-C4
St Michaels Street	C4
Stanford Terrace	B2-B3
Taroveor Road	C3
The Esplanade	B1-C1
The Quay	D2
Tolver Place	C4
Tolver Road	C3-C4
Treassowe Road	C4
Tremenheere Road	B4-C4
Trevean Road	B3
Trewithen Road	A1-B2-B1
Trezela Road	B3
Victoria Place	C2
Voundervour Lane	C2
Wharf Road	D3

Cornish towns

Falmouth Twin fortresses, St. Mawes and Pendennis, guard the harbour entrance and serve as a reminder of Falmouth's once vital strategic importance. Lying in the sheltered waters of the Carrick Roads and provided with one of the world's largest natural harbours, Falmouth prospered on trade until the 19th century. Today the town is popular with holidaymakers.

St Ives is one of the few British towns with a style of painting named after it, for both artists and holidaymakers are drawn to the port, with its charming old quarter known as Down-Long. Regular exhibitions of local painting, sculpture and pottery are held, and the work of sculptor Barbara Hepworth, who spent much of her creative life here, is displayed in the Hepworth Gallery.

Penzance is the first and last town in Britain — it lies at the western extremity of Mounts Bay and basks in a temperate climate and sub-tropical vegetation. Places of interest include the ornate Egyptian House (now a National Trust shop), and steamers and helicopters go to the Scilly Isles.

Newquay Favourite haunt of surfboarders for its Fistral and Watergate beaches, Newquay has a 'Huer's House' where lookouts once warned fishermen of approaching shoals of pilchards. There are fine beaches for holidaymakers, such as Towan, Lusty Glaze and Great Western.

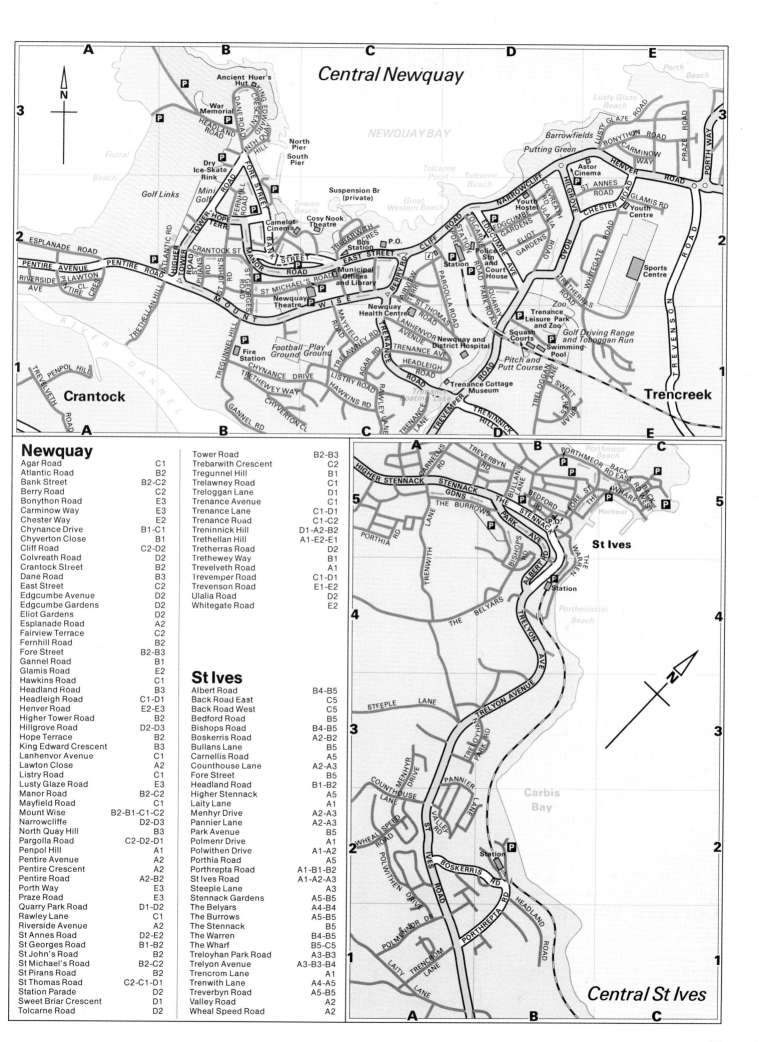

Newquay

St Ives

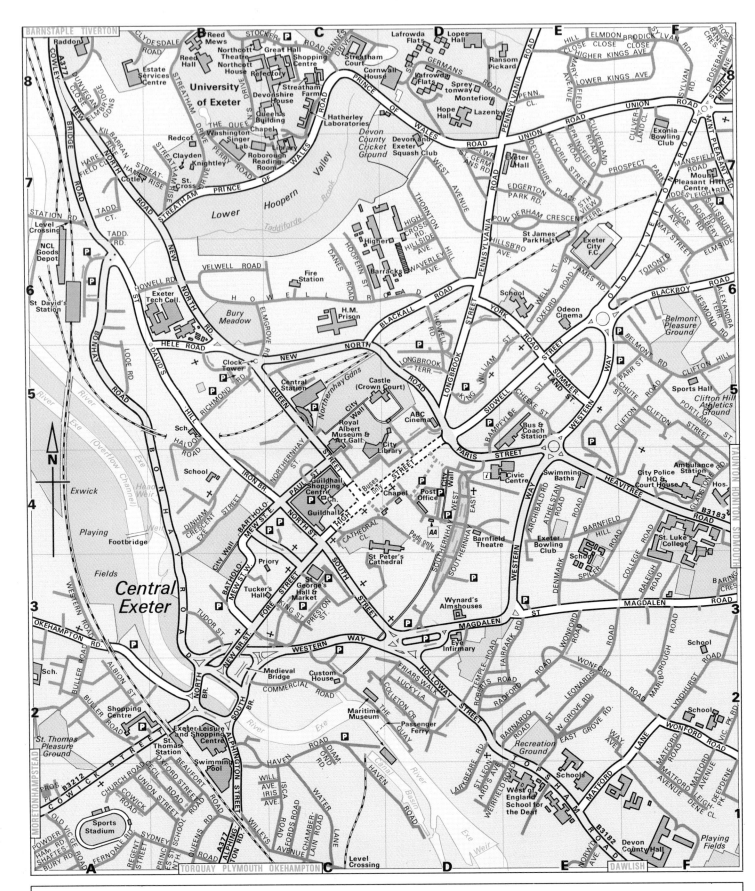

Exeter

The cathedral is Exeter's greatest treasure. Founded in 1050, but rebuilt by the Normans during the 12th century and again at the end of the 13th century, it has many beautiful and outstanding features – especially the exquisite rib-vaulting of the nave. Most remarkable, perhaps, is the fact that it still stood after virtually everything around it was flattened during bombing raids in World War II.

There are still plenty of reminders of Old Exeter, which has been a city since Roman times. Roman and medieval walls encircle parts of the city; 14th-century underground passages can be explored; the Guildhall is 15th-century and one of the oldest municipal buildings in the country; and Sir Francis Drake is said to have met his explorer companions at Mol's Coffee House. Of the city's ancient churches, the most interesting are St Mary Steps, St Mary Arches and St Martin's. Exeter is famous

for its extensive Maritime Museum, with over 100 boats from all over the world. Other museums include the Rougemont House and the Royal Albert Memorial Museum and Art Gallery.

Exmouth has a near-perfect position at the mouth of the Exe estuary. On one side it has expanses of sandy beach, on another a wide estuary alive with wildfowl and small boats, while inland is beautiful Devon countryside.

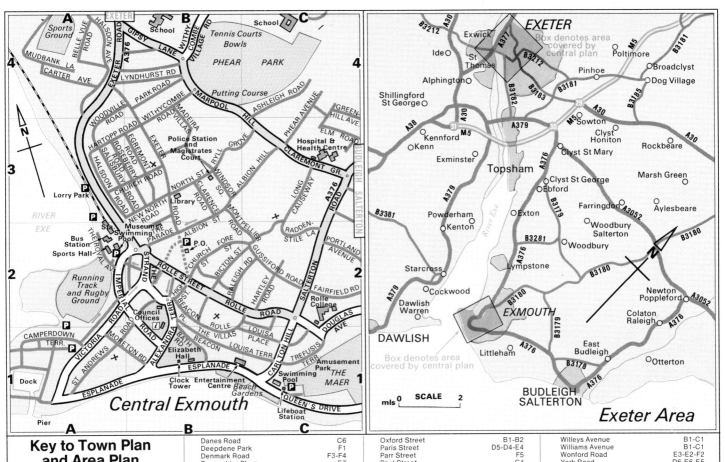

Key to Town Plan and Area Plan

Town Plan

AA Recommended roads
Other roads
Restricted roads
Buildings of interset School
Car Parks P
Churches +
Parks and open spaces

Area Plan

A roads
B roads
Locations
Urban area

Street Index with Grid Reference

Exeter

Albion Street	A2
Alexandra Terrace	F6
Alphington Road	B1
Alphington Street	B1-B2
Archibald Road	E4
Athelstan Road	E4
Bampfylde Street	D4-D5-E5
Baring Crescent	F3
Barnado Road	E2
Barnfield Hill	E4-F4
Bartholomew Street East	B4-C4
Bartholomew Street West	B3
Belmont Road	F6-F5
Blackall Road	C6-D6
Blackboy Road	F6
Bonhay Road	A6-A5-B5-B4-B3-B2
Brodick Close	F8
Buller Road	A2-A3
Cathedral Close	C4-D4
Cecil Road	A1-B1
Chamberlain Road	C1
Cheeke Street	E5
Church Road	A1-A2-B2
Chute Street	E5-F5
Clifton Hill	F5
Clifton Road	E5-F5
Clifton Street	F4-F5
Clydesdale Road	A8-B8
College Road	F3-F4
Colleton Crescent	C2-D2
Commercial Road	B2-C2
Cowick Road	A1
Cowick Street	A1-A2-B2
Cowley Bridge Road	A6-A7-A8
Culverland Close	F7-F8
Culverland Road	E7-E8
Danes Road	C6
Deepdene Park	F1
Denmark Road	F3-F4
Devonshire Place	E7
Diamond Road	C2-C1
Dineham Crescent	B4
Dunvegan Close	A8
East Grove Road	E2
Edgerton Park Road	E7
Elmbridge Gardens	A8
Elmdon Close	E8-F8
Elmgrove Road	B6-C6-B5
Elmside	F6
Exe Street	B4
Fairpark Road	E2-E3
Ferndale Road	A1
Fords Road	C1
Fore Street	B3-C3
Friars Walk	D2
Gladstone Road	F4
Haldon Road	B4-B5
Harefield Close	A7
Haven Road	B1-C1-C2-C1-D1
Heavitree Road	E4-F4
Hele Road	B6-B5
Highcross Road	D7
Higher Kings Avenue	E8-F8
High Street	C4-D4-D5
Hill Close	E8
Hillsborough Avenue	D6-E6
Hillside Avenue	D6
Holloway Street	D2
Hoopern Street	C6-C7
Howell Road	A6-B6-C6-D6-D5
Iddesleigh Road	F7
Iris Avenue	B1-C1
Iron Bridge	B4-C4
Isca Road	C1
Jesmond Road	F6-F5-F6
Kilbarran Rise	A7-A8
King Street	C3
King William Street	D5-E5-E6
Larkbeare Road	D1-D2
Leighdene Close	F1
Longbrook Street	D5-D6
Longbrook Terrace	D5
Looe Road	A5-A6
Lower Kings Avenue	E8-F8
Lower St Germans Road	D7
Lucas Avenue	F7
Lucky Lane	D2
Lyndhurst Road	F2
Magdalen Road	E3-F3
Magdalen Street	D3-E3
Mansfield Road	F7
Marlborough Road	F2-F3
Maryfield Avenue	E8
Matford Avenue	F2-F1-F2
Matford Lane	E1-F1-F2
Matford Road	F1-F2
May Street	F7-F6
Mount Pleasant Road	F8-F7
New Bridge Street—	B2-B3
New North Road	A8-A7-B7-B6-B5-C5-C6-C5-D5
North Bridge	B2
Northernhay Street	C4-C5
North Street	C4
Norwood Avenue	E1
Okehampton Road	A3-A2-B2
Old Tiverton Road	E6-F6-F7-F8
Old Vicarage Road	A1
Oxford Road	E6
Oxford Street	B1-B2
Paris Street	D5-D4-E4
Parr Street	F5
Paul Street	C4
Pennsylvania Close	E8
Pennsylvania Road	D6-D7-E7-E8
Perry Road	B7
Portland Street	F5
Powderham Crescent	D7-E7
Powderham Road	A1
Preston Street	C3
Prince of Wales Road	B7-C7-C8-D8-D7
Princes Street North	B1
Prospect Park	E7-F7
Prospect Place	A1
Queens Road	B1
Queen Street	B5-C5-C4
Radford Road	D2 E2
Raleigh Road	F3
Regent Street	A1
Rennes Drive	C8
Richmond Road	B5
Roberts Road	D2-E2
Rosebank Crescent	E8
Rosebarn Lane	F8
Rosebery Road	F6-F7
St David's Hill	A6-B6-B5-B4
St Germans Road	D8-E8
St James Road	E6
St Leonards Avenue	D1-E1
St Leonards Road	E2-E3
Salisbury Road	F7-F6
School Road	A1
Shaftesbury Road	A1
Sidwell Street	D5-E5-E6
South Bridge	B2
Southernhay East	D3-D4
Southernhay West	D3-D4
South Street	D3
South View Terrace	E7
Spicer Road	E3-E4-F4
Springfield Road	E8-E7
Station Road	A7
Stocker Road	B8-C8
Stoke Hill	F8
Streatham Drive	B7-B8
Streatham Rise	A7-B7
Summerland Street	E5
Sydney Road	A1-B1
Sylvan Road	F8
Taddiforde Court	A7
Taddiforde Road	A6-A7
Temple Road	D2-D3
The Quay	C2-D2
The Queen's Drive	B8
Thornton Hill	D7-D6
Topsham Road	E2-E1-F1
Toronto Road	F6
Tudor Street	B3
Union Road	E7-E8-F8
Union Street	A1-B1
Velwell Road	B6-C6
Victoria Park Road	F2
Victoria Street	E7
Water Lane	C1
Waverley Avenue	C6
Way Avenue	C2
Weirfield Road	D1-E1
Well Street	E6
West Avenue	D7
Western Road	A3
Western Way	E3-E4-E5, C3
West Grove Road	E2
Willeys Avenue	B1-C1
Williams Avenue	B1-C1
Wonford Road	E3-E2-F2
York Road	D6-E6-E5

Exmouth

Albion Hill	B3-C3
Albion Street	B2-B3
Alexandra Terrace	B1-B2
Ashleigh Road	C4
Bath Road	B1-B2
Beacon Place	B2
Belle View Road	A4
Bicton Street	B2-C2
Camperdown Terrace	A1
Carter Avenue	A4
Carlton Hill	C1-C2
Church Road	A3-B3
Church Street	B2
Claremont Grove	C3
Clarence Road	B3
Douglas Avenue	C1-C2
Egremont Road	B3
Elm Road	C3
Esplanade	A1-B1-C1
Exeter Road	B2-B3-B4-A4
Fairfield Road	C2
Fore Street	B2-C2
Gipsy Lane	A4-B4
Green Hill Avenue	C3-C4
Gussiford Road	C2
Halsdon Avenue	A4
Hartley Road	C2
Hartopp Road	A3-B3
Halsdon Road	A3
High Street	B2
Imperial Road	B2-A2-B2-B1
Long Causeway	C3
Louisa Place	B1-C1
Louisa Terrace	B1-C1
Lyndhurst Road	A4-B4
Madeira Villas	B3-B4
Marpool Hill	B4-B3-C3-C4
Montpellier Road	B3-B2-C2
Moreton Road	A1-B1
Mudbank Lane	A4
New North Road	B3
North Street	B3
Park Road	B4
Phear Avenue	C3-C4
Portland Avenue	C2
Queens Drive	C1
Raddenstile Lane	C2
Raleigh Road	B2-C2
Rolle Road	B2-C2
Rolle Street	B2
Rolle Villas	B1-B2
Roseberry Road	A3-B3
Ryll Grove	B3-C3
St Andrews Road	A1-B1-B2
Salisbury Road	A3-B3
Salterton Road	C2-C3
The Beacon	B1-B2
The Parade	B2
The Strand	B2
The Royal Avenue	A2
Trefusis Terrace	C1
Victoria Road	A1-A2-B2
Windsor Square	B3
Withycombe Road	B3-B4
Withycombe Village Road	B4
Woodville Road	A3-A4-B4

93

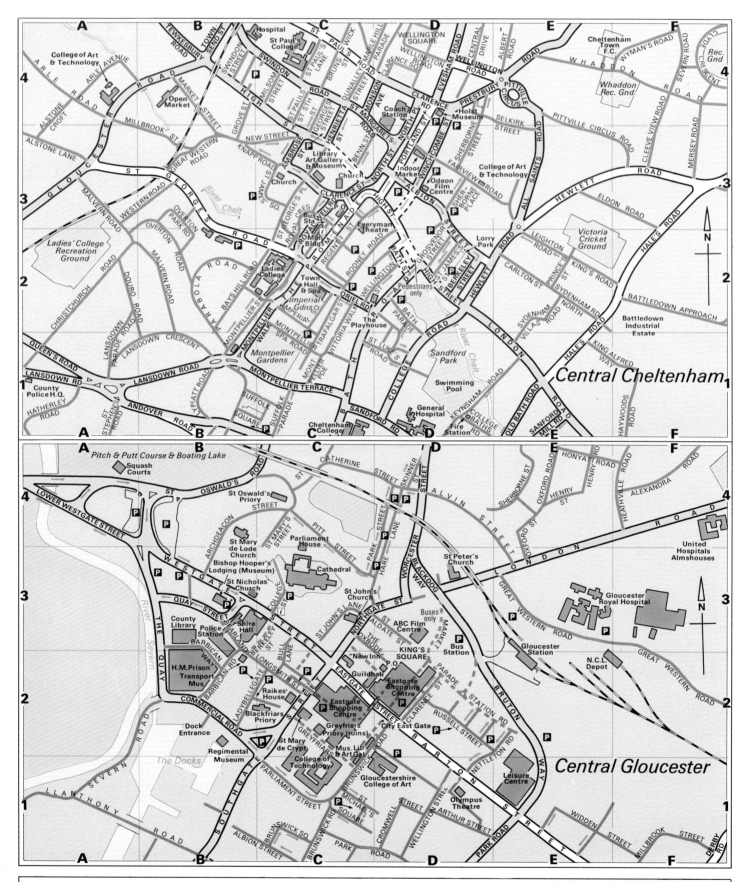

Gloucester

Gloucester's chief asset is its beautiful Norman cathedral. Originally an abbey, the building did not become a cathedral until the reign of Henry VIII and the lovely cloisters enclosing a delightful garden epitomise the tranquil beauty of medieval monastic architecture. The city's four main thoroughfares still follow the cruciform pattern of the original Roman roads built when *Glevum* guarded the

lowest Severn crossing. Since those days Gloucester has been an important inland port and today it is one of the country's major commercial and engineering centres.

Tewkesbury Black-and-white timbered buildings and ancient pubs with crooked roofs and curious names, such as *The Ancient Grudge*, lean haphazardly against each other in Tewkesbury's narrow streets. Rising above them all is the vast and beautiful abbey church, saved from destruction

in the Dissolution of the Monastries by the townsfolk who bought it from Henry VIII.

Cheltenham Elegant Regency architecture arranged in squares, avenues and crescents is Cheltenham's hallmark. The whole town was purpose-built around the medicinal springs discovered in the 18th century, and, under Royal patronage, it became one of the country's most fashionable spas. The composer Gustav Holst was born here and his home is now a museum.

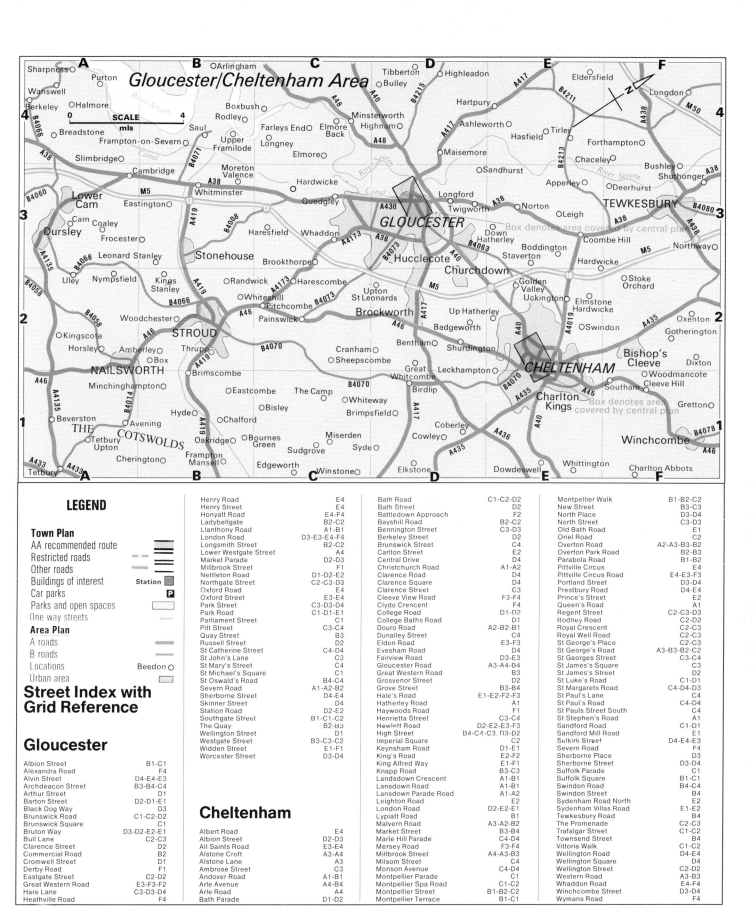

Gloucester/Cheltenham Area

LEGEND

Town Plan
- AA recommended route
- Restricted roads
- Other roads
- Buildings of interest — Station
- Car parks — P
- Parks and open spaces
- One way streets

Area Plan
- A roads
- B roads
- Locations — Beedon ○
- Urban area

Street Index with Grid Reference

Gloucester

Albion Street	B1-C1
Alexandra Road	F4
Alvin Street	D4-E4-E3
Archdeacon Street	B3-B4-C4
Arthur Street	D1
Barton Street	D2-D1-E1
Black Dog Way	D3
Brunswick Road	C1-C2-D2
Brunswick Square	C1
Bruton Way	D3-D2-E2-E1
Bull Lane	C2-C3
Clarence Street	D2
Commercial Road	B2
Cromwell Street	D1
Derby Road	F1
Eastgate Street	C2-D2
Great Western Road	E3-F3-F2
Hare Lane	C3-D3-D4
Heathville Road	F4
Henry Road	E4
Henry Street	E4
Honyatt Road	E4-F4
Ladybellgate	B2-C2
Llanthony Road	A1-B1
London Road	D3-E3-E4-F4
Longsmith Street	B2-C2
Lower Westgate Street	A4
Market Parade	D2-D3
Millbrook Street	F1
Nettleton Road	D1-D2-E2
Northgate Street	C2-C3-D3
Oxford Road	E4
Oxford Street	E3-E4
Park Street	C3-D3-D4
Park Road	C1-D1-E1
Parliament Street	C1
Pitt Street	C3-C4
Quay Street	B3
Russell Street	D2
St Catherine Street	C4-D4
St John's Lane	C3
St Mary's Street	C4
St Michael's Square	C1
St Oswald's Road	B4-C4
Severn Road	A1-A2-B2
Sherborne Street	D4-E4
Skinner Street	D4
Southgate Street	B1-C1-C2
Station Road	D2-E2
The Quay	B2-B3
Wellington Street	D1
Westgate Street	B3-C3-C2
Widden Street	E1-F1
Worcester Street	D3-D4

Cheltenham

Albert Road	E4
Albion Street	D2-D3
All Saints Road	E3-E4
Alstone Croft	A3-A4
Alstone Lane	A3
Ambrose Street	C3
Andover Road	A1-B1
Arle Avenue	A4-B4
Arle Road	A4
Bath Parade	D1-D2
Bath Road	C1-C2-D2
Bath Street	D2
Battledown Approach	F2
Bayshill Road	B2-C2
Bennington Street	C3-D3
Berkeley Street	D4
Brunswick Street	C4
Carlton Street	E2
Central Drive	D4
Christchurch Road	A1-A2
Clarence Road	D4
Clarence Square	D4
Clarence Street	C3
Cleeve View Road	F3-F4
Clyde Crescent	F4
College Road	D1-D2
College Baths Road	D1
Douro Road	A2-B2-B1
Dunalley Street	C4
Eldon Road	E3-F3
Evesham Road	D4
Fairview Road	D3-E3
Gloucester Road	A3-A4-B4
Great Western Road	B3
Grosvenor Street	D2
Grove Street	B3-B4
Hale's Road	E1-E2-F2-F3
Hatherley Road	A1
Haywoods Road	F1
Henrietta Street	C3-C4
Hewlett Road	D2-E2-E3-F3
High Street	B4-C4-C3, D3-D2
Imperial Square	C2
Keynsham Road	D1-E1
King's Road	E2-F2
King Alfred Way	E1-F1
Knapp Road	B3-C3
Landsdown Crescent	A1-B1
Lansdown Road	A1-B1
Lansdown Parade Road	A1-A2
Leighton Road	E2
London Road	D2-E2-E1
Lypiatt Road	B1
Malvern Road	A3-A2-B2
Market Street	B3-B4
Marle Hill Parade	C4-D4
Mersey Road	F3-F4
Millbrook Street	A4-A3-B3
Milsom Street	C4
Monson Avenue	C4-D4
Montpellier Parade	C1
Montpellier Spa Road	C1-C2
Montpellier Street	B1-B2-C2
Montpellier Terrace	B1-C1
Montpellier Walk	B1-B2-C2
New Street	B3-C3
North Place	D3-D4
North Street	C3-D3
Old Bath Road	E1
Oriel Road	C2
Overton Road	A2-A3-B3-B2
Overton Park Road	B2-B3
Parabola Road	B1-B2
Pittville Circus	E4
Pittville Circus Road	E4-E3-F3
Portland Street	D3-D4
Prestbury Road	D4-E4
Prince's Street	E2
Queen's Road	A1
Regent Street	C2-C3-D3
Rodney Road	C2-D2
Royal Crescent	C2-C3
Royal Well Road	C2-C3
St George's Place	C2-C3
St George's Road	A3-B3-B2-C2
St Georges Street	C3-C4
St James's Square	C3
St James's Street	D2
St Luke's Road	C1-D1
St Margarets Road	C4-D4-D3
St Paul's Lane	C4
St Paul's Road	C4-D4
St Pauls Street South	C4
St Stephen's Road	A1
Sandford Road	C1-D1
Sandford Mill Road	E1
Selkirk Street	D4-E4-E3
Severn Road	F4
Sherborne Place	D3
Sherborne Street	D3-D4
Suffolk Parade	C1
Suffolk Square	B1-C1
Swindon Road	B4-C4
Swindon Street	B4
Sydenham Road North	E2
Sydenham Villas Road	E1-E2
Tewkesbury Road	B4
The Promenade	C2-C3
Trafalgar Street	C1-C2
Townsend Street	B4
Vittoria Walk	C1-C2
Wellington Road	D4-E4
Wellington Square	D4
Wellington Street	C2-D2
Western Road	A3-B3
Whaddon Road	E4-F4
Winchcombe Street	D3-D4
Wymans Road	F4

GLOUCESTER
Gloucester Cathedral, one of the Britain's finest buildings, is a splendid example of Norman architecture. The beautiful stained-glass east window is a memorial to local men who fought at Crécy in 1346.

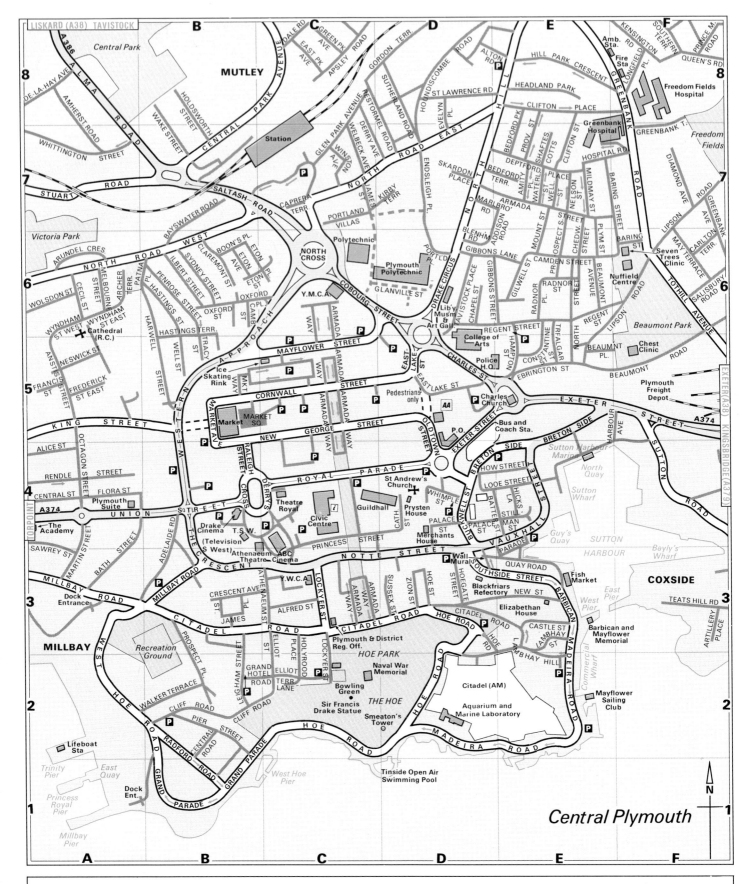

Plymouth

Ships, sailors and the sea permeate every aspect of Plymouth's life and history. Its superb natural harbour – Plymouth Sound – has ensured its importance as a port, yachting centre and naval base (latterly at Devonport) over many centuries. Sir Francis Drake is undoubtedly the city's most famous sailor. His statue stands on the Hoe – where he really did play bowls before tackling the Spanish Armada. Also on the Hoe are Smeaton's Tower, which once formed the upper part of the third Eddystone Lighthouse, and the impressive Royal Naval War Memorial. Just east of the Hoe is the Royal Citadel, an imposing fortress built in 1666 by order of Charles II. North is Sutton Harbour, perhaps the most atmospheric part of Plymouth. Here fishing boats bob up and down in a harbour whose quays are lined with attractive old houses, inns and warehouses. One of the memorials on Mayflower Quay just outside the harbour commemorates the sailing of the *Mayflower* from here in 1620. Plymouth's shopping centre is one of the finest of its kind, and was built after the old centre was badly damaged in World War II. Nearby is the 200ft-high tower of the impressive modern Civic Centre. Some buildings escaped destruction, including the Elizabethan House and the 500-year-old Prysten House. Next door is St Andrew's Church, with stained glass by John Piper.

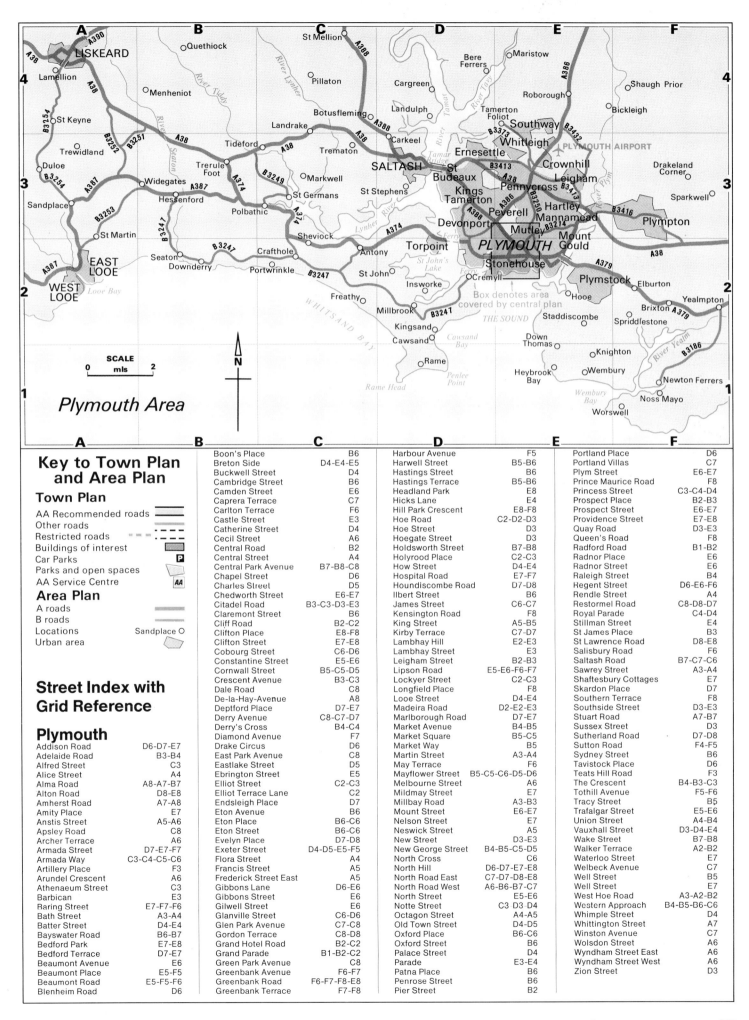

Key to Town Plan and Area Plan

Town Plan

AA Recommended roads ——————
Other roads — — — —
Restricted roads ·······
Buildings of interest ▨
Car Parks Ⓟ
Parks and open spaces ▱
AA Service Centre AA

Area Plan

A roads ══════
B roads ══════
Locations Sandplace ○
Urban area ▱

Street Index with Grid Reference

Plymouth

Addison Road	D6-D7-E7
Adelaide Road	B3-B4
Alfred Street	C3
Alice Street	A4
Alma Road	A8-A7-B7
Alton Road	D8-E8
Amherst Road	A7-A8
Amity Place	E7
Anstis Street	A5-A6
Apsley Road	C8
Archer Terrace	A6
Armada Street	D7-E7-F7
Armada Way	C3-C4-C5-C6
Artillery Place	F3
Arundel Crescent	A6
Athenaeum Street	C3
Barbican	E3
Baring Street	E7-F7-F6
Bath Street	A3-A4
Batter Street	D4-E4
Bayswater Road	B6-B7
Bedford Park	E7-E8
Bedford Terrace	D7-E7
Beaumont Avenue	E6
Beaumont Place	E5-F5
Beaumont Road	E5-F5-F6
Blenheim Road	D6

Boon's Place	B6
Breton Side	D4-E4-E5
Buckwell Street	D4
Cambridge Street	B6
Camden Street	E6
Caprera Terrace	C7
Carlton Terrace	F6
Castle Street	E3
Catherine Street	D4
Cecil Street	A6
Central Road	B2
Central Street	A4
Central Park Avenue	B7-B8-C8
Chapel Street	D6
Charles Street	D5
Chedworth Street	E6-E7
Citadel Road	B3-C3-D3-E3
Claremont Street	B6
Cliff Road	B2-C2
Clifton Place	E8-F8
Clifton Street	E7-E8
Cobourg Street	C6-D6
Constantine Street	E5-E6
Cornwall Street	B5-C5-D5
Crescent Avenue	B3-C3
Dale Road	C8
De-la-Hay-Avenue	A8
Deptford Place	D7-E7
Derry Avenue	C8-C7-D7
Derry's Cross	B4-C4
Diamond Avenue	F7
Drake Circus	D6
East Park Avenue	C8
Eastlake Street	D5
Ebrington Street	E5
Elliot Street	C2-C3
Elliot Terrace Lane	C2
Endsleigh Place	D7
Eton Avenue	B6
Eton Place	B6-C6
Eton Street	B6-C6
Evelyn Place	D7-D8
Exeter Street	D4-D5-E5-F5
Flora Street	A4
Francis Street	A5
Frederick Street East	A5
Gibbons Lane	D6-E6
Gibbons Street	E6
Gilwell Street	E6
Glanville Street	C6-D6
Glen Park Avenue	C7-C8
Gordon Terrace	C8-D8
Grand Hotel Road	B2-C2
Grand Parade	B1-B2-C2
Green Park Avenue	C8
Greenbank Avenue	F6-F7
Greenbank Road	F6-F7-F8-E8
Greenbank Terrace	F7-F8

Harbour Avenue	F5
Harwell Street	B5-B6
Hastings Street	B6
Hastings Terrace	B5-B6
Headland Park	E8
Hicks Lane	E4
Hill Park Crescent	E8-F8
Hoe Road	C2-D2-D3
Hoe Street	D3
Hoegate Street	D3
Holdsworth Street	B7-B8
Holyrood Place	C2-C3
How Street	D4-E4
Hospital Road	E7-F7
Houndiscombe Road	D7-D8
Ilbert Street	B6
James Street	C6-C7
Kensington Road	F8
King Street	A5-B5
Kirby Terrace	C7-D7
Lambhay Hill	E2-E3
Lambhay Street	E3
Leigham Street	B2-B3
Lipson Road	E5-E6-F6-F7
Lockyer Street	C2-C3
Looe Street	D4-E4
Madeira Road	D2-E2-E3
Marlborough Road	D7-E7
Market Avenue	B4-B5
Market Square	B5-C5
Market Way	B5
Martin Street	A3-A4
May Terrace	F6
Mayflower Street	B5-C5-C6-D5-D6
Melbourne Street	A6
Mildmay Street	E7
Millbay Road	A3-B3
Mount Street	E6-E7
Nelson Street	E7
Neswick Street	A5
New Street	D3-E3
New George Street	B4-B5-C5-D5
North Cross	C6
North Hill	D6-D7-E7-E8
North Road East	C7-D7-D8-E8
North Road West	A6-B6-B7-C7
North Street	E5-E6
Notte Street	C3-D3-D4
Octagon Street	A4-A5
Old Town Street	D4-D5
Oxford Place	B6-C6
Oxford Street	B6
Palace Street	D4
Parade	E3-E4
Patna Place	B6
Penrose Street	B6
Pier Street	B2

Portland Place	D6
Portland Villas	C7
Plym Street	E6-E7
Prince Maurice Road	F8
Princess Street	C3-C4-D4
Prospect Place	B2-B3
Prospect Street	E6-E7
Providence Street	E7-E8
Quay Road	D3-E3
Queen's Road	F8
Radford Road	B1-B2
Radnor Place	E6
Radnor Street	E6
Raleigh Street	B4
Regent Street	D6-E6-F6
Rendle Street	A4
Restormel Road	C8-D8-D7
Royal Parade	C4-D4
Stillman Street	E4
St James Place	B3
St Lawrence Road	D8-E8
Salisbury Road	F6
Saltash Road	B7-C7-C6
Sawrey Street	A3-A4
Shaftesbury Cottages	E7
Skardon Place	D7
Southern Terrace	F8
Southside Street	D3-E3
Stuart Road	A7-B7
Sussex Street	D3
Sutherland Road	D7-D8
Sutton Road	F4-F5
Sydney Street	B6
Tavistock Place	D6
Teats Hill Road	F3
The Crescent	B4-B3-C3
Tothill Avenue	F5-F6
Tracy Street	B5
Trafalgar Street	E5-E6
Union Street	A4-B4
Vauxhall Street	D3-D4-E4
Wake Street	B7-B8
Walker Terrace	A2-B2
Waterloo Street	E7
Welbeck Avenue	C7
Well Street	B5
Well Street	E7
West Hoe Road	A3-A2-B2
Western Approach	B4-B5-B6-C6
Whimple Street	D4
Whittington Street	A7
Winston Avenue	C7
Wolsdon Street	A6
Wyndham Street East	A6
Wyndham Street West	A6
Zion Street	D3

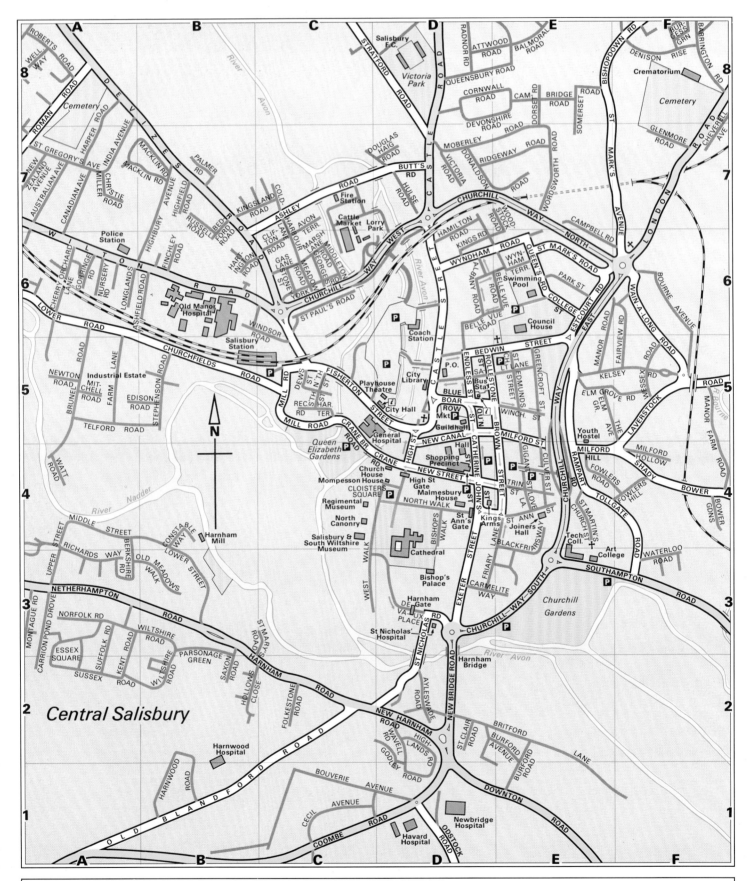

Salisbury

Its attractive site where the waters of the Avon and Nadder meet, its beautiful cathedral and its unspoilt centre put Salisbury among England's finest cities. In 1220 the people of the original settlement at Old Sarum, two miles to the north, moved down to the plain and laid the first stone of the cathedral. Within 38 years its was completed and the result is a superb example of Early English architecture.

The cloisters are the largest in England and the spire the tallest in Britain. All the houses within the Cathedral Close were built for cathedral functionaries, and although many have Georgian façades, most date back to the 13th century. Mompesson House is one of the handsome mansions here and as it belongs to the National Trust, its equally fine interior can be seen. Another building houses the Museum of the Duke of Edinburgh's Royal Regiment. At one time, relations between the clergy and the citizens of Salisbury were not always harmonious, so the former built a protective wall around the Close.

The streets of the modern city follow the medieval grid pattern of squares, or 'chequers', and the tightly-packed houses provide a very pleasing townscape. Salisbury was granted its first charter in 1227 and flourished as a market and wool centre; there is still a twice-weekly market in the spacious square.

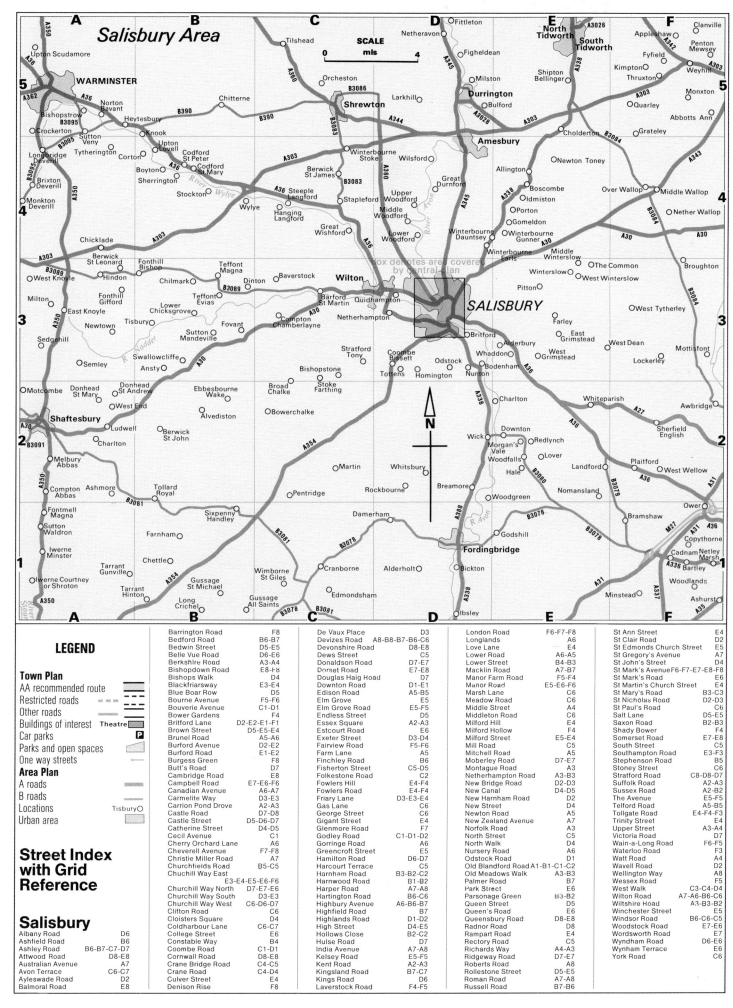

Salisbury Area

SCALE
mls
0   4

Box denotes area covered by central plan

N

LEGEND

Town Plan
AA recommended route
Restricted roads
Other roads
Buildings of interest — Theatre
Car parks — P
Parks and open spaces
One way streets

Area Plan
A roads
B roads
Locations — Tisbury○
Urban area

Street Index with Grid Reference

Salisbury

Albany Road	D6
Ashfield Road	B6
Ashley Road	B6-B7-C7-D7
Attwood Road	D8-E8
Australian Avenue	A7
Avon Terrace	C6-C7
Ayleswade Road	D2
Balmoral Road	E8
Barrington Road	F8
Bedford Road	B6-B7
Bedwin Street	D5-E5
Belle Vue Road	D6-E6
Berkshire Road	A3-A4
Bishopdown Road	E8-F8
Bishops Walk	D4
Blackfriarsway	E3-E4
Blue Boar Row	D5
Bourne Avenue	F5-F6
Bouverie Avenue	C1-D1
Bower Gardens	F4
Britford Lane	D2-E2-E1-F1
Brown Street	D5-E5-E4
Brunel Road	A5-A6
Burford Avenue	D2-E2
Burford Road	E1-E2
Burgess Green	F8
Butt's Road	D7
Cambridge Road	E8
Campbell Road	E7-E6-F6
Canadian Avenue	A6-A7
Carmelite Way	D3-E3
Carrion Pond Drove	A2-A3
Castle Road	D7-D8
Castle Street	D5-D6-D7
Catherine Street	D4-D5
Cecil Avenue	C1
Cherry Orchard Lane	A6
Cheverell Avenue	F7-F8
Christie Miller Road	A7
Churchfields Road	B5-C5
Chuchill Way East	E3-E4-E5-E6-F6
Churchill Way North	D7-E7-E6
Churchill Way South	D3-E3
Churchill Way West	C6-D6-D7
Clifton Road	C6
Cloisters Square	D4
Coldharbour Lane	C6-C7
College Street	E6
Constable Way	B4
Coombe Road	C1-D1
Cornwall Road	D8-E8
Crane Bridge Road	C4-C5
Crane Road	C4-D4
Culver Street	E4
Denison Rise	F8
De Vaux Place	D3
Devizes Road	A8-B8-B7-B6-C6
Devonshire Road	D8-E8
Dews Street	C5
Donaldson Road	D7-E7
Dorset Road	E7-E8
Douglas Haig Road	D7
Downton Road	D1-E1
Edison Road	A5-B5
Elm Grove	E5
Elm Grove Road	E5-F5
Endless Street	D5
Essex Square	A2-A3
Estcourt Road	E6
Exeter Street	D3-D4
Fairview Road	F5-F6
Farm Lane	A5
Finchley Road	B6
Fisherton Street	C5-D5
Folkestone Road	C2
Fowlers Hill	E4-F4
Fowlers Road	E4-F4
Friary Lane	D3-E3-E4
Gas Lane	C6
George Street	C6
Gigant Street	E4
Glenmore Road	F7
Godley Road	C1-D1-D2
Gorringe Road	A6
Greencroft Street	E5
Hamilton Road	D6-D7
Harcourt Terrace	C5
Harnham Road	B3-B2-C2
Harnwood Road	B1-B2
Harper Road	A7-A8
Hartington Road	B6-C6
Highbury Avenue	A6-B6-B7
Highfield Road	B7
Highlands Road	D1-D2
High Street	D4-E5
Hollows Close	B2-C2
Hulse Road	D7
India Avenue	A7-A8
Kelsey Road	E5-F5
Kent Road	A2-A3
Kingsland Road	B7-C7
Kings Road	D6
Laverstock Road	F4-F5
London Road	F6-F7-F8
Longlands	A6
Love Lane	E4
Lower Road	A6-A5
Lower Street	B4-B3
Macklin Road	A7-B7
Manor Farm Road	F5-F4
Manor Road	E5-E6-F6
Marsh Lane	C6
Meadow Road	C6
Middle Street	A4
Middleton Road	C6
Milford Hill	E4
Milford Hollow	F4
Milford Street	E5-E4
Mill Road	C5
Mitchell Road	C6
Moberley Road	D7-E7
Montague Road	A3
Netherhampton Road	A3-B3
New Bridge Road	D2-D3
New Canal	D4-D5
New Harnham Road	D2
New Street	D4
Newton Road	A5
New Zealand Avenue	A7
Norfolk Road	A3
North Street	C5
North Walk	D4
Nursery Road	A6
Odstock Road	D1
Old Blandford Road	A1-B1-C1-C2
Old Meadows Walk	A3-B3
Palmer Road	B7
Park Street	E6
Parsonage Green	B3-B2
Queen Street	D5
Queen's Road	E6
Queensbury Road	D8-E8
Radnor Road	D8
Rampart Road	E4
Rectory Road	C5
Richards Way	A4-A3
Ridgeway Road	D7-E7
Roberts Road	A8
Rollestone Street	D5-E5
Roman Road	A7-A8
Russell Road	B7-B6
St Ann Street	E4
St Clair Road	D2
St Edmonds Church Street	E5
St Gregory's Avenue	A7
St John's Street	D4
St Mark's Avenue	F6-F7-E7-E8-F8
St Mark's Road	E6
St Martin's Church Street	E4
St Mary's Road	B3-C3
St Nicholas Road	D2-D3
St Paul's Road	C6
Salt Lane	D5-E5
Saxon Road	B2-B3
Shady Bower	F4
Somerset Road	E7-E8
South Street	C5
Southampton Road	E3-F3
Stephenson Road	B5
Stoney Street	C6
Stratford Road	C8-D8-D7
Suffolk Road	A2-A3
Sussex Road	A2-B2
The Avenue	E5-F5
Telford Road	A5-B5
Tollgate Road	E4-F4-F3
Trinity Street	E4
Upper Street	A3-A4
Victoria Road	D7
Wain-a-Long Road	F6-F5
Waterloo Road	F3
Watt Road	A4
Wavell Road	D2
Wellington Way	A8
Wessex Road	F5
West Walk	C3-C4-D4
Wilton Road	A7-A6-B6-C6
Wiltshire Road	A3-B3-B2
Winchester Street	E5
Windsor Road	B6-C6-C5
Woodstock Road	E7-E6
Wordsworth Road	E7
Wyndham Road	D6-E6
Wynham Terrace	E6
York Road	C6

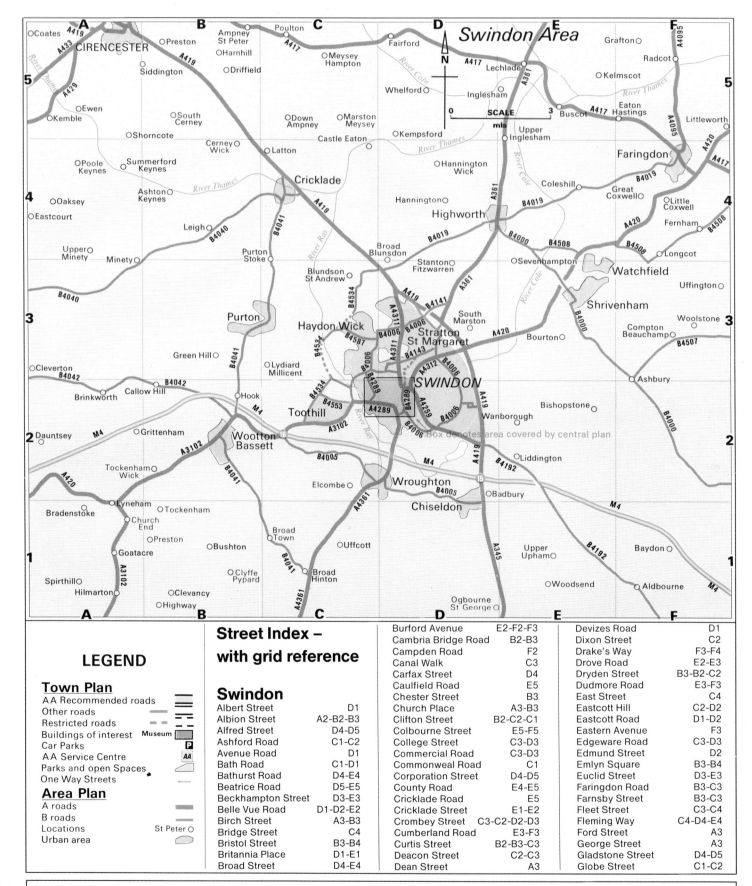

Swindon Area

SCALE
0 — 3
mls

Box denotes area covered by central plan

Swindon

Brunel's decision in 1841 to build the Great Western Railway's workshops here transformed Swindon from an agricultural village into a major industrial centre. The surviving buildings of the original railway village have been restored.

Regrettably the fortunes of the BR Engineering Ltd locomotive and other workshops (the heart of the Great Western system and renowned for

locomotives such as the King George V) have declined considerably and even face complete closure — but modern Swindon has seen a remarkable revival. Plans were made in the 1950s to reduce the town's dependence on one industry, and with the combination of development aid and improved road access via the M4, Swindon has seen the arrival of a wide range of manufacturing industries and a near doubling of its population, to 150,000. Aptly chosen for the relocation of

the British Rail's Western Region Headquarters from Paddington, the town now boasts a modern shopping complex, a regional theatre and the impressive Oasis Leisure Centre, while an illustrious past is recalled in the Great Western Railway Museum.

Outside Swindon are 19th-century Lydiard Mansion, standing in 150 acres of parkland, the leisure facilities of Coate Water, and a museum on naturalist and writer Richard Jeffries.

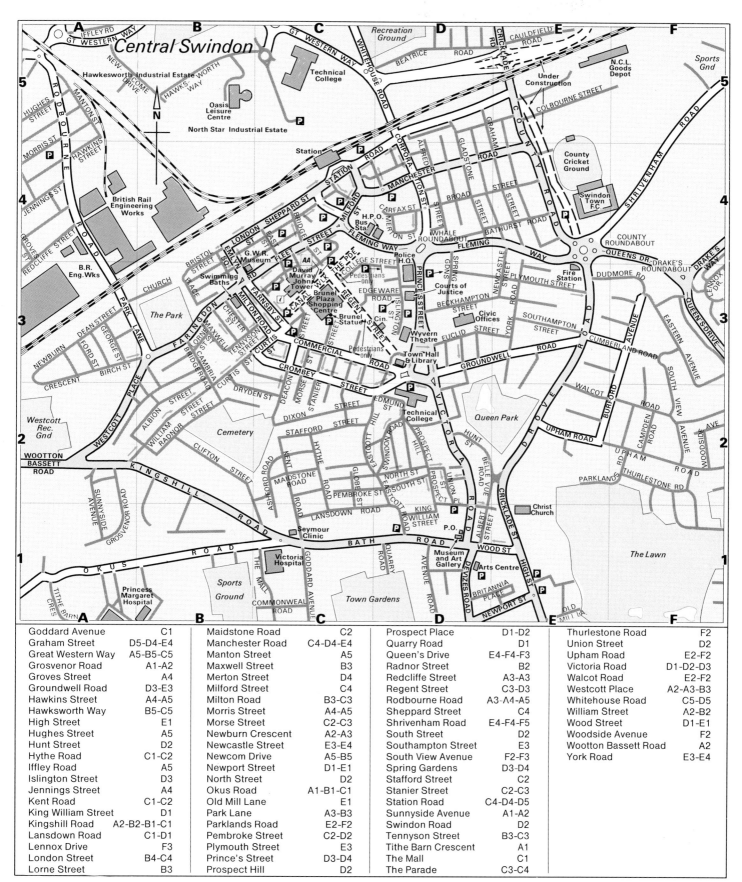

Central Swindon

Goddard Avenue	C1	Maidstone Road	C2	Prospect Place	D1-D2	Thurlestone Road	F2
Graham Street	D5-D4-E4	Manchester Road	C4-D4-E4	Quarry Road	D1	Union Street	D2
Great Western Way	A5-B5-C5	Manton Street	A5	Queen's Drive	E4-F4-F3	Upham Road	E2-F2
Grosvenor Road	A1-A2	Maxwell Street	B3	Radnor Street	B2	Victoria Road	D1-D2-D3
Groves Street	A4	Merton Street	D4	Redcliffe Street	A3-A3	Walcot Road	E2-F2
Groundwell Road	D3-E3	Milford Street	C4	Regent Street	C3-D3	Westcott Place	A2-A3-B3
Hawkins Street	A4-A5	Milton Road	B3-C3	Rodbourne Road	A3-A4-A5	Whitehouse Road	C5-D5
Hawksworth Way	B5-C5	Morris Street	A4-A5	Sheppard Street	C4	William Street	A2-B2
High Street	E1	Morse Street	C2-C3	Shrivenham Road	E4-F4-F5	Wood Street	D1-E1
Hughes Street	A5	Newburn Crescent	A2-A3	South Street	D2	Woodside Avenue	F2
Hunt Street	D2	Newcastle Street	E3-E4	Southampton Street	E3	Wootton Bassett Road	A2
Hythe Road	C1-C2	Newcom Drive	A5-B5	South View Avenue	F2-F3	York Road	E3-E4
Iffley Road	A5	Newport Street	D1-E1	Spring Gardens	D3-D4		
Islington Street	D3	North Street	D2	Stafford Street	C2		
Jennings Street	A4	Okus Road	A1-B1-C1	Stanier Street	C2-C3		
Kent Road	C1-C2	Old Mill Lane	E1	Station Road	C4-D4-D5		
King William Street	D1	Park Lane	A3-B3	Sunnyside Avenue	A1-A2		
Kingshill Road	A2-B2-B1-C1	Parklands Road	E2-F2	Swindon Road	D2		
Lansdown Road	C1-C2	Pembroke Street	C2-D2	Tennyson Street	B3-C3		
Lennox Drive	F3	Plymouth Street	E3	The Mall	C1		
London Street	B4-C4	Prince's Street	D3-D4	The Parade	C3-C4		
Lorne Street	B3	Prospect Hill	D2				

SWINDON
Making waves at the Oasis Leisure Centre 'free-shaped' pool — under the biggest glazed dome in Britain, the water drops away gradually from inches-deep for paddling to a portholed diving area, and is fringed with tropical shrubs.

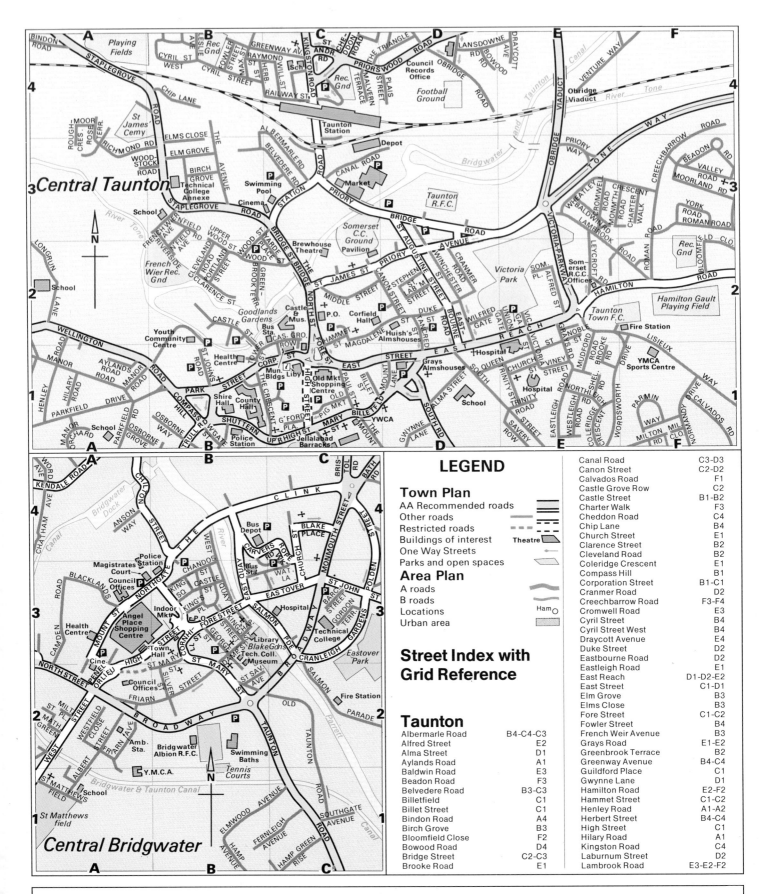

LEGEND

Town Plan

AA Recommended roads
Other roads
Restricted roads
Buildings of interest — Theatre
One Way Streets
Parks and open spaces

Area Plan

A roads
B roads
Locations — Ham○
Urban area

Street Index with Grid Reference

Taunton

Albermarle Road	B4-C4-C3
Alfred Street	E2
Alma Street	D1
Aylands Road	A1
Baldwin Road	E3
Beadon Road	F3
Belvedere Road	B3-C3
Billetfield	C1
Billet Street	C1
Bindon Road	A4
Birch Grove	B3
Bloomfield Close	F2
Bowood Road	D4
Bridge Street	C2-C3
Brooke Road	E1
Canal Road	C3-D3
Canon Street	C2-D2
Calvados Road	F1
Castle Grove Row	C2
Castle Street	B1-B2
Charter Walk	F3
Cheddon Road	C4
Chip Lane	B4
Church Street	E1
Clarence Street	B2
Cleveland Road	B2
Coleridge Crescent	E1
Compass Hill	B1
Corporation Street	B1-C1
Cranmer Road	D2
Creechbarrow Road	F3-F4
Cromwell Road	E3
Cyril Street	B4
Cyril Street West	B4
Draycott Avenue	E4
Duke Street	D2
Eastbourne Road	D2
Eastleigh Road	E1
East Reach	D1-D2-E2
East Street	C1-D1
Elm Grove	B3
Elms Close	B3
Fore Street	C1-C2
Fowler Street	B4
French Weir Avenue	B3
Grays Road	E1-E2
Greenbrook Terrace	B2
Greenway Avenue	B4-C4
Guildford Place	C1
Gwynne Lane	D1
Hamilton Road	E2-F2
Hammet Street	C1-C2
Henley Road	A1-A2
Herbert Street	B4-C4
High Street	C1
Hilary Road	A1
Kingston Road	C4
Laburnum Street	D2
Lambrook Road	E3-E2-F2

Taunton

The hub of Somerset, surrounded by the rolling, wooded Quantocks and the Blackdown Hills, Taunton lies on the River Tone in the fertile Vale of Taunton Dene. Famous for its thriving local cider industry, the town is also a lively commercial and agricultural centre whose livestock market rivals Exeter's as the most important in the West Country. In the past it was a major centre of the wool trade.

As befits a county town, Taunton is the headquarters of Somerset's entertaining and successful cricket team. It also offers National Hunt racing, has no fewer than three public schools and, somewhat improbably, the British Telecom Museum where antique telephone equipment is kept. There has been a castle in the town since Norman times: now it is home for the Somerset County and Military Museums.

Bridgwater, an industrial centre, was a busy port until Bristol overshadowed it. Twice a day a bore – a great tidal wave – surges up the River Parrett from Bridgwater Bay; the times are posted on the bridge in the town centre for those who want to see it.

In 1695 the rebel Duke of Monmouth is reputed to have surveyed the field before the Battle of Sedgemoor from the town's church tower. Dating from the 14th century, the Church of St Mary has some particularly fine Jacobean screenwork.

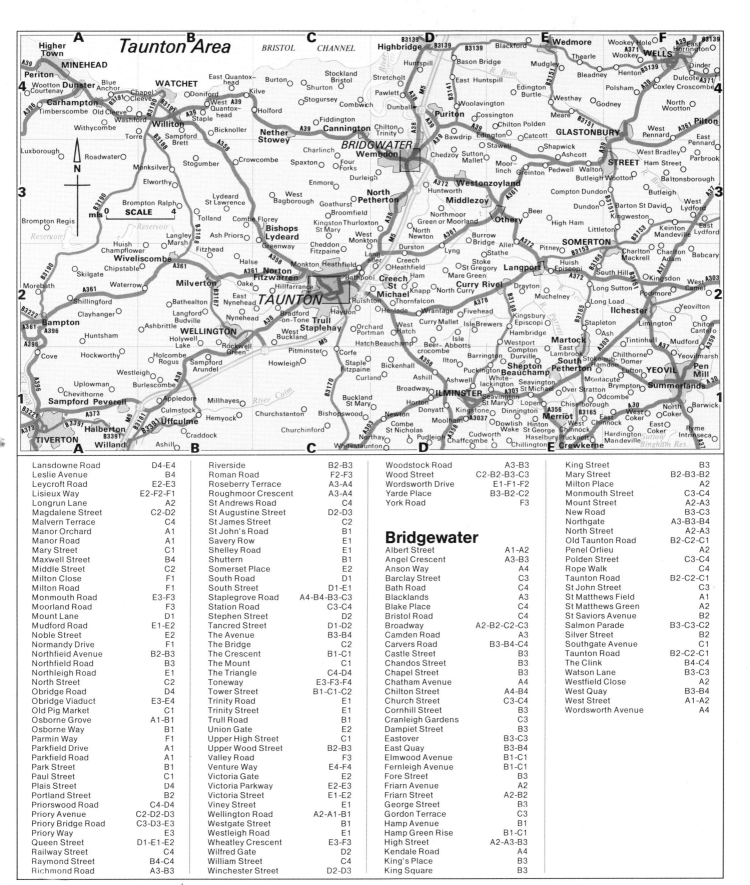

Taunton Area

TAUNTON
Taunton School, an attractive rambling building in Staplegrove Road, is one of the town's three public schools for boys. This is the largest of the three in terms of numbers of pupils and is inter-denominational.

103

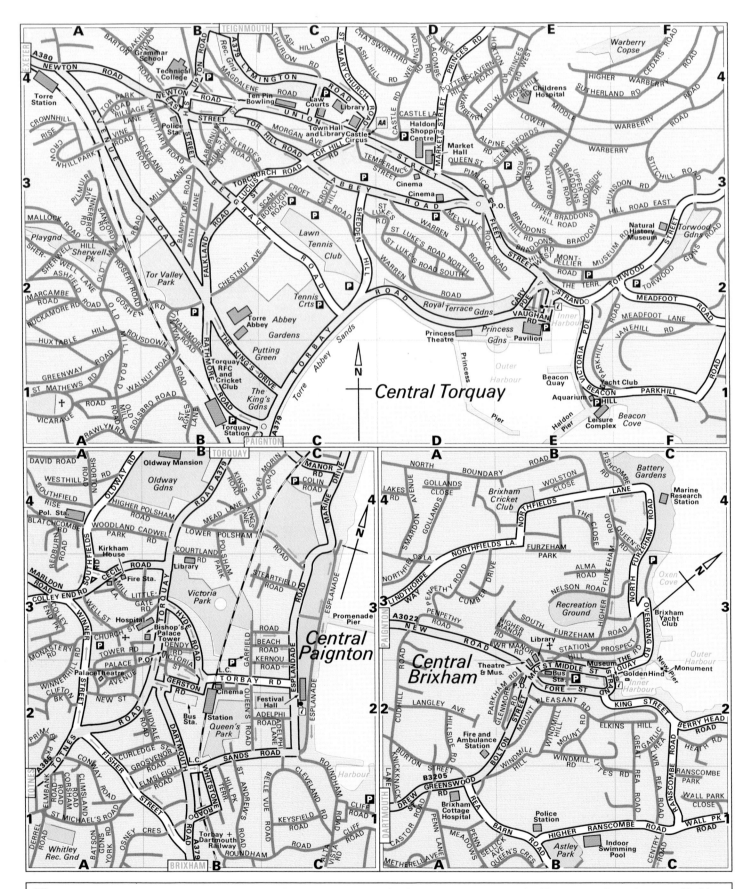

Torquay

With its sparkling houses, colourful gardens and sub-tropical plants set among the limestone crags of the steep hillside, Torquay has the air of a resort on the French Riviera – an impression strengthened by the superb views of sea and coast from Marine Drive, the 'corniche' road that sweeps around the rocky headland. Torquay is undoubtedly the queen of the Devon coast, a resort carefully planned in the early 19th century to cater for the wealthy and discriminating visitor. It had begun to be popular with naval officers' families during the Napoleonic wars when no one could travel to the continent, and this burgeoning popularity was exploited by the Palk family through two generations. Sir Robert Palk inherited an estate which included Torquay, and he and his descendants set about transforming it into the town of today.

Paignton, set on the huge sweep of Tor Bay south of Torquay, continues the range of holiday amenities and has good, sandy beaches.

Brixham, which lies a little further down the coast, falls into two parts – the old village on the hill slopes – and the fishing village half a mile below. Less commercialised than its neighbours, it is popular with holidaymakers.

Newton Abbot lies on the River Teign. It is a busy market town and has been an important railway junction since the mid 19th century.

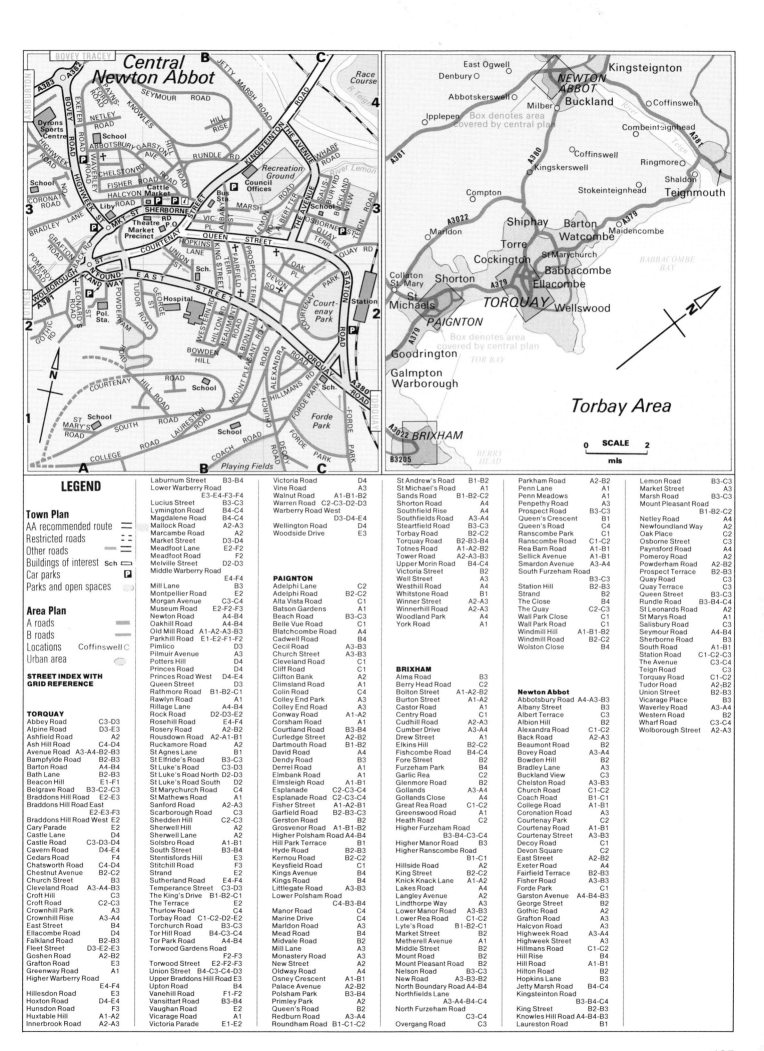

LEGEND

Town Plan

AA recommended route
Restricted roads
Other roads
Buildings of interest   Sch
Car parks   P
Parks and open spaces

Area Plan

A roads
B roads
Locations   Coffinswell ○
Urban area

STREET INDEX WITH GRID REFERENCE

TORQUAY

Abbey Road	C3-D3
Alpine Road	D3-E3
Ashfield Road	A2
Ash Hill Road	C4-D4
Avenue Road	A3-A4-B2-B3
Bampfylde Road	B2-B3
Barton Road	A4-B4
Bath Lane	B2-B3
Beacon Hill	E1-F1
Belgrave Road	B3-C2-C3
Braddons Hill Road	E2-E3
Braddons Hill Road East	E2-E3-F3
Braddons Hill Road West	E2
Cary Parade	E2
Castle Lane	D4
Castle Road	C3-D3-D4
Cavern Road	D4-E4
Cedars Road	F4
Chatsworth Road	C4-D4
Chestnut Avenue	B2-C2
Church Street	B3
Cleveland Road	A3-A4-B3
Croft Hill	C3
Croft Road	C2-C3
Crownhill Park	A3
Crownhill Rise	A3-A4
East Street	B4
Ellacombe Road	D4
Falkland Road	B2-B3
Fleet Street	D3-E2-E3
Goshen Road	A2-B2
Grafton Road	E3
Greenway Road	A1
Higher Warberry Road	E4-F4
Hillesdon Road	E3
Hoxton Road	D4-E4
Hunsdon Road	F3
Huxtable Hill	A1-A2
Innerbrook Road	A2-A3
Laburnum Street	B3-B4
Lower Warberry Road	E3-E4-F3-F4
Lucius Street	B3-C3
Lymington Road	B4-C4
Magdalene Road	B4-C4
Mallock Road	A2-A3
Marcambe Road	A2
Market Street	D3-D4
Meadfoot Lane	E2-F2
Meadfoot Road	F2
Melville Street	D2-D3
Middle Warberry Road	E4-F4
Mill Lane	B3
Montpellier Road	E2
Morgan Avenue	C3-C4
Museum Road	E2-F2-F3
Newton Road	A4-B4
Oakhill Road	A4-B4
Old Mill Road	A1-A2-A3-B3
Parkhill Road	E1-E2-F1-F2
Pimlico	D3
Pilmuir Avenue	A3
Potters Hill	D4
Princes Road	D4
Princes Road West	D4-E4
Queen Street	D3
Rathmore Road	B1-B2-C1
Rawlyn Road	A1
Rillage Lane	A1
Rock Road	D2-D3-E2
Rosehill Road	E4-F4
Rosery Road	A2-B2
Rousdown Road	A2-A1-B1
Ruckamore Road	A2
St Agnes Lane	B1
St Elfride's Road	B3-C3
St Luke's Road	C3-D3
St Luke's Road North	D2-D3
St Luke's Road South	D2
St Marychurch Road	E2
St Mathews Road	A1
Sanford Road	A2-A3
Scarborough Road	C3
Shedden Hill	C2-C3
Sherwell Hill	A2
Sherwell Lane	A2
Solsbro Road	A1-B1
South Street	B3-B4
Stentisfords Hill	E3
Stitchill Road	F3
Strand	E2
Sutherland Road	E4-F4
Temperance Street	C3-D3
The King's Drive	B1-B2-C1
The Terrace	E2
Thurlow Road	C4
Torbay Road	C1-C2-D2-E2
Torchurch Road	B3-C3
Tor Hill Road	B4-C3-C4
Tor Park Road	A4-B4
Torwood Gardens Road	F2-F3
Torwood Street	E2-F2-F3
Union Street	B4-C3-C4-D3
Upper Braddons Hill Road	E3
Upton Road	B4
Vanehill Road	F1-F2
Vansittart Road	B3-B4
Vaughan Road	E2
Vicarage Road	A1
Victoria Parade	E1-E2
Victoria Road	D4
Vine Road	A3
Walnut Road	A1-B1-B2
Warren Road	C2-C3-D2-D3
Warberry Road West	D3-D4-E4
Wellington Road	D4
Woodside Drive	E3

PAIGNTON

Adelphi Lane	C2
Adelphi Road	B2-C2
Alta Vista Road	C1
Batson Gardens	A1
Beach Road	B3-C3
Belle Vue Road	C1
Blatchcombe Road	A4
Cadwell Road	B3
Cecil Road	A3-B3
Church Street	A3-B3
Cleveland Road	C1
Cliff Road	C1
Clifton Bank	A2
Climsland Road	A1
Colin Road	C4
Colley End Park	A3
Colley End Road	A3
Conway Road	A1-A2
Corsham Road	A1
Courtland Road	B3-B4
Curledge Street	A2-B2
Dartmouth Road	B1-B2
David Road	A4
Dendy Road	B3
Derrel Road	A1
Elmbank Road	A1
Elmsleigh Road	A1-B1
Esplanade	C2-C3-C4
Esplanade Road	C2-C3-C4
Fisher Street	A1-A2-B1
Garfield Road	B2-B3-C3
Gerston Road	B2
Grosvenor Road	A1-B1-B2
Higher Polsham Road	A4-B4
Hill Park Terrace	B1
Hyde Road	B2-B3
Kernou Road	B2-C2
Keysfield Road	C1
Kings Avenue	B4
Kings Road	B4
Littlegate Road	A3-B3
Lower Polsham Road	C4-B3-B4
Manor Road	C4
Marine Drive	C4
Marldon Road	A3
Mead Road	B4
Midvale Road	B2
Mill Lane	A3
Monastery Road	A3
New Street	A2
Oldway Road	A4
Osney Crescent	A1-B1
Palace Avenue	A2-B2
Polsham Park	B3-B4
Primley Park	A2
Queen's Road	B2
Redburn Road	A3-A4
Roundham Road	B1-C1-C2

Second index column (Torquay / Paignton continued & Brixham / Newton Abbot)

St Andrew's Road	B1-B2
St Michael's Road	A1
Sands Road	B1-B2-C2
Shorton Road	A4
Southfield Rise	A4
Southfields Road	A3-A4
Steartfield Road	B3-C3
Torbay Road	B2-C2
Torquay Road	B2-B3-B4
Totnes Road	A1-A2-B2
Tower Road	A2-A3-B3
Upper Morin Road	B4-C4
Victoria Street	B2
Well Street	A3
Westhill Road	A4
Whitstone Road	B1
Winner Street	A2-A3
Winnerhill Road	A2-A3
Woodland Park	A4
York Road	A1

BRIXHAM

Alma Road	B3
Berry Head Road	C2
Bolton Street	A1-A2-B2
Burton Street	A1-A2
Castor Road	A1
Centry Road	C1
Cudhill Road	A2-A3
Cumber Drive	A3-A4
Drew Street	A1
Elkins Hill	B2-C2
Fishcombe Road	B4-C4
Fore Street	B2
Furzeham Park	B4
Garlic Rea	C2
Glenmore Road	B2
Gollands	A3-A4
Gollands Close	A4
Great Rea Road	C1-C2
Greenswood Road	A1
Heath Road	C2
Higher Furzeham Road	B3-B4-C3-C4
Higher Manor Road	B3
Higher Ranscombe Road	B1-C1
Hillside Road	A2
King Street	B2-C2
Knick Knack Lane	A1-A2
Lakes Road	A4
Langley Avenue	A2
Lindthorpe Way	A3
Lower Manor Road	A3-B3
Lower Rea Road	C1-C2
Lyte's Road	B1-B2-C1
Market Street	B2
Metherell Avenue	A1
Middle Street	B2
Mount Road	B2
Mount Pleasant Road	B2
Nelson Road	B3-C3
New Road	A3-B3-B2
North Boundary Road	A4-B4
Northfields Lane	A3-A4-B4-C4
North Furzeham Road	C3-C4
Overgang Road	C3

NEWTON ABBOT

Abbotsbury Road	A4-A3-B3
Albany Street	B3
Albert Terrace	C3
Albion Hill	B2
Alexandra Road	C1-C2
Back Road	A2-A3
Beaumont Road	B2
Bovey Road	A3-A4
Bowden Hill	B2
Bradley Lane	A3
Buckland View	C3
Chelston Road	A3-B3
Church Road	C1-C2
Coach Road	B1-C1
College Road	A1-B1
Coronation Road	A3
Courtenay Park	C2
Courtenay Road	A1-B1
Courtenay Street	A3-B3
Decoy Road	C1
Devon Square	C2
East Street	A2-B2
Exeter Road	A4
Fairfield Terrace	B3
Fisher Road	A3-B3
Forde Park	C1
Garston Avenue	A4-B4-B3
George Street	B2
Gothic Road	A2
Grafton Road	A3
Halcyon Road	A3
Highweek Road	A3-A4
Highweek Street	A3
Hillmans Road	C1-C2
Hill Rise	B4
Hill Road	A1-B1
Hilton Road	B2
Hopkins Lane	B3
Jetty Marsh Road	B4-C4
Kingsteinton Road	B3-B4-C4
King Street	B2-B3
Knowles Hill Road	A4-B4-B3
Laureston Road	B1
Lemon Road	B3-C3
Market Street	A3
Marsh Road	B3-C3
Mount Pleasant Road	B1-B2-B2-C2
Netley Road	A4
Newfoundland Way	A3
Oak Place	C2
Osborne Street	C3
Paynsford Road	A4
Pomeroy Road	A2
Powderham Road	A2-B2
Prospect Terrace	B2-B3
Quay Road	C3
Quay Terrace	C3
Queen Street	B3-C3
Rundle Road	B3-B4-C4
St Leonards Road	A2
St Marys Road	A1
Salisbury Road	C2
Seymour Road	A4-B4
Sherborne Road	B3
South Road	A1-B1
Station Road	C1-C2-C3
The Avenue	C3-C4
Teign Road	C3
Torquay Road	C1-C2
Tudor Road	A2-B2
Union Street	B2-B3
Vicarage Place	B3
Waverley Road	A3-A4
Western Road	B2
Wharf Road	C3-C4
Wolborough Street	A2-A3

NEWTON ABBOT (additional roads)

Parkham Road	A2-B2
Penn Lane	A1
Penn Meadows	A1
Penpethy Road	A3
Prospect Road	B3-C3
Queen's Crescent	B1
Queen's Road	C4
Ranscombe Park	C1
Ranscombe Road	C1-C2
Rea Barn Road	A1-B1
Sellick Avenue	A1-B1
Smardon Avenue	A3-A4
South Furzeham Road	B3-C3
Station Hill	B2-B3
Strand	B2
The Close	B4
The Quay	C2-C3
Wall Park Close	C1
Wall Park Road	C1
Windmill Hill	A1-B1-B2
Windmill Road	B2-C2
Wolston Close	B4

105

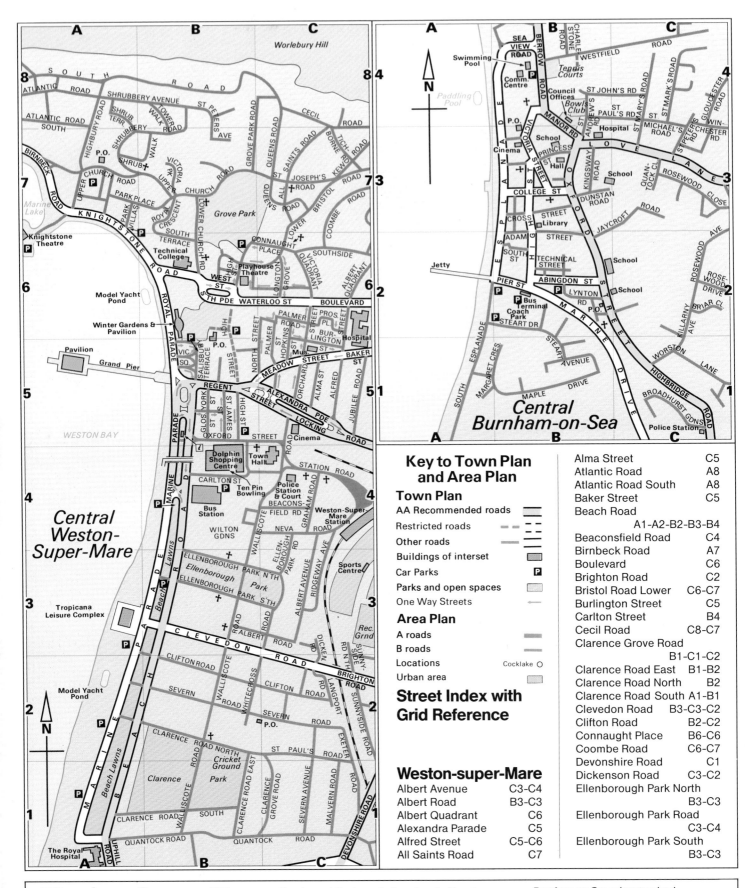

Key to Town Plan and Area Plan

Town Plan

AA Recommended roads	
Restricted roads	
Other roads	
Buildings of interset	
Car Parks	P
Parks and open spaces	
One Way Streets	←

Area Plan

A roads	
B roads	
Locations	Cocklake ○
Urban area	

Street Index with Grid Reference

Weston-super-Mare

Albert Avenue	C3-C4
Albert Road	B3-C3
Albert Quadrant	C6
Alexandra Parade	C5
Alfred Street	C5-C6
All Saints Road	C7

Alma Street	C5
Atlantic Road	A8
Atlantic Road South	A8
Baker Street	C5
Beach Road	A1-A2-B2-B3-B4
Beaconsfield Road	C4
Birnbeck Road	A7
Boulevard	C6
Brighton Road	C2
Bristol Road Lower	C6-C7
Brighton Road	C2
Burlington Street	C5
Carlton Street	B4
Cecil Road	C8-C7
Clarence Grove Road	B1-C1-C2
Clarence Road East	B1-B2
Clarence Road North	B2
Clarence Road South	A1-B1
Clevedon Road	B3-C3-C2
Clifton Road	B2-C2
Connaught Place	B6-C6
Coombe Road	C6-C7
Devonshire Road	C1
Dickenson Road	C3-C2
Ellenborough Park North	B3-C3
Ellenborough Park Road	C3-C4
Ellenborough Park South	B3-C3

Weston-Super-Mare

Elegant piers, promenades and hotels mark Weston-Super-Mare's 19th-century transformation into a flourishing seaside resort. At one time nothing more than a small fishing village, the town now boasts several attractive parks and gardens, and near the beach are numerous entertainment and leisure centres.

Havens for children are the Winter Garden Complex and Tropicana, both equipped with water slides, swimming pools and solaria. Madeira Cove attracts visitors to its Marine Lake, aquarium and model village, and Knightstone Island nearby provides further entertainments.

The High Street has been turned into a pedestrian area for easy shopping, and tucked away down a cobbled street is the Woodspring Museum full of nostalgic memories of a town which still retains its character and charm.

Burnham-on-Sea enjoys two local breweries, responsible for supplying the real ales which are exclusive to the pubs in this area. Developed into a resort as early as the 18th century, Burnham-on-Sea also offers many other amenities, including a mild Somerset climate, acres of sandy beaches, a Leisure Park and a pier which was built in 1856 as a terminal for passing steamers and the railway. Live entertainment can be seen at Princess Hall.

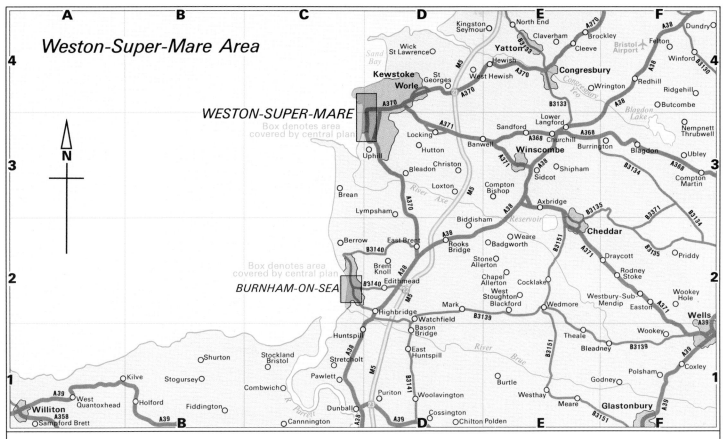

Weston-Super-Mare Area

WESTON-SUPER-MARE
Box denotes area covered by central plan

BURNHAM-ON-SEA
Box denotes area covered by central plan

Exeter Road	C2-C1	Royal Crescent	B7	Whitecross Road	B2-C2-C3
Gloucester Street	B5	Royal Parade	B6-B5	Wilton Gardens	B4
Graham Road	C4	St James Street	B5	York Street	B5
Grove Park Road	B7-B8-C8	St Joseph's Road	C7		
Highbury Road	A7-A8	St Paul's Road	C2-C1		
High Street	B6-B5	St Peter's Avenue	B8-B7		
Hopkin Street	C5-C6	Salisbury Terrace	B5		
Jubilee Road	C5	Severn Avenue	C1-C2		
Kew Road	C7	Severn Road	B2-C2		
Knightstone Road	A7-A6-B6	Shrubbery Avenue	A8-B8	**Burnham-on-Sea**	
Langport Road	C2	Shrubbery Road	A7-B7-B8	Abingdon Street	B2
Locking Road	C5-C4	Shrubbery Terrace	A8	Adam Street	B2-B3
Longton Grove	C6	Shrubbery Walk	A7-B7	Berrow Road	B4
Lower Church Road	B7-B6	South Parade	B6	Briar Close	C2
Malvern Road	C1	South Road	A8-B8	Broadhurst Gardens	C1
Marine Parade		Southside	C6	Charlestone Road	B4
	A1-A2-A3-B3-B4-B5	South Terrace	B7-B6	College Street	B3
Meadow Street	B5-C5	Station Road	C4	Cross Street	B3
Neva Road	B4-C4	Sunnyside Road	C2	Dunstan Road	B3
North Street	B5-C5-C6	Sunnyside Road North		Esplanade	A2-B2-B3-B4
Orchard Street	C5-C6		C3-C2	Gloucester Road	C4
Oxford Street	B5-C5	Tichbourne Road	C7	Highbridge Road	C1
Palmer Road	C6	Tower Walk	B8	High Street	B2-B3
Palmer Street	C5-C6	Upper Church Road	A7-B7	Jaycroft Road	B2-B3-C3
Park Place	A7-B7	Victoria Park	B7	Kilarny Avenue	C1-C2
Park Villas	A7	Victoria Square	B5	Kingsway Road	B3
Prospect Place	C6	Victoria Quadrant	C6	Love Lane	B3-C3
Quantock Road	A1-B1-C1	Walliscote Road		Lynton Road	B2
Queens Road	C7-C8		B1-B2-B3-B4-C4-C5	Manor Road	B4-B3
Regent Street	B5-C5	Waterloo Street	B6-C6	Maple Drive	B1
Ridgeway Avenue	C3-C4	West Street	B6	Margaret Crescent	A1-B1
				Marine Drive	B2-B1-C1
				Oxford Street	B3-B2-C2-C1

Pier Street	B2
Princess Street	B3
Quantock Close	C3
Rosewood Avenue	C2-C3
Rosewood Close	C3
Rosewood Drive	C2
St Andrew's Road	B3-B4
St John's Road	B4-C4
St Marks Road	C4
St Mary's Road	C3-C4
St Michael's Road	C4-C3
St Paul's Road	B4-C4
St Peter's Road	C3-C4
Sea View Road	B4
South Esplanade	A1-A2
South Street	B2
Steart Avenue	B2-B1
Steart Drive	A2-B2
Technical Street	B2
Victoria Street	B4-B3
Westfield Road	B4-C4
Winchester Road	C4-C3
Worston Lane	C1

WESTON-SUPER-MARE
The piers and good beaches of Weston-Super-Mare attract over three million visitors a year, and town spectaculars such as the aircraft displays of Great Weston Air Day and the summer carnival are another powerful draw.

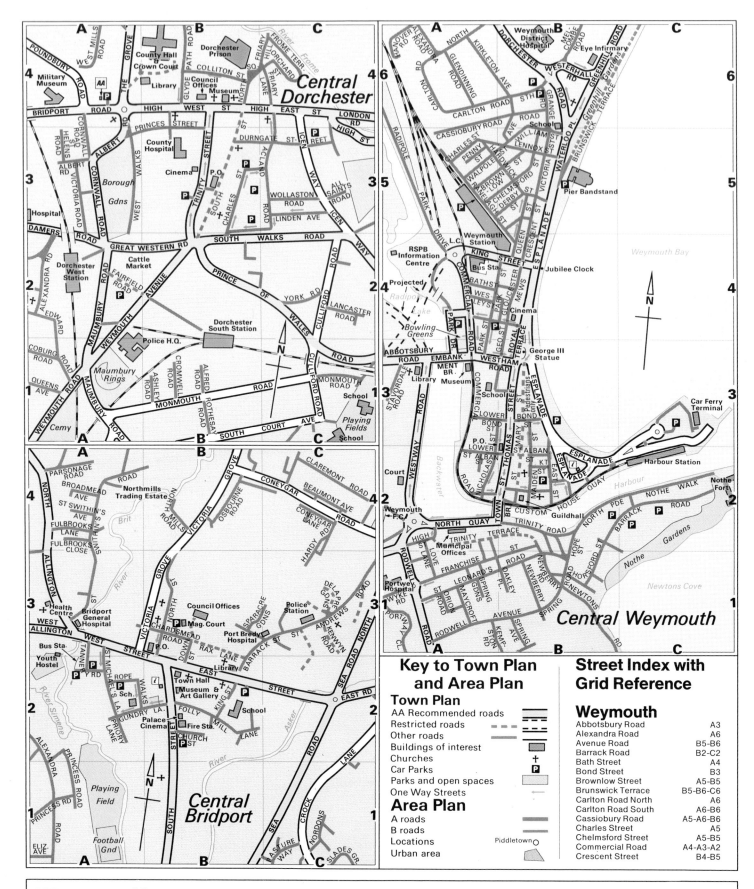

Central Dorchester

Central Weymouth

Central Bridport

Key to Town Plan and Area Plan

Town Plan

AA Recommended roads

Restricted roads

Other roads

Buildings of interest

Churches

Car Parks

Parks and open spaces

One Way Streets

Area Plan

A roads

B roads

Locations — Piddletown

Urban area

Street Index with Grid Reference

Weymouth

Abbotsbury Road	A3
Alexandra Road	A6
Avenue Road	B5-B6
Barrack Road	B2-C2
Bath Street	A4
Bond Street	B3
Brownlow Street	A5-B5
Brunswick Terrace	B5-B6-C6
Carlton Road North	A6
Carlton Road South	A6-B6
Cassiobury Road	A5-A6-B6
Charles Street	A5
Chelmsford Street	A5-B5
Commercial Road	A4-A3-A2
Crescent Street	B4-B5

Weymouth

King George III favoured the ancient port of Weymouth and as a result the town aquired a certain fashionable status as a resort in the late 18th century. Still popular with holidaymakers, it offers good bathing, fishing and golf, and it is also a busy Channel Islands ferry port. Georgian houses – many of which have been turned into guest houses – overlook the broad esplanade, but near the harbour older buildings line narrow, picturesque streets and alleyways. One of the 17th-century houses in Trinity Street has been restored and refurnished in contemporary style, and another place of interest is the museum in Westham Road.

Dorchester is essentially still the busy market town Thomas Hardy featured in many of his novels. He was born at nearby Higher Bockhampton and several of his personal possessions are displayed in the Dorset County Museum in Dorchester. A series of fires in the 17th and 18th centuries left the town rather short of historic buildings, although St Peter's Church, which dates back to the 1400s, survived, as did the Old Shire Hall – scene of the trial of the Tolpuddle Martyrs in 1834.

Bridport's wide pavements used to be called 'ropewalks' because new ropes were laid out on them for twisting and drying. The 750-year-old industry continues to this day, and relics of the old trade are kept in the museum in South Street.

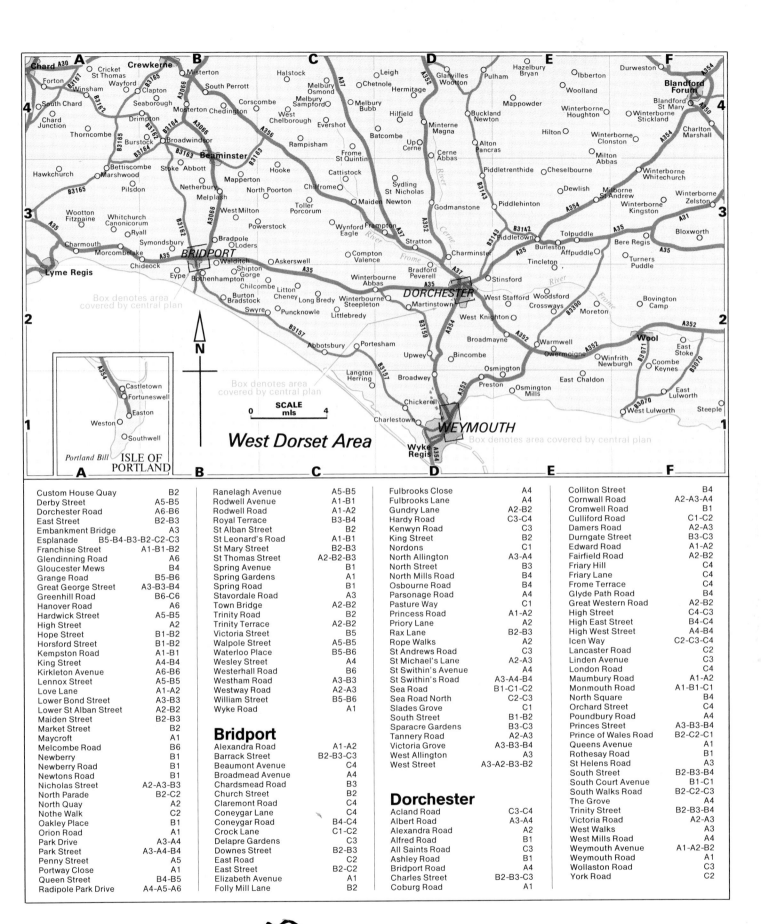

West Dorset Area

SCALE
mls
0 — 4

Box denotes area covered by central plan

ISLE OF PORTLAND
Portland Bill
Castletown
Fortuneswell
Weston
Easton
Southwell

Custom House Quay	B2	Ranelagh Avenue	A5-B5
Derby Street	A5-B5	Rodwell Avenue	A1-B1
Dorchester Road	A6-B6	Rodwell Road	A1-A2
East Street	B2-B3	Royal Terrace	B3-B4
Embankment Bridge	A3	St Alban Street	B2
Esplanade	B5-B4-B3-B2-C2-C3	St Leonard's Road	A1-B1
Franchise Street	A1-B1-B2	St Mary Street	B2-B3
Glendinning Road	A6	St Thomas Street	A2-B2-B3
Gloucester Mews	B4	Spring Avenue	B1
Grange Road	B5-B6	Spring Gardens	A1
Great George Street	A3-B3-B4	Spring Road	B1
Greenhill Road	B6-C6	Stavordale Road	A3
Hanover Road	A6	Town Bridge	A2-B2
Hardwick Street	A5-B5	Trinity Road	B2
High Street	A2	Trinity Terrace	A2-B2
Hope Street	B1-B2	Victoria Street	B5
Horsford Street	B1-B2	Walpole Street	A5-B5
Kempston Road	A1-B1	Waterloo Place	B5-B6
King Street	A4-B4	Wesley Street	A4
Kirkleton Avenue	A6-B6	Westerhall Road	B6
Lennox Street	A5-B5	Westham Road	A3-B3
Love Lane	A1-A2	Westway Road	A2-A3
Lower Bond Street	A3-B3	William Street	B5-B6
Lower St Alban Street	A2-B2	Wyke Road	A1
Maiden Street	B2-B3		
Market Street	B2	**Bridport**	
Maycroft	A1		
Melcombe Road	B6	Alexandra Road	A1-A2
Newberry	B1	Barrack Street	B2-B3-C3
Newberry Road	B1	Beaumont Avenue	C4
Newtons Road	B1	Broadmead Avenue	A4
Nicholas Street	A2-A3-B3	Chardsmead Road	B3
North Parade	B2-C2	Church Street	B2
North Quay	A2	Claremont Road	C4
Nothe Walk	C2	Coneygar Lane	C4
Oakley Place	B1	Coneygar Road	B4-C4
Orion Road	A1	Crock Lane	C1-C2
Park Drive	A3-A4	Delapre Gardens	C3
Park Street	A3-A4-B4	Downes Street	B2-B3
Penny Street	A5	East Road	C2
Portway Close	A1	East Street	B2-C2
Queen Street	B4-B5	Elizabeth Avenue	A1
Radipole Park Drive	A4-A5-A6	Folly Mill Lane	B2

Fulbrooks Close	A4	Colliton Street	B4
Fulbrooks Lane	A4	Cornwall Road	A2-A3-A4
Gundry Lane	A2-B2	Cromwell Road	B1
Hardy Road	C3-C4	Culliford Road	C1-C2
Kenwyn Road	C3	Damers Road	A2-A3
King Street	B2	Durngate Street	B3-C3
Nordons	C1	Edward Road	A1-A2
North Allington	A3-A4	Fairfield Road	A2-B2
North Street	B3	Friary Hill	C4
North Mills Road	B4	Friary Lane	C4
Osbourne Road	B4	Frome Terrace	C4
Parsonage Road	A4	Glyde Path Road	B4
Pasture Way	C1	Great Western Road	A2-B2
Princess Road	A1-A2	High Street	C4-C3
Priory Lane	A2	High East Street	B4-C4
Rax Lane	B2-B3	High West Street	A4-B4
Rope Walks	A2	Icen Way	C2-C3-C4
St Andrews Road	C3	Lancaster Road	C2
St Michael's Lane	A2-A3	Linden Avenue	C3
St Swithin's Avenue	A4	London Road	C4
St Swithin's Road	A3-A4-B4	Maumbury Road	A1-A2
Sea Road	B1-C1-C2	Monmouth Road	A1-B1-C1
Sea Road North	C2-C3	North Square	B4
Slades Grove	C1	Orchard Street	C4
South Street	B1-B2	Poundbury Road	A4
Sparacre Gardens	B3-C3	Princes Street	A3-B3-B4
Tannery Road	A2-A3	Prince of Wales Road	B2-C2-C1
Victoria Grove	A3-B3-B4	Queens Avenue	A1
West Allington	A3	Rothesay Road	B1
West Street	A3-A2-B3-B2	St Helens Road	A3
		South Street	B2-B3-B4
Dorchester		South Court Avenue	B1-C1
		South Walks Road	B2-C2-C3
Acland Road	C3-C4	The Grove	A4
Albert Road	A3-A4	Trinity Street	B2-B3-B4
Alexandra Road	A2	Victoria Road	A2-A3
Alfred Road	B1	West Walks	A3
All Saints Road	C3	West Mills Road	A4
Ashley Road	B1	Weymouth Avenue	A1-A2-B2
Bridport Road	A4	Weymouth Road	A1
Charles Street	B2-B3-C3	Wollaston Road	C3
Coburg Road	A1	York Road	C2

WEYMOUTH
Little has changed along the town's seafront since George III first came to the resort in the late 18th century to try out a new-fangled contraption called a bathing machine. A statue of the King stands on the esplanade.

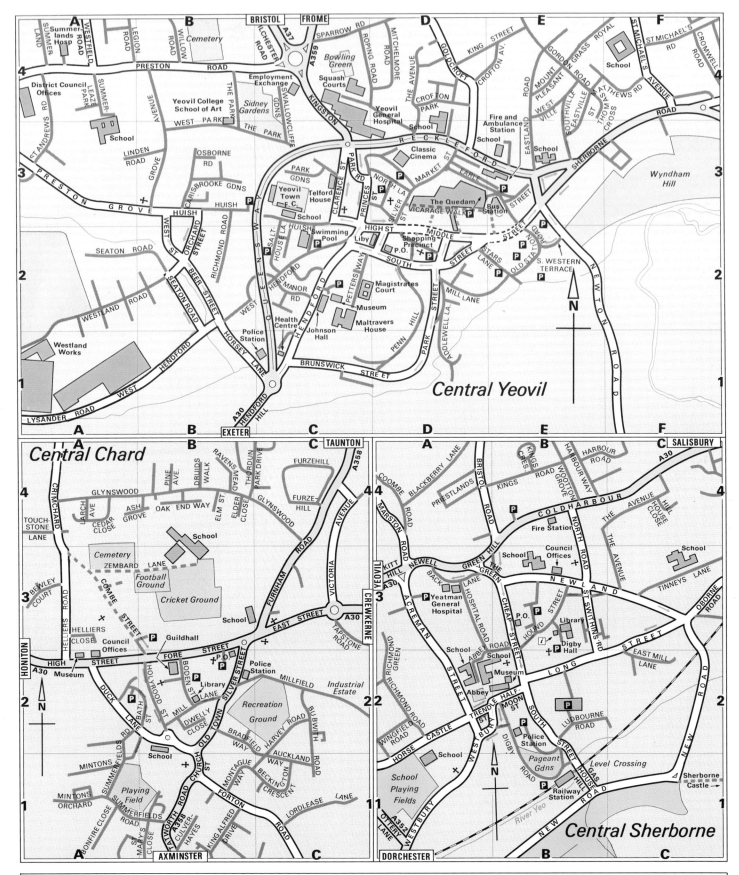

Yeovil

Home of the Westland helicopter and aircraft factory — as a result of which it suffered bomb damage in the Second World War — and six miles south of the Fleet Air Museum at Yeovilton, the market town of Yeovil is also known for its more homely glovemaking. There is a fine 14th-century church, and a collection of firearms and local interest items at Hendford Manor.

Sherborne Full of medieval buildings built in the golden Ham Hill stone, Sherborne has a magnificent, mainly 15th-century, abbey church. Of the town's two public schools, the 1550 boys' school occupies some of the abbey buildings, and the abbey gatehouse has a museum.

East of the town are two castles: a Norman structure which was partly destroyed after the Civil War, and the 'new' castle, a fine Elizabethan house built and occupied by Sir Walter Raleigh, and full of treasures.

Chard was the scene of one of Judge Jeffreys' Bloody Assizes, held in the courthouse (built 1590) here after the Monmouth Rebellion of 1685. The town's grammar school was founded in 1671, the Choughs Hotel is Elizabethan and the porticoed Town Hall dates back to 1834. All stand in the main street, from which streams flow north to the Bristol Channel and south to the English Channel — at 400ft (122m), this is the county's highest town.

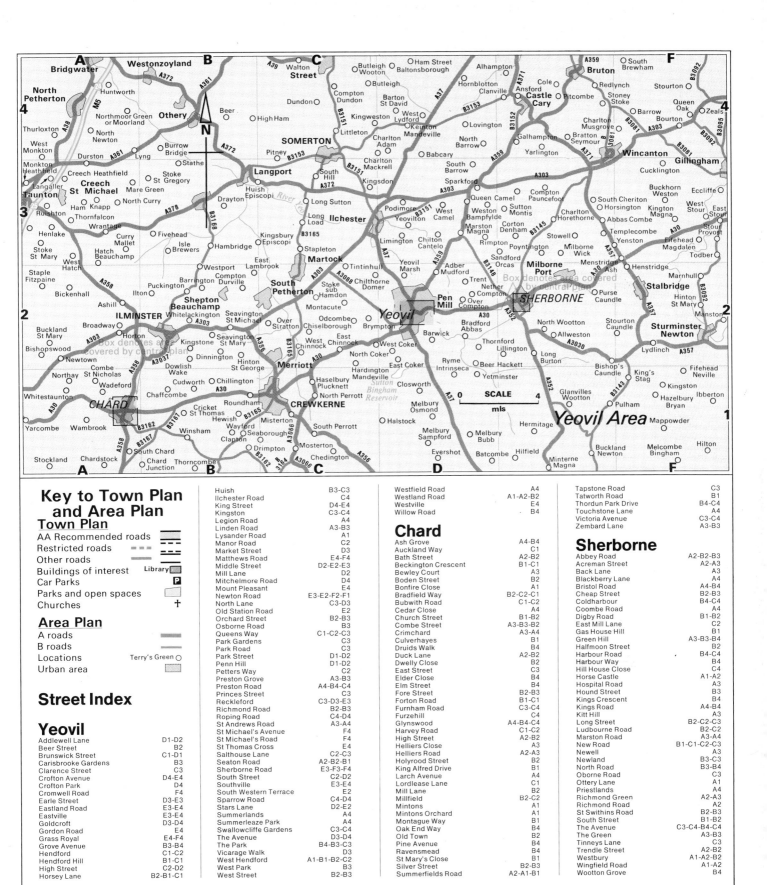

SHERBORNE
The 'new' castle was built by Sir Walter Raleigh in 1594, and is said to be the place where a servant, horrified at the sight of smoke rising from his newfangled tobacco pipe, promptly doused him with ale to 'put out the fire'.

Legend to Atlas

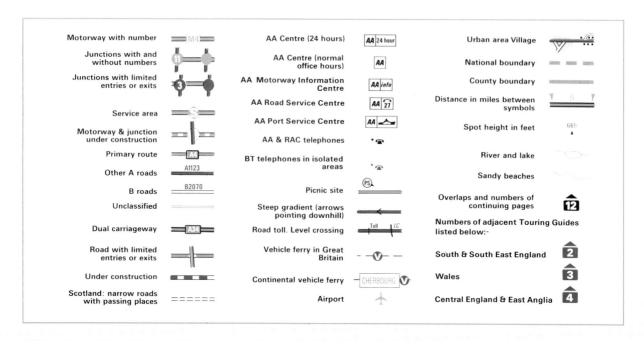

Motorway with number	Urban area Village
Junctions with and without numbers	National boundary
Junctions with limited entries or exits	County boundary
Service area	Distance in miles between symbols
Motorway & junction under construction	Spot height in feet
Primary route	River and lake
Other A roads	Sandy beaches
B roads	Overlaps and numbers of continuing pages
Unclassified	Numbers of adjacent Touring Guides listed below:-
Dual carriageway	
Road with limited entries or exits	South & South East England
Under construction	Wales
Scotland: narrow roads with passing places	Central England & East Anglia

AA Centre (24 hours)
AA Centre (normal office hours)
AA Motorway Information Centre
AA Road Service Centre
AA Port Service Centre
AA & RAC telephones
BT telephones in isolated areas
Picnic site
Steep gradient (arrows pointing downhill)
Road toll. Level crossing
Vehicle ferry in Great Britain
Continental vehicle ferry
Airport

Abbey or Cathedral	Coastal Launching Site	Nature Trail
Ruined Abbey or Cathedral	Surfing	Wildlife Park (mammals)
Castle	Climbing School	Wildlife Park (birds)
House and Garden	County Cricket Ground	Zoo
House	Gliding Centre	Forest Drive
Garden	Artificial Ski Slope	Lighthouse
Industrial Interest	Golf Course	Tourist Information Centre
Museum or Collection	Horse Racing	Tourist Information Centre (summer only)
Prehistoric Monument	Show Jumping/Equestrian Centre	Long Distance Footpath
Famous Battle Site	Motor Racing Circuit	AA Viewpoint
Preserved Railway or Steam Centre	Cave	Other Place of Interest
Windmill	Country Park	Boxed symbols indicate tourist attractions in towns
Sea Angling	Dolphinarium or Aquarium	

The National Grid

The National Grid provides a system of reference common to maps of all scales. The grid covers Britain with an imaginary network of 100 kilometre squares. Each square is identified by two letters, *eg* TR. Every 100 kilometre square is then subdivided into 10 kilometre squares which appear as a network of blue lines on the map pages. These blue lines are numbered left to right 0-9 and bottom to top 0-9. These 10 kilometre squares can be further divided into tenths to give a place reference to the nearest kilometre.

Key to Road Maps

Thurso

Wick

Stornoway

Outer
Hebrides

Ullapool

Portree

Banff

Inverness

Peterhead

Aberdeen

Fort
William

Pitlochry

Oban

Perth

Dundee

Edinburgh

Largs

Glasgow

Berwick

Peebles

Campbeltown

Ayr

Dumfries

Newcastle
upon Tyne

Stranraer

Workington

Middlesbrough

Isle of
Man

Kendal

Scarborough

Douglas

Lancaster

York

Blackpool

Leeds

Hull

Grimsby

Liverpool

Manchester

Sheffield

Caernarfon

Chester

Lincoln

Stoke

Nottingham

King's Lynn

Shrewsbury

Leicester

Norwich

Peterborough

Great
Yarmouth

Aberystwyth

Birmingham

Coventry

Northampton

Cambridge

Worcester

Fishguard

Carmarthen

Hereford

Felixstowe

Gloucester

Pembroke

Swansea

20/21

22/23

Oxford

Chelmsford

Cardiff

Bristol

Reading

LONDON

16/17

18/19

Maidstone

Barnstaple

Guildford

Dover

Folkestone

14/15

Taunton

Salisbury

Southampton

Brighton

Newhaven

8/9

10/11

12/13

Exeter

Weymouth

Bournemouth

4/5

6/7

Truro

Plymouth

2/3

Scilly
Isles

Shetland
Islands

Orkney
Islands

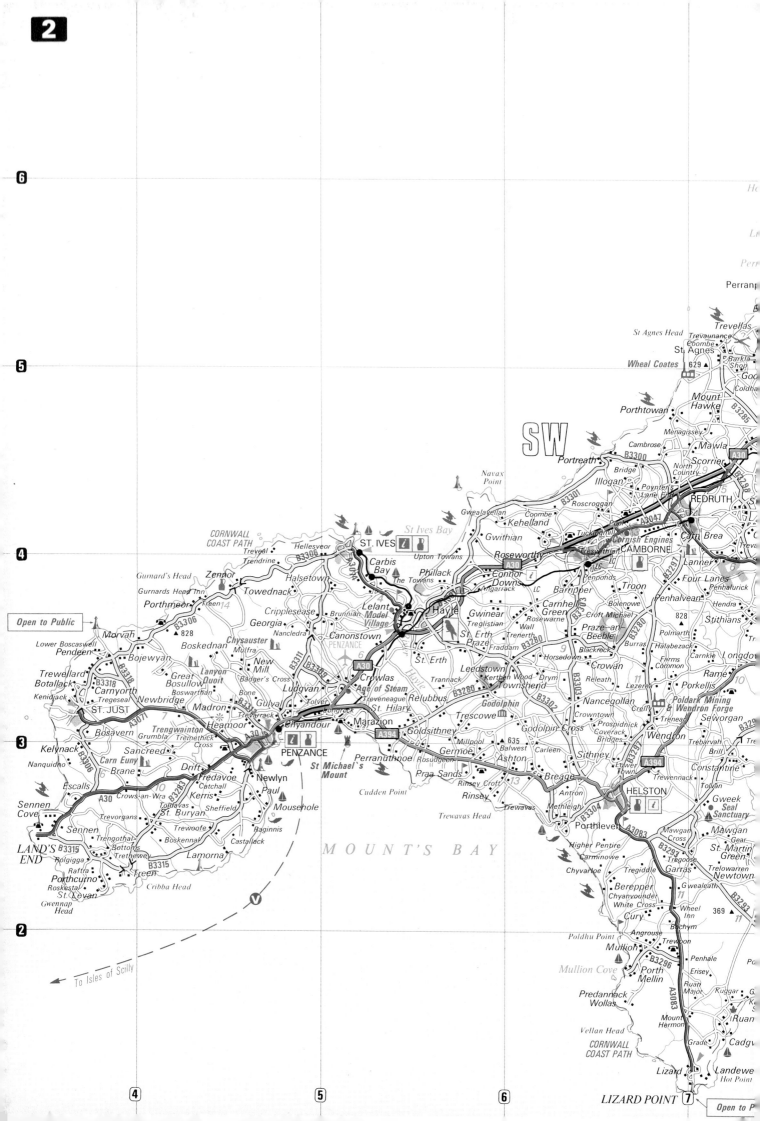

SCALE

0 1 2 3 4 5 miles

0 1 2 3 4 5 kilometres

SW

Gunver Head

TREVOSE HEAD

Open to Public

CORNWALL COAST PATH

243 Trevose

Constantine Bay

Watergate Bay

Newquay Bay

NEWQUAY

BAY

Widemouth Bay

Dizzard Point · Dizzard

Poundstock · Trevolter · Tregole

St. Gennys · Coxford · Trewint

Crackington Haven · Trevigue · Sweets · Trencreek · Wainhouse Corner

Hill · Pencuke · A39

Fire Beacon Point · Benny · B3263 · Trevillian · Marshgate

Boscastle · Trewannion · Otterham · Trelash

Tintagel Head · Bossiney · Trethevey · Trevalga · Treworld · Lesnewth · Hallworthy · A395

Tintagel · Treforda · Halgabron · Trenale · Davidstow · Trewassa · Tremail

1009 · Trewarmett · Pennathy · B3266 · Trela · Trevivian · Cold North

Start Point (PS) · Trebarwith · Upton · Trefrew · A39 · Collan's Cross · St. Clether · Woolgarden

Trecarne · Treligga · Delabole · Trevia · Tregoodwell · Bowithick

Westdowns · Pengelly · Trewalder · Langteglos · Camelford · 1377 · Wesley

Port Quin Bay · Portreath · Trelights · St. Teath · Knightshill · Watergate · Highertown · BROWN WILLY

Port Isaac · Portgaverne · Trewetha · Pendoggett · Treveighan · Michaelstow · Codda · Bolventor · BODMIN MOOR

New Polzeath · Polzeath · Plain Street · Treharrock · St. Endellion · Trenewth · St. Breward · Row · Bradford

Rumps Point · Pentire Point · Treglines · B3314 · St. Kew · Trelill · Trequite · Trewen · Hengar · Tregarrick · Blisland · Temple

Trebetherick · Tredrizzick · Trevanger · St. Minver · Chapel Amble · Hendra · Brighter · St. Tudy · Lank · Pensont · Waterloo

Rock · Pityme · Trewethern · Lower Amble · St. Kew Highway · Wenfordbridge · Tregenna · A30

Crugmeer · Cellissick · Splatt · Stoptide · Trevelver · Bodieve · St. Mabyn · Tredethy · Trewint · Millpool · Maidenwell

Trevone · Harlyn Bay · St. Cadoc · Treator · Dinas · Padstow · Trewarnon · Tregunna · Wadebridge · Cronford · Helland · Trezance · Cabilla · Warleggan

Towan · Windmill · Trevelver · Trevanson · Whitecross · Egloshayle · Pencarrow · Cardinham · Treslea · Fawton

St. Merryn · Tregance · St. Issey · A389 · Sladesbridge · Washaway · Norton · Penbugle · Welltown · Mount

Treyarnon · Treburrick · Trevisker · Little Petherick · St. Breock · Burlawn · Polbrock · Lane End · Cooksland

Trehemborne · Carnevas · Trevorrick · Penrose · Trenance · Tredinnick · Tredruston · Dunmere Bridge · BODMIN · A38 · Glynn · Doublebois

Porthcothan · Trevethan · St. Ervan · Rumford · Trelow · No Man's Land · St. Jidgey · Brocton · Boscarne · St. Nicholas · Fletchersbridge · Coldwin

Trevemedar · Engollan · Carnewas · Downhill · Treven900 · Cannalidgey · Ruthernbridge · Nanstallon · St. Lawrence · Kirland · Middledrift · East Taphouse

Park Head · Berry's Point · Trenance · Mawgan Porth · Trevilledor · Rosenannon · Tregustick · Tregawne · Withielgoose · Lidcutt · Lanhydrock · West Taphouse · Penfrane

Trevarrian · Denzell · Trewallack · Treliver · Tremore · Lamorick · Tregullon · Cutmadoc · Braddock · Wilton

Tregurrian · St. Mawgan · Trembleath · St. Wenn · Withiel · Retire · Lanivet · Trebyah · Fairy Cross · Restormel · Boconnoc

Carloggas · Gluvian · B3274 · Demelza · 744 · St. Ingunger · Bodwin · Redmoor · Polscoe · Sandylake · Bara · Herod

St. Columb Minor · Trebelzue · St. Columb Major · Tregonetha · Belowda · Victoria · Bokiddick · Maudlin · Trevellion · Lanlivery · Penhale · Brooks · LOSTWITHIEL · 683

Porth · Colan · Trevithick · Trebudannon · Ruthvoes · Tregoss · Higher Town · Lockengate · Sweetshouse · Trewether · Castle · 1644 · Bottallick · Bocaddon

Mountjoy · A392 · Trevarren · A30 · Bilberry · Carbis · Molinnis · Bodwen · Tredinnick · Milltown · Langunnett · Lanreath

Quintrell Downs · St. Columb Road · Toldish · Enniscaven · Carne · Roche · Bugle · Bodiggo · Rosevean · Penpillick · Lerryn

Kestle Mill · Lane · Indian Queens · B3279 · St. Dennis · Carnsmerry · Stenalees · Treverbyn · Luxulyan · Cliff · Carwen · Trenewan

Trerice · Lappa Valley Railway · Fraddon · Blue Anchor · Whitemoor · Yonderrtown · Penwithick · Trethurgy · Tregrehan · A390 · Lanreath Highway

St. Enoder · Retew · Nanpean · Carthew · Stents · Tregrehan Mills · Tywardreath Highway · Golant · Penpoll · Trenewan

Newlyn East · Summercourt · Burthy · Treviscoe · Foxhole · Wheal Martyn Museum · St. Blazey · Tywardreath · Torfrey · St. Veep · Penpol

Cargoll · Rejerrah · Trevilson · 490 · Meledon · Burgotha · High Street · Carclaze · Biscovey · St. Blazey Gate · Lombard · Trefrawl · Tregarrick

Fiddlers Green · Mitchell · Brighton · Trethosa · Carbalia · ST. AUSTELL · Par · A3082 · FOWEY · Bodinnick · Lanteglos Highway

Shepherds · Carland Cross · New Mills · Trelion · Gwindra · Trewoon · Boscoppa · Polkerris · Crumplehorn

Goonhavern · Trelassick · St. Stephen · Lanjeth · Hay · A3058 · AA 96 · Charlestown · St Catherine's · Polruan

B3285 · Zelah · Killiserth · Treveal · Coombe · St. Mewan · Trelowth · Boscoppa · Carlyon Bay · Menabilly · Lansallos

St. Allen · Ladock · Halzey · Polgooth · London Apprentice · Porthpean · St Austell Bay · Polrun

Trispen · Tregear · Grampound Road · Sticker · Hewas Water · Rescorla · Towan · Gribbin Head · CORNWALL COAST PATH

Treworgan · Treverbyn · Probus · A390 · Grampound · Nantellan · Leyalsa Meor · Trenarren · Black Head

Gwarnick · Bodrean · Tresillian · County Demonstration · Creed · Tregidgeo · Pentewan

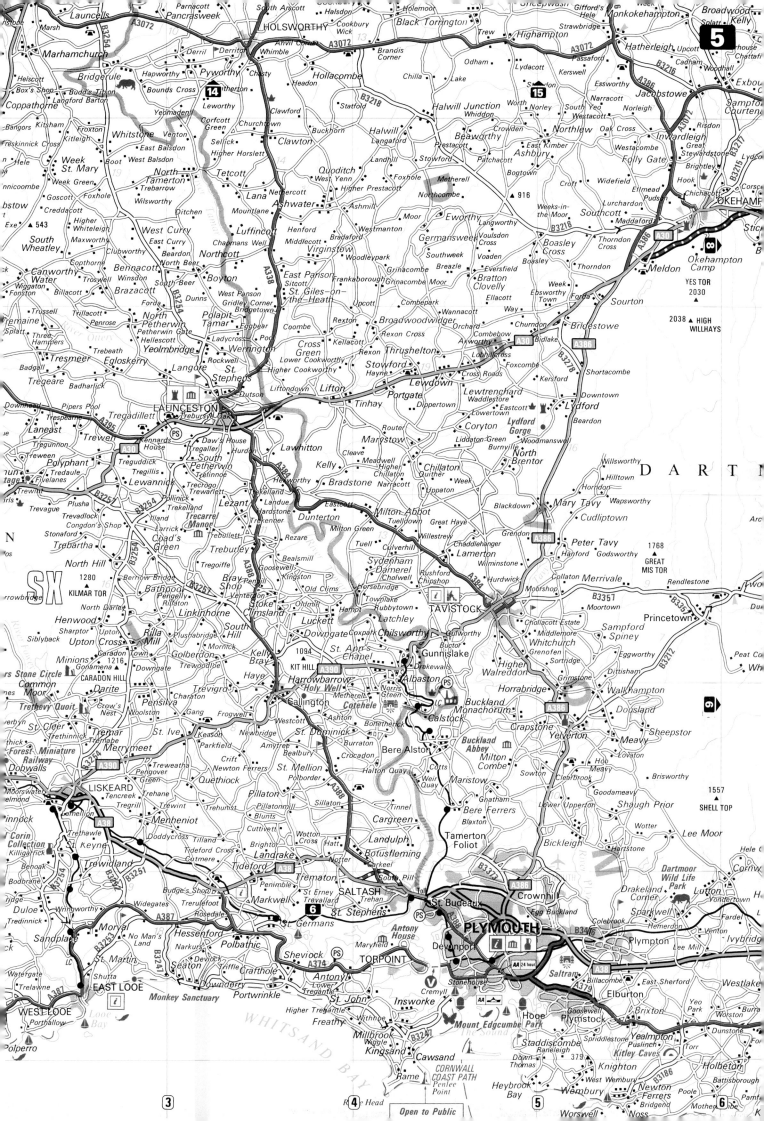

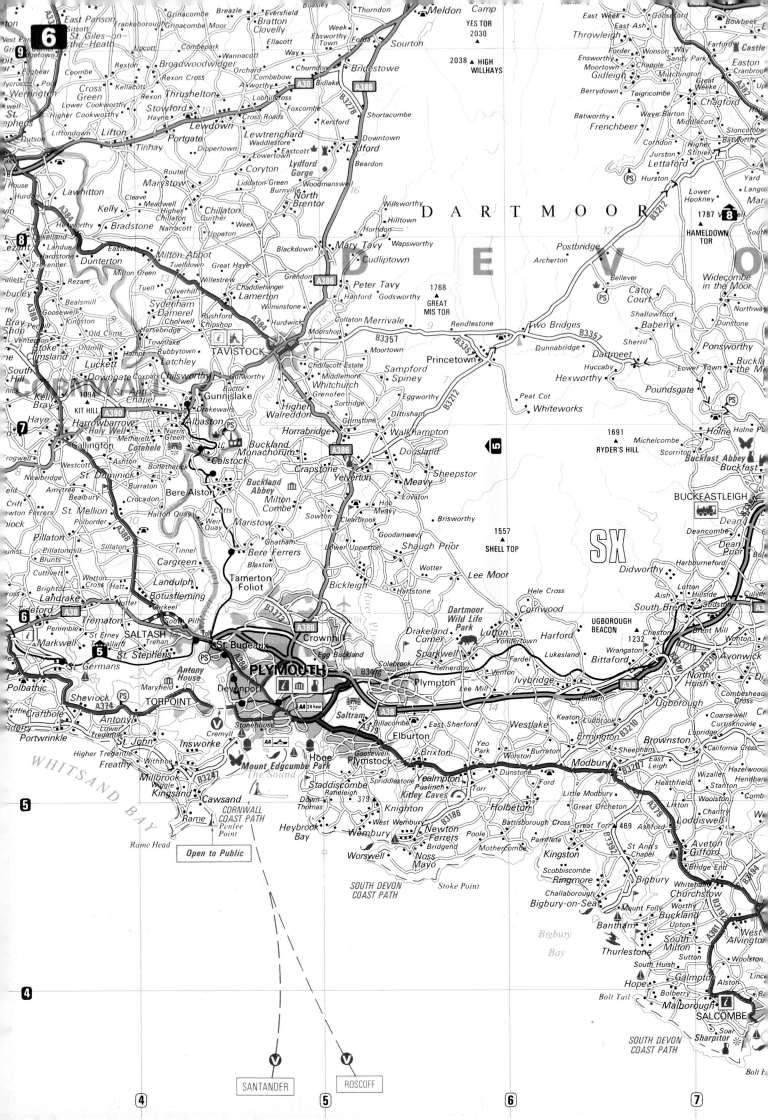

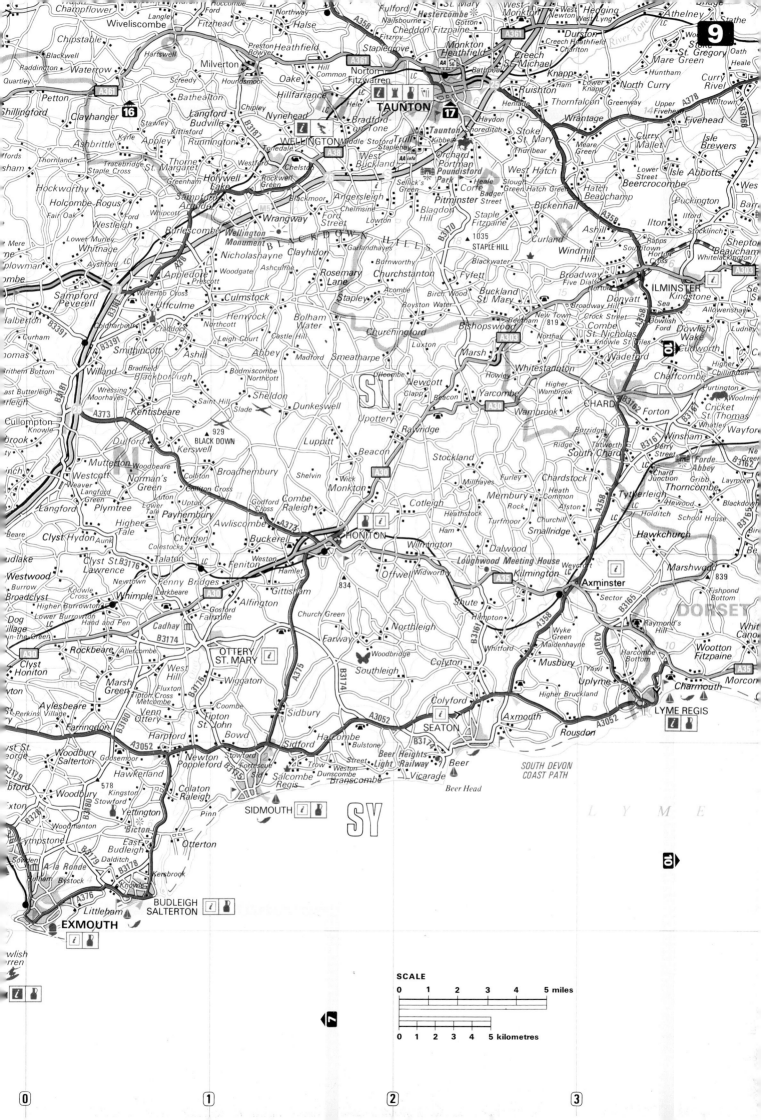

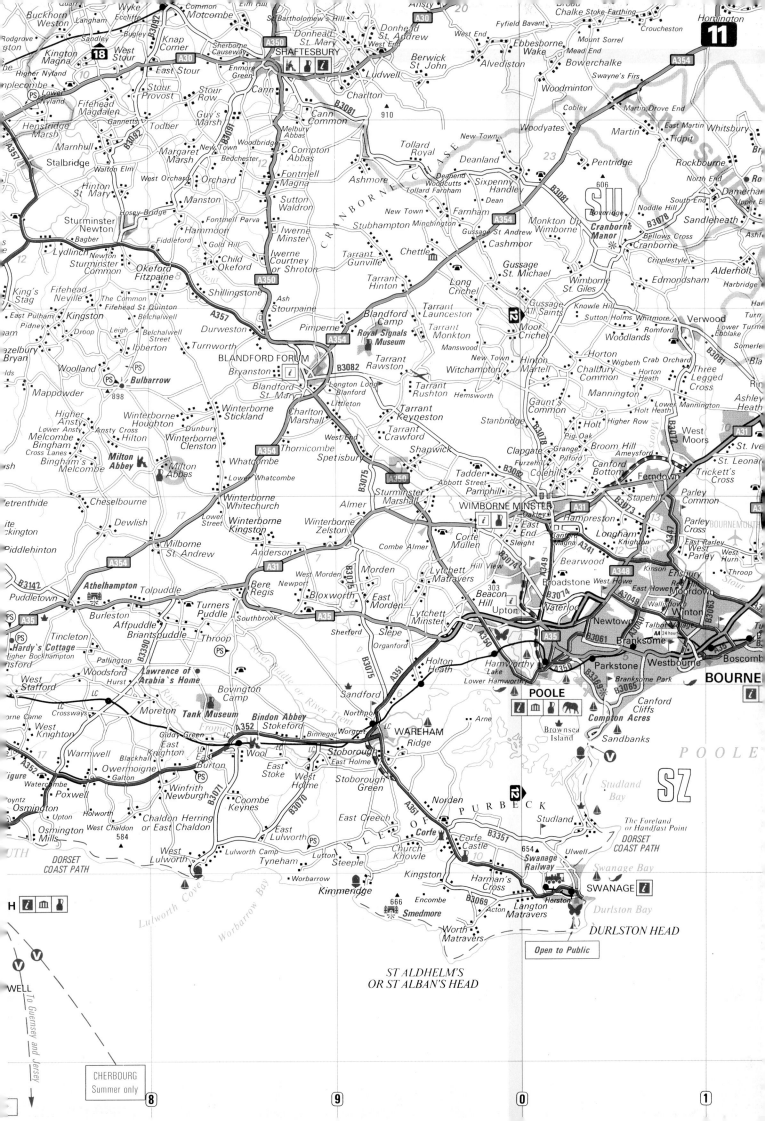

INDEX

As well as the page number of each place name the index also
includes an appropriate atlas page number together with a four figure
map reference (see National Grid explanation on page 112).

In a very few instances place names appear without a map reference.
This is because either they are not shown on the atlas or they lie just
outside the mapping area of the guide. However, each tour does
include a detailed map which highlights the location of all places
mentioned on the route.

T

	page	map		

U

	page	map		

V

	page	map		

W

	page	map		

Y

	page	map		

Z

	page	map		